The Investor's Quotient

The Investor's Quotient

SECOND EDITION

The Psychology of Successful Investing in Commodities & Stocks

Jake Bernstein

John Wiley & Sons, Inc.

New York • Chichester • Brisbane • Toronto • Singapore

This publication is designed to provide accurate and
authoritative information in regard to the subject
matter covered. It is sold with the understanding that
the publisher is not engaged in rendering legal, accounting,
or other professional services. If legal advice or other
expert assistance is required, the services of a competent
professional person should be sought. *From a Declaration
of Principles jointly adopted by a Committee of the
American Bar Association and a Committee of Publishers.*

Library of Congress Cataloging in Publication Data:

Bernstein, Jacob
    The investor's quotient : the psychology of successful investing
in commodities and stocks / Jake Bernstein. — 2nd ed.
        p.   cm.
    Includes bibliographical references and index.
    ISBN 0-471-55876-1 (cloth) 0-471-38362-7 (paper)
    1. Investments.   2. Investments—Psychological aspects.
  I. Title.
HG4521.B444   1993
332.6'78—dc20   93-18785

Printed in the United States of America.

10 9 8 7

This book is dedicated to traders and investors everywhere
who have, through their struggles, come to understand
that success in the markets is more dependent upon
their own behavior and personal psychology than
upon any system, method, program, computer, or advisor.

Preface

The first edition of *The Investor's Quotient* was published in 1980. Since then I have authored more than 16 books on stock and futures trading, but the one book which continues to stimulate questions, comments, and letters of praise from traders the world over is the original IQ book. The reason for this was not too difficult to understand.

There are thousands of traders and investors who are aware of the single most important investment fact: Psychological factors are paramount in the struggle for success in the markets. These individuals are in touch with the problem and they are seriously seeking solutions. Their search has brought them to the IQ book, where they have found explanations, consolations, realizations, directions, and insights.

But the serious trader and investor are never entirely satisfied with existing answers. Whether the answers are those that provide more and possibly better ways to make money in the markets or whether they provide new and more meaningful understandings of self, the search for the best continues.

As the stock and futures markets have become more volatile than ever before, thousands of newcomers have joined the ranks of the knowledge seekers. I have always maintained that the trader is more important than the system, that self-discipline and self-control are the key ingredients to success, and that the trader is the weakest link in the chain. The years that have passed since my first IQ book have proven undoubtedly that this is true. But the 1980s and early 1990s have further reaffirmed what we have always known. Whether we study the writings of Jesse Livermore, Gerald Loeb, W. D. Gann, or Bernard Baruch, we always arrive at the inescapable conclusion that profitable trading in stocks and futures can only be achieved by individuals who are either extremely fortunate or extremely disciplined. Since those who are extremely fortunate are clearly in the minority, then those who are highly disciplined comprise the vast majority of successful traders, investors, and speculators.

Discipline, however, is a term with broad implications. A trader who follows his or her rules is not necessarily a disciplined trader. It is necessary for the trader to first know the rules and for the rules to be those which are consistent with or which facilitate success. Discipline is a rubric under which are subsumed such quintessential skills and qualities as self-control, consistency, organization, persistence, direction, insight, and the ability to take action when necessary. These are the skills which traders seek to develop to their fullest. Unfortunately, they are skills which cannot be learned easily or quickly. There are no shortcuts to success other than for the fortunate few.

In order to solve a problem, it is first necessary to recognize that a problem exists. We must first know that we do not know. And then we must know what it is we do not know. Regrettably, there are many traders who do not know that they do not know. Nor are they remotely aware of what it is that they need to know. It's been said that there are several levels of ignorance. The first or true ignorance is characterized by the individual not knowing that they are ignorant. The second level of ignorance is knowing that one does not know. The third level of ignorance is knowing that you do not know, and knowing what it is that you do not know. The fourth level of ignorance is knowing all of the above and wanting to do something to improve, but not knowing what to do. The fifth level of ignorance is knowing that you do not know, knowing what to do about it, but being unable to act. And finally, comes what I call the oxymoron stage of ignorance, the highest level of ignorance, which is knowing that you do not know, knowing what to do about it and taking action, which is desirable ignorance (hence the oxymoron).

The hundreds of letters and calls I've received from those who have read the original IQ book, as well as the wonderful conversations and long hours I've spent talking to those readers who have called me or whom I've chanced to meet in an airport, on a plane, or on fishing trips, have given me a good sense of what's needed now. Hence, I've decided to rewrite the original IQ book, updating it to reflect the needs and wants of traders and investors in the 1990s. Additionally, *The Investor's Quotient (Second Edition)* contains new insights acquired during my last ten years as an observer of my own trading, as well as the trading of others.

What follows contains the old, the new, and above all, the true. What follows is derived from extensive personal experience in trading the most volatile and demanding markets in history. What follows springs from the mind and heart of a futures and stock trader who is older, wiser, more compassionate but more cynical, more concerned but less serious, and more relaxed but more frustrated. In short, I have changed. I prefer to think that my changes have been for the better and that they will help you find your way on the road to consistently profitable trading.

I will, at the outset, make a few seemingly immodest but totally honest assumptions, and I will give you some guarantees. The regulations that are imposed on me by our "wise" professional and bureaucratic agencies prohibit me from guaranteeing you monetary profits. And while the disinflationary years since 1980 have brought with them the usual trend toward increased conservatism and erosion of personal freedoms, I am still not prohibited from giving you other guarantees. I will exercise these rights while I still have them. Here are a few things that reading, studying, and applying this book will do for you:

1. Your losses should decrease and your profits should increase. At first you will notice that you are losing less on your bad trades and making more on your profitable trades.

2. Eventually you will be trading and/or investing profitably. Yes, there will still be losses. They are a necessary part of the game. There can be no profits without losses, but the losses may be minimized, and that's the name of the game.

3. Your attitudes about yourself will be considerably more positive. You will take pride in your skills and you will apply your self-knowledge toward positive ends, both in the markets and in your personal life.

4. Your self-confidence will increase. You will listen to and follow your own good work rather than relying upon the advice of others whether they be considered experts or not.

5. You will become more consistent, more organized, and more thorough in applying your market knowledge. In doing so, you will achieve positive results even if you fail at first. Through failure, you can discover what's working for you and what's not.

6. You will search for and find trading systems and methods which best suit your temperament, finances, and personality.

7. You will not take your market work too seriously, however, you will not assign it an inferior position. In other words, you will strike the correct balance of market studies vs. personal and family activities. You will not be a slave to the market, rather you will

become one of its masters. You will do so not by actually mastering the market, but rather by mastering yourself.

8. You will make fewer errors either of poor judgment, subversion, or perversion of your own trading rules. You will recognize your potential errors early in their development, and you will squelch them before they take their toll, both in emotions and in profits.

9. You will understand more clearly the relationship between news, fundamentals, other traders, yourself, and the market. You will know your place most of the time.

10. While you will still err on occasion, you will do so less frequently and you will rarely repeat the same blunders.

11. You will be less concerned with the success of others than with your own success. Your competition will be your own performance.

12. You will have conquered the need to trade for the sake of the game. In other words, you will trade only when the opportunity for profit is clear.

13. Finally, you will determine your position as a trader whether long-term, short-term, intermediate term or otherwise.

The changes and benefits I've just mentioned, may prove to be just the tip of the iceberg. There are many additional benefits that may result from the synergism stimulated in turn by your studies and self-analysis. I cannot give you any guarantees of success. I can, however, guarantee that if you are successful in changing your personal psychology; your relationship with yourself and those around you and your perception and relationship with the markets, you will thus become more successful than you ever dreamed possible.

After more than 20 years in the markets, I am absolutely convinced that few great traders are born great; they're created either as a result of their own intense efforts or as a result of work with others.

After more than 20 years as a futures and stock trader, I am convinced that it is the *TRADER* and not the *SYSTEM* that brings success. A good system can go a long way to foster self-confidence and, as a result, success. However, a good system in the hands of an undisciplined trader is like a race car in the hands of an inexperienced driver; the car will go fast, it will handle well, but the driver who cannot control the car and who does not know how to manage the car on the track can be seriously injured or worse.

So let's forget about systems for a while. Let's forget about the eye-catching ads with headlines of great promise. Let's forget about the "Holy Grail" trading systems, those fabulous equity curves, and those high percentage accuracies. Not a single one of them will do you any good unless you are emotionally and behaviorally fit to meet the challenge.

My first task is to share with you some of my personal background in the markets. Although my first experiences as a trader have not changed, my perception and understanding of them has. Hence, the personal background I am about to give you is similar to what appeared in the first version of this book. I have, however, made some important changes based on my personal growth since the IQ book was first published.

Contents

1 My Story   1

2 Many Markets—Many Similarities   13

3 Psychology and the Markets: Similarities and Differences   21

4 Psychoanalytic Theory—Do Childhood Experiences Affect Behavior?   31

5 Learning Theory: Is All Learning Stimulus-Response?   40

6 The Response Sector   51

7 The Consequences of Behavior   58

8 The Discovery Process—How to Know Yourself   69

9 How to Rectify Trading Errors   79

10 Further Details on Dealing with Trading Problems   92

11 Scheduling and Self-Discipline   98

12 The Importance of Trading with the Trend   104

13 The Role of Advisory Services   114

14 Is This You?   123

15 Can a Positive Mental Attitude Facilitate Consistent Success?   128

16 The Broker-Client Relationship   135

17 Putting It All Together—Where You Fit   144

18 Social Psychology and the Markets   151

19 Some Psychological Trading Rules   164

20 The Perceptual Factor   168

21 Subliminal Perception—Response without Awareness   180

22 Minimize Stress—Maximize Health and Profits   195

23 Often-Asked Questions   203

24 Sex and the Markets: Fact or Fantasy   223

25 Using Psychology to Maximize Investment Success   230

26 Writings of the Masters: Study History to Learn
        about the Future   233

27 Creative Visualization and Guided Imagery   239

28 Overcome Your Worst Fears: How Psychology
        Facilitates Success   250

29 Why Too Many Traders and Investors Lose   259

30 Modeling the Behavior of Successful Traders   264

31 Facing the Challenges of Today's and Tomorrow's
        Markets   268

32 Some Closing Thoughts: Facing the Challenges of
        Today and Tomorrow   272

Bibliography   276

Overview of "Trading Masters"   279

Index   287

1

My Story

As a college student I became interested in stocks. My college roommate, several years younger than I, had been brought up with the market, trained intensively and extensively by his father, an accomplished and extremely knowledgeable investor. My friend, John, convinced me to open an account at the local brokerage firm in Champaign, Illinois, our college town. Since John was under age, he could not open a brokerage account on his own, and so we stuck a deal: I would open the account, he would fund it, and he would teach me how to invest in stocks. His knowledge was impressive. We began trading gold mining stocks, John's favorite at the time. The year was 1968.

John was convinced that gold mining stocks were likely to go considerably higher. We bought 100 shares of Wright-Hargreaves Mines (WRT), a small Canadian gold mining firm listed on the American Stock Exchange. As I recall, the stock was trading at about $3 per share. In those days of low inflation, some stocks like WRT traded in sixteenth's of a point. Several times a week we'd venture down to the brokerage firm and, feeling important, we'd sit and watch the ticker tape like seasoned investors, breathlessly anticipating every tick. Even a gain of 3/16 was exciting!

From WRT, we expanded into mobile home stocks, electronics stocks, and the budding computer industry. We had some great successes and we had our share of failures as well. But it was the thrill of the game that was the most exciting aspect of the stock market. I wasn't making much money but I was learning a great deal.

John was and most likely still, a fabulous market technician. Although we parted company many years ago, the market lessons I learned from him will never be forgotten. His technical knowledge was vast and his perspective on market history was truly amazing. He devoured virtually everything he could read about the market.

The one major bit of knowledge I failed to acquire in my early trading days was that the most important market skills I would need, could not be learned from John, or for that matter, from anyone else. John was too busy wrestling with his own inner conflicts to help me with mine. He was too involved in understanding the reasons for his own psychological limitations to give me insight regarding mine. And while we both spent hundreds of hours researching market indicators and trends, we both knew that there was something lurking in the depths of our minds that was much more important than trends or indicators, much more valuable than trading systems or methods; much more dangerous than mere dollar losses, and much more potentially profitable than tips or inside information. Yet, we couldn't express our thoughts and feelings clearly enough to bring them to awareness.

I went off to pursue a career in clinical psychology and John continued his market work. After John graduated, we became roommates again and lived in Chicago with his older brother, who also shared an interest in the markets. Our apartment was crammed with market related materials; charts, graphs, books, reports, and Wall Street Journals. We were our own good work, long on research but short on psychology and self-awareness. We knew that the market work was good, but we weren't always able to follow our own good work. I found myself growing tired of stocks, blaming the market and not myself for my failures. I failed to realize that it was not the market that was wrong, but rather I was wrong. I began to look elsewhere for trading opportunities.

Will Eggs Hit the Moon?

One weekend, while reading *Barron's,* an advertisement for commodity futures trading attracted my attention. The ad, very clever and seductive, depicted a rocket ship on its way to the moon. Inside the rocket was a basket of eggs. A caption on the ad read: "Will Egg Futures Hit the Moon This Year?" The ad was rich in psychological and symbolic messages, so much so that it lured me into requesting more information. Lo and behold, several days later a fast-talking charismatic commodity broker called me. His sales technique was well-polished, but wasted on me, since I had only $1000 to my name.

Being very persistent and high-pressured, as brokers are apt to be, he called time and time again, until at last he had enticed me to open a futures trading account. My last few dollars went his way. I had no unrealistic expectations in spite of the promises. I expected, in fact, to lose what little money I had managed to scrape together.

By now you're probably sure you know the outcome of my story: a small loss, some margin calls, and a bigger loss. But you're wrong, for I was more fortunate—at least initially. Luck was on my side. Within several weeks, my friendly broker (let's call him Joe) phoned to tell me that my $1000 had turned into $3500. My original $1000 was being returned. I owed my good fortune to Joe and his knowledge of the egg futures market. Herein, my story gets even better. Within several months, the original investment grew to over $6000.

As the days passed, the profits swelled. The winners were many and large; the losers few and small. All the while, I knew nothing about the futures market (called the commodity market back then), but each day I received confirmation sheets in the mail—"We have today for your account and risk bought 5 Sep 69 Eggs. . . ." and the profits continued to grow. Winners continued to outnumber losers. The profits were rolling in. Joe and I were very happy. As far as I was concerned, the game was easy.

Joe had taken just a little time to explain to me how the game worked. He told me that the egg market was a weather market; that chickens were very sensitive to hot weather. "The hotter it gets the unhappier chickens get" explained Joe. "Then, when it gets too hot, they die," he added. "And when chickens die, there's fewer eggs. When there's fewer eggs, the price goes up. That, my little buddy, is what we call the law of supply and demand" he concluded.

Finding My Niche

The commodity market was just the right place for me. After all, I grew up in poverty, raised in the slums of Montreal, Canada, by parents who barely spoke English. My parents were concentration camp survivors, who knew well the meaning of persistence and refusal to quit even under the most adverse of conditions. While my parents couldn't provide me with material things, they did instill in me a high degree of motivation. I was quick to recognize an opportunity when I saw one. I witnessed my parents working hard all of their lives, waking at 4:00 AM and working until well after 10:00 PM to earn a meager living. I was determined not to go down the same path.

The commodity game soon pushed my studies in clinical psychology into the background. I visited the local library and checked out several books on the commodity markets. After some hours of study and a little creative thought, I developed a system. It was based on support and resistance. The books made it all look so easy with 20/20 hindsight; buy at support and sell at resistance. That's all there was to it! I gave it dry-run tests on several markets, and soon I was ready for the "acid test."

Buy Them Bellies

After some intensive chart analysis and study of lines on charts, I concluded that the day had come to double my money in pork bellies. I called Joe to place an order just before boarding a commuter train to downtown Chicago. I was on my way to the Merc, the Chicago Mercantile Exchange. I wanted to be there when the market made me rich.

Today, when I think back to that day, I can only wonder how I could have been so naive, so blind-sided, so jaded. I know well enough today, that such excessive self-confidence, the "King-Kong" feeling is a sure sign of trouble. "Joe," I said in a self-assured voice, "buy 15 Feb bellies on the open with a stop loss 10 points from limit down. Place an order to liquidate at limit up OCO." (I was proud to show off my market knowledge in such a professional way.)

Aghast, after regaining his composure he replied, "Jake, you don't want to trade the belly market, stick with eggs, we know the market, if you trade bellies you'll get creamed . . . besides that, you've never even traded before, don't buy 15 right off the bat!" I refused to listen to reason. "Just buy them bellies," I commanded. "But Jake, you don't know the market. You think that just by reading one book and having a system you'll profit. Believe me, it's not that easy, or I would have done it myself. Don't do it . . . You'll be sorry . . . OK, let's buy just a few bellies, not 15; or better yet let's open a second account with some money from this one. Then you can lose it slowly."

But his pleas fell on deaf and overconfident ears. I had allowed a larger percentage gain, none of which came from my own efforts, to get in the way of logic and good sense. "Joe, if you don't buy those bellies, I'll close my account. I know what I'm doing. I have a trading system. I know I can double the money today . . . so just put in those damn orders and I'll be down there in about an hour to watch the fun." He hesitated a bit, then replied: "OK, Jake, but you'll be sorry, very sorry."

I boarded the train from Chicago's northern suburbs to downtown. With a copy of *The Wall Street Journal* in hand and wearing my best pair of blue jeans, I sat and observed all the businessmen in suits. Everyone of them looked alike to me—unhappy, going nowhere in their humdrum jobs, void of excitement and potential. As for me, delusions of grandeur danced in my head. "What a dull life these people must lead," I said to myself as I glanced over the commodity section of the Journal. "No need for me to wear a suit. I'm making money in the market. All I need worry about is how to spend it. . . . What color should my Jaguar be?"

Before long, the train chugged its way into the Canal Street station and I boarded a taxi to the Chicago Mercantile Exchange. As I entered this realm of fast money and fast markets, I felt more at home. This was a game I understood . . . and it had been so easy to learn! I must be a natural at this; a born winner. My anticipation was beyond control. This game was so very easy, once you knew the ropes. It was almost boring, I thought.

I add here parenthetically that I had, by this time, lost every remnant of common sense, good sense, market sense, self sense, and logic. I had clearly entered a fantasy world that was being fed by my own delusional system, by my own wish fulfillment, and by my own mental masturbation. And I can tell you that I have never been back to that place since. The fate that awaited me was a classic case of what learning psychologists call *one trial learning*—an experience whose consequences are so intense, so extreme that the lesson is learned immediately and never forgotten.

It was only a quick elevator ride up to Joe's office and into the "boiler room." My sophistry continued all the way up the elevator. I knew that the market had already opened and half way expected a cheer to well up in the roomful of brokers as I made my grand entrance. But a distinctly different reception awaited me. I looked for Joe's smiling face but I didn't find it. In fact, Joe didn't look so good. "What's up, Joe," I quipped. "Not bellies," he answered as he handed me several order tickets showing where I had bought my bellies and where I had been sold out. In disbelief I looked at the tickets several times. I was out of most of my position at limit down, but I was unable to get filled on several contracts since the market was "locked" at limit down.

This was a new experience for me. I had no idea that a market could stop trading due to a lack of buyers. I was unable to sell my remaining bellies for two more days. Then, finally, when the market started trading again I sold out, glad to be out at the low price for the day. I called Joe for the damage report. The news was brief and devastating, but not unexpected; I had been wiped out on my very first trade!

The End and the Beginning

The story ends here. But it also begins here. For this was the real beginning of my commodity education. How much I made or lost was not the important thing. What was significant was the lesson itself. I was much more fortunate than many stock and commodity traders. For I, at least, had lost back only what I had made. There are countless others who daily lose much more than they can afford. And despite their charts, graphs, inside information, tips, systems, and news, their losses keep rising.

Having no speculative funds left, I fortunately had no choice but to stay out of the market. This was a blessing in disguise. In my thirst for knowledge and in my efforts to intellectualize the loss, I was driven to the writings of Bernard M. Baruch, Jesse Livermore, W. D. Gann, Burton Pugh, Arthur Cutten, and others. The resulting education was not in technique, which is very important, but in self-awareness. My experience did not indicate that my technique itself was at fault, but rather my attitude was at the base of this loss, as it is for virtually every loss. Had I traded only one contract, I might have had many other opportunities to prove the system, but the system did not get a valid test because of my personal shortcomings. By being overconfident, by fantasizing that I was a modern day Jesse Livermore, I became blind to the truth. By ignoring the basics of "know thyself," I became an instant loser. In the sense that we are all subject to emotion, we are all vulnerable to losses.

The painful lesson I had learned only needed to be learned once. It marked the beginning of my career as a serious futures trader and it marked the end of my days as a totally undisciplined trader. Today, more than 22 years after my painful experience, I am still struggling with issues of self-discipline, but the struggle becomes less difficult with each completed trade. The fight against emotion will never end. It will always haunt traders and it will always lurk in the background as a deteriorating influence. The best we can hope for is to limit its negative influences.

Systems and Traders

A trading system is an inanimate scheme that cannot win or lose. A car without a driver is only a shell consisting of metal and mechanical parts. It can go nowhere without a driver. It can only stand in one spot and look attractive. A car with a destructive driver becomes an instrument of death. It can be driven into a brick wall, and despite all its beauty and mechanical perfection, it has served no one well. However, in the hands of an experienced driver, a car can achieve unbelievable feats of speed and performance.

Trading systems are vehicles that must be piloted skillfully through the traffic and carefully through the curves and highways. The advanced computer hardware and software technology of the 1990s has given us powerful tools for finding and testing trading systems, signals, and timing indicators. But the effort is for naught unless the results can be applied in a disciplined and consistent fashion.

What follows in this book is about traders, not systems. Systems have no feelings, no emotions, and no faults. They are what they are. Traders can take good systems and turn them into outstanding results, acceptable results, or deplorable results. A good system in the hands of a fool is a worthless system. A mediocre system in the hands of a skilled practitioner is an excellent system.

Stock and futures trading depends more upon the ability of the trader or investor more than any other single variable. But none of this will do you any good unless you can recognize problems, evaluate potential solutions, and apply those solutions consistently. Not too many years ago, I had the good fortune to spend a few hours privately with W. Clement Stone, a man who, beginning with less than nothing in his childhood, managed to build one of the largest and most wealthy insurance empires in the world. In response to my queries about the secret of his success, Clem responded:

> in order to achieve success you need to see, think, and do . . . you need to let yourself see objectively the opportunities and problems which exist . . . you need to think about solutions or opportunities, but most important of all, you need to take action.

Without action, the possibility of positive change is extremely limited. There are few things in life that take care of themselves. Problems, if left to themselves, will most often go from bad to worse. Trading problems must first be recognized as problems. Potential solutions must then be evaluated, and finally, action must be taken.

The Need to Take Risk

Since the first days of recorded history, the urge or need to speculate has been a driving factor in the development of humankind. Although the cultural growth and technological advancement of civilizations have liberated us from the more crude forms of risk taking, many of us are still risk takers at heart, although we may not be willing to admit to it. In fact, many of us are not consciously aware of how risk-laden our lives really are. Risk is an inherent aspect of life. The primordial roots of what we today term "speculation" are found in prehistoric man's struggle against a multiplicity of foes—animal, human, and climatic.

Since the earliest days of recorded history, the farmer who has set seed in the ground or raised animals on the hoof has been constantly engaged in gambling on nature. Should he plant early? Will there be sufficient moisture to support a crop of corn? Will there be an early frost? Are prices now best for marketing his crop? Will there be demand for my animals? Will weight gains be slowed by extreme weather? Will disease strike my animals? And in more recent years, the producer has been plagued by questions such as: Will government actions adversely affect prices for my products? Will my banker lend me the money to support my operations? Will my bank fail? If they do, will I get my money back? How can international events affect prices? What's the economic outlook?

We often fail to realize the risk and uncertainty in our daily lives. In fact, we are by nature speculative beings. Living as we do in a world of constant change, instability, aggression, and uncertainty, we must be willing to accept the potentially ephemeral nature of our existence. To drive an automobile, fly in a plane, or even walk on the streets, we must be willing to speculate on the outcome of our actions and of those around us. Consider the menace of the drunk driver or the action of terrorists against planes. And with the growing threat of AIDS, even sexual activities have become more dangerous than ever before. Check into a hospital and the statistics show you have a considerable risk of infection, death, mismedication, and/or unnecessary treatment and misdiagnosis.

And some of us consciously seek an even higher degree of risk. Driven by a variety of needs—emotional, physical, and financial—some of us attempt to increase our personal wealth, knowing all the while that we are attempting to do so in a way that could jeopardize what we now possess. For many, the freely accepted challenge of the markets provides a high-risk game of financial life and death. For some, the markets offer a profession, providing steady and above-average income. For the very few, they are a mighty engine which can, with skill, be used to create vast wealth.

What are the motivating factors that drive individuals to speculate? What are the traits that differentiate successful speculators from those destined to failure? Are there, indeed, ways in which speculative performance can be improved? What, if any, are the psychological forces that underlie success or failure in the world of stocks and futures? Can the necessary and appropriate behaviors be learned? Is successful speculation more a product of the speculator than of the system he or she is employing? How can one determine his or her standing in the speculative world?

Inasmuch as my original training and profession were in the area of clinical psychology, it was not difficult for me to recognize the numerous emotional and psychological factors involved in the markets and in the mind of the trader. My experience as a futures trader, combined with my experience as a psychologist helped me recognize the existence of a very close relationship between speculation, success, and emotional stability.

After spending considerable time in the study of human behavior and personality, I was attracted, quite fortuitously, to the futures and stock markets. At first I saw little, if any, relationship between my profession as a clinical psychologist and my market hobby. As the days passed and my losses increased, I reached an awareness that changed not only my life, but my fortunes as well. Once I recognized the close relationship between these two seemingly diverse fields—psychology and trading— the road to personal and financial success was considerably easier to travel and better defined. Until then, I felt like most traders—a small and anxious child attempting to be heard above the loud voices of traders in the pit.

Traders, Investors, and Success

Regardless of education, background, intellectual ability, and effort, there are some individuals who are extremely successful in the markets. On the other hand, there are those who spend virtually every free moment studying the ups and downs of prices only to fail time and time again. I have personally known traders who had little or no understanding of the fundamentals behind price movements, but who, despite this seeming liability, have acquired considerable wealth through trading the markets. I have known traders who similarly had no understanding of the markets and who lost repeatedly. I have always been intrigued by what I perceived as an inverse relationship between intellectual ability and success in the markets. It seemed to me that the less intelligent traders I knew, were more consistently successful than those I knew, who were intellectually and analytically inclined. If this was indeed the case, then I was certainly interested in determining why.

What differentiates losers from winners? The question is not only intriguing, but also very valuable in the lessons it can teach us. Why did legendary speculators such as Livermore, Baruch, and Gann place such great emphasis on personal development, self-control, and emotional stability? Were these qualities the real reasons behind their success? Is it possible to be a market winner without thorough knowledge of the market? Is an education in the self more important than an education in market techniques, systems, or methods? What are the more valuable lessons a trader can learn? How can these lessons be learned and applied in a consistent, money-making fashion?

Invariably, there will be those one-time winners who strike it rich in the markets or in real estate ventures. But such successes by novices are few and far between. Lasting success in the market, or for that matter in any other venture, is most often a function of experience, insight, and self-discipline. While some individuals appear to come by these skills naturally, it is more likely that they acquire them through subtle and direct learning experiences, most of which occur in the formative childhood years. An individual who does not acquire these skills during childhood, is not locked in to a life of failure. The good news is that these skills can be acquired at virtually any time given appropriate learning and understanding.

Much has been said in support of the genetic argument for financial success. There are those who take refuge in deterministic ideas, claiming, for example, that certain ethnic groups or nationalities have a predisposition for success; that they control the markets; that they have inherited the ability to trade effectively, or that they are doomed to failure as a result of their ancestry. While it is true that genetic differences exist, it is also true that learning plays a very important part in the success equation. It is virtually impossible to separate the effects of heredity from those of the environment.

Hence the issue is primarily an academic one. Unfortunately, there are those who use the issue to rationalize their own failures or to explain away the successes of others. Taking solace in such excuses is a waste of effort as well as a psychological mechanism used to avoid dealing with reality. These issues will be discussed in considerable detail later on.

In addition to the abuse of genetic arguments as a rationalization for failure, some skeptics claim that speculation in stocks and/or futures is merely a form of legalized gambling, and this may very well be true in some cases. Although those who know both themselves, as well as the markets, there is virtually no relationship between gambling and speculation in stocks or futures. I will devote considerable attention later in this book to the gambling versus speculation controversy.

The Philosophers' Words

I'd venture to say that few of my readers will be familiar with the works and life of G. I. Gurdjieff or his fellow theosophist philosophers such as Ouspensky, Blavatsky, or C. W. Leadbetter. In fact, the theosophical school of philosophy is unfamiliar to even a vast majority of those with "higher" educations. This is likely so, because the teachings of theosophy are so basic that they threaten the psychological stability of all but the most well-developed minds. Many of the more popular philosophical movements have rejected theosophy for a variety of reasons, all of which are open to debate. Gurdjieff has been criticized as a charlatan and Blavatsky rejected as a fraud. Yet there are staunch supporters of theosophy who are well respected. It is certain that the conflicts will never be resolved.

My studies of Gurdjieff and Ouspensky have helped me discover many truths about myself and about life. I will share some of these with you later on. However, before beginning, I'd like to briefly mention one of the insights I achieved through my readings of Gurdjieff. The system which he proposed for achieving self knowledge was complex and difficult to accomplish. It required years of study, several under the direct supervision of the master himself. Once Gurdjieff was approached by a frustrated and dejected student who complained about the difficult physical and mental tasks which were part of his self-education. "Why must this work be so difficult?" asked the disgruntled student. Upon brief reflection, Gurdjieff replied confidently "so that your future will not be the same as your past". And I give the same answer to those who ask why they must work hard at self understanding in order to achieve lasting and consistent success in the markets. If you are pleased with your results, and if your market performance has been consistent, then you do not need to read any further. If, however, you feel that you can do better; that you are not achieving your full potential as a trader or as an investor; that you are missing some key ingredients in the formula or success; then you must read on.

What I've Seen and What I'm Doing about It

After years of watching traders defeat themselves, and after years of watching myself become my own instruments of destruction, I have learned that we alone are responsible for most of our failures and/or successes. I have been guilty of repetition in telling you that the self is the single most important variable in the equation for success. But by the time you have finished this book I will be guilty of even more repetition. Why? Because it is impossible to drive this point home as fully as necessary without repetition. Self is the most difficult thing to understand; more difficult than understanding the objective sciences and more difficult to understand than mathematics. Self is elusive, ever-changing and worst of all, defensive. Self consists of many selves. No person is always the same self. What prompts a trader to act in a particular way in one situation on a given day, may evoke an entirely different reaction in the same situation on another day. It is this seeming inconsistency which makes self so difficult to understand. In order to objectively evaluate virtually any situation, we must stand away from it and evaluate it with clarity and reasonable objectivity. It is difficult, at times impossible, to stand away from the self and evaluate it objectively.

The chapters that follow are, therefore, intended to provide a road map to the self. The Bible says "know thyself," and in this sense my writings are designed to be a chapter in the trader's bible to self-knowledge. Note that I have set only a modest goal. I seek to write only a chapter in the bible of self knowledge. I do so since I understand well the immense complexity and intricacy which constitutes self knowledge. If you can add to your library of self knowledge my chapter, then you will likely be that much closer to your goal. In knowing where you stand psychologically, you will know how to get where you want to be financially via the most direct and successful route.

2

Many Markets—
Many Similarities

In writing the first edition of this book, it was necessary for me to ignore many of the golden rules held for so many years by so many investors and traders. In writing this edition, I find that it is still necessary for me to part company with the traditional, focusing instead on the basic unfiltered truth about the markets. Some of my ideas and points of view may arouse controversy, anger, and fear . . . and you may reject them as useless. I suggest, however, that you give them serious consideration before reaching your conclusions. Remember, my ideas are not new; in fact, they are among the oldest known. What's different, is that I seek to define the most basic aspects of all markets; aspects that are a function of human interaction and emotion, as opposed to economic principle and theory. Investing, trading, buying, selling, "scalping," spread trading, options trading, options writing, options strategies, and arbitrage in their various forms are all variations on one theme: They are all forms of betting on the future. They have one goal—profit. They are all forms, therefore, of *speculation.*

Speculation has been with us since the earliest recorded history. Speculation and life are so intimately intertwined that not to speculate means not to exist. The true success of the words I write can be measured only by their ability to awaken in others those sleeping giants waiting to express themselves. Let but one loser rise up and become a winner, and my work will have been done.

Knowledge is power, according to a well-worn truism. This statement is too general. It is more meaningful to say that self-knowledge is power. It is self-knowledge that I will discuss in detail throughout this book. If you believe that I or anyone else can provide you with a sure-fire formula for wealth and success in the markets, then you are wrong. If you believe that those who have acquired vast fortunes in the marketplace have done so through well-protected secrets, then you are also incorrect. If you believe that you can attain market success through a positive, self-confident attitude, through emotional control and appropriate motivation, then you are on the right track and are likely to find some very meaningful answers in the pages that follow. In placing only minor emphasis on the basics of trading, market fundamentals, and economic factors, I am not discounting their importance. I am, however, departing from the old tradition of technique and placing major emphasis on the individual person who must act upon the information. We are not all fortunate enough to be Baruchs, Wykoffs, or Livermores. We must learn *how to* rather than *why to*. Economics can tell us why things happen. Indeed, economics may tell us that things are going to happen, but it won't tell us how to make the future work for us. Knowing how to make the future into a reality that is beneficial financially requires the type of education not offered heretofore between the covers of a single book. True, knowledge of the masters has been available in bits and pieces, but a work devoted exclusively to the psychological aspects of trading and investment has had to wait for its time. And that time is now.

A Brief Overview of the Markets

The operational principles of all markets are similar. Whether involved in stocks, futures, real estate, or even retail marketing, buyers and sellers respond to many of the same economic influences, fundamental factors, and news items. Traders respond to their own perceptions of reality. And perceptions differ, at times markedly, from one individual to another. Perceptions are also modified by factors that are internal to the individual. Traders must cope with forces and conflicts within themselves. This is why the basic facts of trading, as they have been taught or understood traditionally, are relatively unimportant. Perhaps a different perspective about market basics will help us achieve a more functional psychological understanding as opposed to a purely academic orientation. What follows, therefore, is my view of the markets from a psychological point of view, designed as a prerequisite to our analysis of trader and investor behavior.

Since I will focus primarily on the individual and the group rather than the market, only a general overview of traditional market terminology is necessary. Virtually every operational aspect of the markets has psychological and behavioral correlates. "Operational aspects" in this case refers to things such as trading volume, open interest, chart patterns, price orders, the role of brokers, the mechanics of pit or floor trader behavior, fundamental reports, news, market sentiment, short sales, price limits, and a host of other market-related facts, behaviors and phenomena. On a purely operational level, each of these factors has an objective and relatively mechanical definition. However, their ramifications in actual practice go well beyond the simple operational definitions.

Consider, for example, the term *daily price limit.* In futures trading, the daily price limit is defined simply as the maximum permissible price fluctuation in points, dollars, or cents from the previous daily closing price. A move of 150 points up or down from the previously daily close in live cattle futures, is the daily price limit for this market. While this definition is specific, its ramifications are immense. For one thing, the mere mention of "daily price limit" stimulates fear and panic in the mind of many traders. Fear of what? Fear of being "locked in" to a market on the wrong side. A limit move in one direction or another frequently forces a trading halt at the limit price since there are no traders willing to sell at limit up or to buy at limit down. Although this happens rarely, it is a fact of life in futures trading. And some markets, orange juice in particular, have had a history of locked limit moves for several days in succession.

What are the psychological implications of limit moves? Being locked into the market is a nearly universal fear among traders. The idea of not being able to exit a position that has gone against you is akin to being locked into a closet or to being locked into an airplane for takeoff. There is a sense of no control, of being powerless, and of having your destiny determined by others. To some traders, the fear of being locked into a market is so intense that it affects trading decisions. The fear can easily cause a trader to avoid trades that might otherwise have been profitable. Many traders are fearful of buying near limit down or of selling short near limit up. While the fear of being locked into the market is their main concern, the facts tell quite a different story. Limit moves up often, but not always, come near the end of a move up and limit moves down often occur near the bottom of a bear market. Yes, there are notable exceptions. But there are specific ways to avoid the dangers of limit moves and, furthermore, the incidence of successive limit moves is rare and often specific to certain markets such as orange juice, pork bellies, and live hogs. Some markets have no trading limits. Does the absence of trading limits in given markets make them more or less palatable to those who are fearful of being locked in? As a matter of fact, this alternative is often considered unacceptable as well. Why? Because the market could move sharply in one direction or another without offering the "protection" of a limit. In this case, there are other fears such as bad price fills on stop orders and the negative fantasy of a virtually "unlimited" loss. But there are specific ways in which these fears and risks can be minimized provided one's thinking is clear and objective.

To the emotion-driven trader, objective alternatives to such fears are relatively meaningless. And they will remain meaningless until the true relationship between self and the markets has been understood. This example which, by the way, has been explored thus far only in minimal detail demonstrates the significant differences between cold, hard market facts, and their emotional or behavioral consequences and correlates. Detailed analyses of other emotional correlates to market facts will be given later.

Stocks, Futures, and Other Markets— Similarities and Differences

In theory, the price of all goods and services in a free market rises and falls in magnitude as a function of what buyers, at any one time and place offer to pay, and what sellers, at the same time and place, demand to receive for them. It is generally assumed that economic conditions, supply, demand, sales, corporate management ability, governmental policy, international conditions, weather, and corporate profits all influence the movement of stock prices up and down. And, we are told many of the same influences, but in particular weather, crop conditions, as well as supply and demand, influence the price movements in the futures markets.

The object of all trading and investing is to either buy low and sell high, to buy high and sell higher, to sell short at a high price and buy back at a lower price, to sell at a low price and buy back at a still lower price, or to engage in any number of combinations and variations on these themes using various vehicles such as stock or futures options, spreads, option strategies, arbitrage, and so on. Regardless of which market vehicle we examine, the principles of operation are similar and, above all, the elements of psychology are similar.

The real estate market, for example, one to which many individuals can relate, is basically no different from the stock market. One buys and sells properties either to make a profit or to avoid a larger loss. Instead of a single, central exchange, these properties, either vacant land, farmland, residential or commercial buildings, are bought and sold through commissioned real estate brokers. Real estate brokers are tested, regulated, and licensed, as are stock and futures brokers.

The real estate market moves more slowly than the stock market, but in most other aspects the two are similar. In the stock market, one can borrow money from one's broker in order to purchase a stock. This loan, called *margin,* allows the buyer increased *leverage* (the ability to buy more for less). In real estate, the prospective buyer borrows from a bank. This allows the purchase of a home or piece of property for about 10 to 30 percent of its selling price.

Futures trading is somewhat more complex but is also closely related to stocks and real estate. Instead of buying and selling pieces of property, shares in a company, or land, traders exchange contracts for the delivery of goods (commodities) at some point in the future. Hence the term *futures contract.* The individual who buys a futures contract at a given price stands to profit if the price rises. As in the case of stocks and real estate, the object is to buy at a low price and/or to sell at a high price, or more often, to buy at a high price and sell at an even higher price. Margin is also used. With futures, however, only 1 to 5 percent of the total purchase money is necessary to complete the transaction. Consequently, a much smaller amount of a buyer's money is necessary to make or to lose large money. In comparison with other markets, futures trading is the most speculative and most dynamic. It is also the most potentially dangerous and potentially profitable.

One of the key differences between stocks and futures in comparison to real estate is the ability to sell short. There is no way, as yet, to sell a piece of property short and, as a result, there is no way to make money in a declining real estate market. Perhaps this is what makes real estate slumps last so long and hurt so much.

All of the financial markets have common elements. First and foremost, they involve the exchange of money for goods. Second, they can all result in a profit or a loss. And third, they all depend in varying degrees on human beings for their fluctuation and liquidity. The act of buying or selling must be performed by people. While computers can replace people, human involvement is necessary at some point in the chain. There are those who claim that all the functions involved in investing and speculation can be performed by computer; I however, am extremely skeptical and doubt that such a day will ever come. The human element is the quintessential aspect of all markets, particularly its emotional factor. It is the human element that is the single common thread among all markets. To understand people is, therefore, to understand the markets. Once you understand yourself, your motivation, and the motivation of others, you will understand all markets no matter what their specific product may be.

While the mechanical aspects of market operation are simple to understand, requiring only study and memorization of various facts, the motivating factors behind market movements are less definitive and require considerably more study. People move markets. To understand people, one must first understand oneself. Hence, it is not only necessary to know the basics of market terminology and operation, but, in order to invest successfully, it is also necessary to be familiar with the workings of the human mind, as well as the principles of human behavior.

Success in the Market

Each market has its unique terminology. To acquire a better working knowledge of each market's basic instruments, you will need to read and study intensively. But don't be fooled into thinking that such knowledge assures success in the markets. Many traders have been able to achieve an outstanding depth of knowledge about the markets, yet they are losers. On the other hand, there are many traders who have virtually no understanding of the markets, but who have managed to achieve great success in spite of what seems to be a limitation of considerable importance. Furthermore, an understanding of the fundamental factors that drive the markets is also unnecessary for success.

A number of years ago, I had the good fortune to meet a floor trader from the Chicago Mercantile Exchange who helped me understand this point. His specialty was the futures market in Treasury bills. After briefly discussing our common market interests, I asked his opinion about the long-term outlook for interest rates. "What's an interest rate?" he replied. "What do you mean 'what's an interest rate?'" I retorted in amazement. "I don't know what an interest rate is," he reiterated. "I know that interest rates have something to do with T-bills, but I'm not quite sure how they're related," he explained. "But if you don't know what interest rates are and how they're related to Treasury bill futures, how can you trade the market?" I asked in total disbelief. "Oh, that's easy," he quipped, "all I need to know is that a one point move in T-bills is worth $25."

This true story tells in simple form what might take many months to teach. Here is the case of a very successful floor trader who buys and sells futures contracts many times daily, but who has no knowledge other than how to buy and sell. He is basically ignorant of the many fundamental facts that affect prices. This information vacuum, in a sense, has been a friend to our floor trader. He can relate to the market only as he sees it, without external and often extraneous influences.

This is not to say that a thorough knowledge of the markets and the factors that influence them cannot facilitate success. However, my example demonstrates that there are other important qualities that may be necessary if the investor or trader is to achieve consistent success. I have deviated from the traditional explanations of stock and futures trading. I have chosen, rather, to place only limited emphasis on the mechanics, definitions, fundamentals, explanations, and trading systems that are held so near and dear by so many traders. There are many books about trading and investing that can serve as excellent reference works in this area, but there are few good books about the internal aspect of trading.

My emphasis in this book will be almost exclusively on the internal and external processes of human behavior as they relate to the ultimate profit or loss of trading. I will assume that you have acquired the prerequisite working knowledge of trading and investing. I will attempt to convince you that the individual seeking to improve his or her investment success need not spend hours studying the theories of economics, the details of market supply and demand, or the rules of price charting. My experiences as a trader, and my observation of traders have convinced me that your time will be best spent studying the theories and principles of human and animal psychology. It is from this understanding that lasting success as an investor or speculator can be achieved.

REVIEW

1. Stocks, futures, and real estate all function on the same basic economic principles.
2. Aside from the basics of how to place orders, vocabulary, terminology, and knowledge of the risks involved, no further understanding of the markets is required in order for success to be achieved.

3. A trader may profit handsomely as well as consistently in the financial markets with only a working knowledge of the markets themselves.

4. More important than any of the above is the trader's ability to know and remain in touch with him or herself. The emotional factors that comprise the markets are perhaps the only factors that must be known fully if success is to follow.

5. Those who do not have a very basic understanding of market functioning should acquire it prior to reading the remaining chapters.

3

Psychology and the Markets: Similarities and Differences

Although this book is not a psychology text, several basic psychological concepts and historical developments in the study of human behavior must be understood before the markets themselves can be viewed from a psychological perspective. This introduction is a general discussion about the psychological functioning of organisms, human and nonhuman. For a more detailed picture, you can read one of many comprehensive, contemporary texts (see Bibliography).

Scientists, theologians, occultists, and others have, for thousands of years, advanced theories to explain human behavior. Their hypotheses have ranged from the astrological on one extreme to medical on the other. Explanations have varied from demonic possession to self-determinist. And in every case, the popular theories have been very much a reflection of the times. What is considered deviant behavior in some societies is not even noteworthy in others. In fact, aberrant human behavior is very much a function of the society in which it occurs. Certain pathological behaviors are society specific. Still other behaviors appear to remediate themselves when left "untreated" and "unnamed." The mere act of designating a behavior as deviant by naming it appears to perpetuate its prevalence and persistence.

The complex interaction of life experiences and social structures molds an even more complex picture of human behavior. At times, the factors affecting human beings appear so numerous and varied that any attempt to understand them seems futile. And yet on another level, human behavior can be seen as nothing more than a series of stimulus response connections and interactions. Indeed, the behavioral school of

21

psychology has viewed human behavior in terms of stimulus-response theories.

During the Dark Ages, the mysteries of human behavior were no less a problem than they are today. In attempting to deal with the demons that supposedly arose from within, human beings employed peculiar and sadistic techniques during the dark ages—techniques that persisted for many years beyond the "enlightened age" of the Renaissance. Whether in the form of trephining (drilling a hole in one's head to release the evil spirits) or bloodletting, they were doomed to failure. We take false comfort in the erroneous conclusion that as the human race became more "enlightened" and abandoned magical cures, we adopted practices that were more humane, more reasonable, more logical, more likely to be effective. To a certain extent this is true. Yet, even today we still use such techniques as electroconvulsive therapy that "shocks" patients back to reality, or insulin coma therapy which overdoses patients with insulin, thereby inducing a temporary coma that is expected to reverse the psychotic processes.

The root cause of barbarism and sadism administered in the name of psychological treatment is a painfully evident lack of knowledge about what stimulates and maintains human behavior. If we knew more about what "makes" behavior happen perhaps we'd know more about how to change it or how to control it, assuming that change and control are desirable.

Through years of trial and error (mostly error), systems and theories of human psychology were developed to explain behavior and to treat behavior gone astray. At best, the theories have seemed reasonable, however, in most cases, treatments arising from these theories has been no more effective than the black-magic cures of shamans. In fact, until recently, researchers have been content to merely explain behavior realizing that their state of ignorance would not yet allow the prediction and control of human behavior. The ethics of these issues have further complicated the situation.

Generally, the journey toward an effective understanding of the human psyche has been a slow and difficult one encompassing hundreds of years. Despite dramatic technological advances in other sciences, psychology and psychiatry are still very much in their youth. This is perhaps due to the fact that humankind is resistant to finding out the truth about itself. There is a desire to avoid the pain that often comes with truth. The true facts may produce stress and pain rather than the bliss of ignorance—and so it is with many traders and investors. Roadblocks, self-imposed to be sure, are constantly being thrown in our paths. The enemy lies not in the external environment, rather it dwells within. Fortunately, there has been steady progress in the study of human psychology since the 1970s. We have developed more definitive techniques for understanding and changing behavior.

In the modern psychological world, there are essentially two dichotomous schools of thought, which are theoretically similar to the two divergent schools of thought currently popular in the trading world. Traders and investors generally align themselves with either the technical or fundamental approach to market analysis. Some traders, whose methods are not pure enough for either group, employ a hybrid approach to the decision-making process. Since many investors can relate well to the continuum of technician versus fundamentalist, I will introduce the two divergent schools of psychological thought within the framework of technical versus fundamental.

In the futures and stock markets, the fundamentalist point of view focuses exclusively on economically based indicators which, it is believed, facilitate the process of price forecasting or trade selection. The various fundamental indices are incorporated either individually or in combination to arrive at trading decisions. Such basic factors as crop size, weather conditions, supply and demand statistics, economic forecasts, interest rates trends. Federal Reserve policy, export statistics, plantings, breeding intentions, housing starts, cross currency rates, government programs, and consumption are taken into account. The essence of this approach is to determine the balance of supply and demand in order to determine how it will affect future prices.

The purpose of fundamental analysis is to determine what the price of a given stock or futures market may be in several days, weeks, months or years. The accuracy of the decisions depends to a great extent on the availability and accuracy of information. It also depends to a certain degree upon the prevalence of "normal" conditions. Any exaggerated shift or aberration in conditions can distort the data and, therefore, the outcome as well.

Real estate investors are subject to the same limitations and potential problems when analyzing fundamentals. There may be new fundamentals that have not played an important role in the past, or not all of the fundamentals may be known. Furthermore, the fundamentals may be incorrect or may be incorrectly interpreted.

The technician, on the other hand, makes judgments by purely mechanical and/or mathematical rules. The technician is not concerned with the economy, supply, demand, crop size, earnings, or weather. Technicians study specific chart formations, mathematical indicators, moving average signals, geometric formations, cyclical events, and so forth. Even those who trade the markets according to astrology are technicians of a sort because they follow very specific guidelines in arriving at decisions. Insofar as they are true to their principles, technicians do not consider any inputs other than their data when reaching trading decisions. The avowed chartist is a technician dedicated to following specific kinds of chart patterns. Chartists will ideally refuse to waste time either reading or discussing the fundamentals. Such information can only confuse the issue.

Being a market technician has certain advantages: it permits greater objectivity; it allows for more mechanical execution of trades; and it deals with the true data and its derivatives, namely, prices, volume, and open interest, and mathematical derivations of these indicators. On the negative side, the technical approach isolates the trader from worldwide events, which can and do impact on markets significantly. For the technician, this limitation is more of an asset than a liability inasmuch as it excludes from the calculations unquantifiable fundamental developments.

Ultimately, the relative success of each market orientation seems to be more a function of the trader than of the approach itself. In fact, despite the seeming objectivity of technical trading rules and of fundamental statistics, the end result is almost entirely dependent on who interprets the data. This point will be covered in considerable detail later on.

There is a third and less well-defined school of market forecasting. It consists of traders who are either too uncertain about the two major techniques or who are too insecure about being totally committed to one side to the exclusion of the other. Their eclectic approach leads them to accept input from as many sources as possible, both technical and fundamental. The rationale behind this approach is very simple. Since information from any source may be helpful, it is prudent to gather as much of it as possible. "Open all the floodgates," such traders reason, "and we're in a better position to isolate the best trades and trends." Those who favor this approach subscribe to as many publications, advisory services, and newsletters as their budgets will permit.

There would be nothing wrong with this approach if market fluctuations did indeed correlate closely with the information that traders study. The major drawback to this type of market analysis is that very often the amount of information available is overwhelming, contradictory, and confusing. Frequently, when all indicators are in agreement, the opposite event occurs. And all too often, weak traders are paralyzed by the sheer magnitude of information that confronts them.

There is yet one more category of market analysis that is not really a category at all—in fact, it is a nontechnique. Those who trade or invest in the markets using this nontechnique attend selectively to whatever they desire. One day they may buy for a reason that will be used as a rationale for selling the very next day. They do not justify their trading on any basis other than "gut feeling." Typically, floor traders fall into this category. Their seat-of-the-pants, dead-reckoning technique works well—but only for them. The trading public has little understanding of how the pit trader trades. In actuality, the trading goal and style of the floor trader is distinctly different from the goals and methods of the general public.

There is little to be said either pro or con about this nontechnique. If it succeeds, then it is good; if it fails, then it is not useful. The importance of this approach is not whether it is a successful method or one doomed to failure. It is important by virtue of two distinct facts. First, it is a well-known fact that a vast majority of traders use no trading system whatsoever, whether technical or fundamental. Second, it is this nontechnique that allows the trader or investor to succeed or fail almost exclusively as a result of his or her trading discipline which is an outgrowth of trader psychology.

The science of price forecasting is relatively young. In fact, there is doubt as to whether it can indeed be called a science. Some individuals and research groups have constructed complex econometric models to assist in their prediction efforts, and they find it possible, through the use of computer technology, to forecast economic trends well in advance. This technique has also spilled over to the stock and commodity markets. In essence, it is a fundamental method that still requires interpretation. Despite recent advances, the relative infancy of economic forecasting makes it clear that we have much more to learn. This same youthful awkwardness is found in the science of psychology. In fact, psychologists and psychiatrists typically align themselves along a continuum comparable to that of investors.

In any academic field, there are usually many schools of thought. The extreme points of view are found at opposite ends and variations on each theme are found between the two poles. This model can be used to represent anything from religious groupings to political affiliation. Market fundamentalists and pure technicians fall at opposite poles while other types of market analysts cluster at different points somewhere inbetween.

And so it is with psychologists and psychiatrists. On one extreme, we find the traditional Freudians while on the other reside the behaviorists.

The traditional psychologist is essentially similar to the market fundamentalist. He studies what he believes to be the underlying causes of human behavior. He is concerned with such issues as:

- Why do people act the way they do?
- What are the underlying causes of behavior and mental disturbance?
- How can we use the life history of an individual to help him?
- What motivates people to act in certain ways?
- What are the sexual conflicts, desires, and their developmental aspects that stimulate behavior?
- What are the unconscious processes that stimulate behavior?

These questions are very similar to those asked by the market fundamentalist. By seeking to determine the why of price movement and the underlying causes of market fluctuation, the fundamentalist is of the same general orientation as the traditional psychologist.

The behavioral psychologist, on the other hand, studies only overt and clearly measurable behavior. The behaviorist is interested in the following aspects of behavior:

- How often does a certain behavior occur?
- What are the events that maintain behavior?
- What happens before and after a given behavior?
- Can the behavior be changed by manipulation of environmental conditions?
- How long does it take to change behavior using certain methods?
- How long has the current behavior been present?

In asking these questions, the behaviorist is working on an essentially technical level. He is interested in measurement, detection of specific trends, frequency counts, and the application of operational techniques. This is very similar to the specific trend detection and measurement methods employed by market technicians. Although they cannot control or change market behavior, they look for overt symptoms and not underlying causes. The fundamental trader and the traditional psychologist are both concerned with underlying causes whereas the technician and behavioral psychologist are concerned with overt behavior.

Traditional Psychiatry and Psychology

The founders of traditional psychiatry were Josef Breuer and Sigmund Freud, two physicians who were in medical practice in Vienna at the end of the nineteenth century. During the early 1900s, Freud formulated a theory of human behavior by studying early childhood experiences and various theoretical structures of the human mind. Most actions, he felt, were the consequence of unconscious impulses and processes. His complete theory is complex, intricate, and difficult to explain in a limited amount of space. Freud and his followers felt that most behavior was shaped by the interaction of internal mechanisms.

The dream and its symbols were used as tools in the understanding of mental processes and behavior. An elaborate list of symbolic meanings was devised by some Freudians. In so doing it was theorized, the psychiatrist could ascertain the true reasons for an individual's behavior. By talking with the patient and employing various techniques, among them hypnosis, the conflicts could theoretically be resolved by getting the patient to see his behavior in relation to the underlying drives and attempts at repression. Whatever may have been troubling the patient could be "cured" given the proper use of this technique. This method was termed "psychoanalysis," otherwise known as the "talking cure."

The study and development of psychoanalysis and psychiatry spanned many years and immeasurable amounts of effort. Since this is not intended to serve as a text on the history or theory of psychology, my coverage of psychological principles will be limited. Those who wish to pursue the subject in greater detail will find a Bibliography at the end of this book. My sole intent in this ultra-brief overview is to familiarize readers with the most basic concepts in order to advance to the subject at hand—investor and trader psychology.

The Freudian school of psychiatry stimulated the growth of many other theoretical concepts. The Adlerians, Jungians, and Rankians are all followers of Freud's basic concepts to an extent, each rooted in a unique variation on Freud's theme. Each school has survived, and all have followers today. The most popular however, still remain the Freudian and neo-Freudian schools. The essence of Freudian-type theories rests in their reliance on "underlying cause." Their approach is therefore similar to the fundamentalist approach in speculation and investing. Each aspect of market movement has a specific explanation.

A market goes up because supply is small and demand is large; crops are poor; weather is bad. Prices go down because crops are large; export demand is slow; earnings are poor; sales are lagging, and so on. A patient acts anxious because of an early childhood trauma; he fears the vengeful arm of authority because he is fearful of his father; he fears his father because he has guilt about his own sexual attraction toward his mother; he fears punishment from his father. The Freudian approach to understanding human beings and the fundamentalist approach to market analysis rest on ascertaining and understanding underlying causes or fundamentals. In this respect, they are similar. As a matter of fact, the shortcomings, as well as the potential advantages of each approach are similar.

The Freudian school of human psychology is based on the "medical model" of treatment and analysis. In the same way that a physician attempts to isolate a germ or organic dysfunction as the causative agent in disease, the medically oriented therapist seeks to uncover the causes of undesirable behavior in order to "cure" the patient. This orientation is reflected in the medical training that all psychiatrists must have in order to practice. It is also seen in the medical approach to treatment of behavior disorders. Contemporary reliance on drugs and medication are outgrowths of the belief that medical treatments must alter the underlying cause of a disease or dysfunction. And the cause must be internal. And if the cause is internal, then it can probably be treated or helped with medicine. Hence the large number of tranquilizers and sleep medications taken by Westerners. The term "medical model" derives from its medical focus.

While the medical model of disease made significant inroads in medical treatment, many of its procedures have come into question since the 1980s. It has been shown that many human beings are disposed to certain diseases by genetic components and/or by psychological factors. Stress, depression, and negative self-concept tend to debilitate the immune system. Some theorists argue that cancer is exacerbated by psychological factors. And it has also been shown that psychological attitudes can either facilitate or limit the efficacy of medications. There is still much to learn about the interaction of behavior, genetics, environment, and the medical model of disease.

Behavioral Psychology

On the other extreme, we have the so-called behaviorists, beginning with John B. Watson, B. F. Skinner, Edward Lee Thorndike, and others. Their theories will be discussed in considerable detail later. For now, suffice it to say that their point of view is one that deals exclusively with symptoms and not with causes per se. Whereas the medically oriented practitioner will examine such things as guilt, unconscious processes, sexual fantasies, castration fears, and defense mechanisms, the behaviorist looks only at outward behavior or symptoms, believing that the only problems that can be treated are those we can see or otherwise describe. We cannot empirically observe unconscious processes but we can study the behavior that is produced by unconscious processes. And through the study of behavior, and behavior alone, we can determine what it is we want to change and the techniques we will use to change it. Behavioral treatment is based upon the application of conditioning or learning techniques according to the principles of Skinner, Watson, and Pavlov. The treatment techniques used by behavioral psychologists are primarily mechanical and have, therefore, been subjected to considerable criticism by those aligned with the medical model.

The numerous variations on the behavioral theme are closely related in their underlying theory. The essence of the behavioral model is very simple. It is assumed that the environment acts on or stimulates an organism. The organism then responds. Depending on the results of the organism's response, behavior becomes habitual or it is terminated. If the behavior brings about desirable consequences, then its likelihood of future repetition is good. If it does not bring the desired result, then a new behavior is attempted. In short, behavior is maintained as a function of its consequences.

The behavioral orientation is similar to the market orientation of the technician. Remember that the true technician watches for clues and symptoms of market direction. He acts upon the meaning of his signals and is totally unconcerned about the underlying cause or causes. Figure 3.1 characterizes the two extreme points of view regarding market analysis and human psychology.

With this simplified background in the basics of each approach to speculation and psychology, let's examine some of the other relevant aspects of psychology as they relate to speculation. There are many different areas within the field of psychology. One can devote a lifetime

Fundamentalist   Technician
Freudian   Behaviorist
Medical model   Conditioning model

Figure 3.1 Fundamentalist-technician continuum.

to studying the numerous theories and concepts or, alternatively the controversies and disagreements. So vast is this quasi-science that my discussion must be limited to those topics necessary to provide a working knowledge of the material presented here. If you are already familiar with the field, or even if you have had only an introductory course in psychology, then this is really all the information you need in order to benefit from this book.

My concern is primarily with those concepts and theories that can be applied to successful speculation. Here is the general plan I will follow. First, I will familiarize you with some of the positive aspects of various psychological approaches. I will then explain the mechanisms that regulate investor behavior in psychological terms. And finally, I will present an overview of how we can best use the teachings of psychology and psychiatry to maximize our success in speculation and investing.

REVIEW   Why study psychology in relation to speculation? Let me use my personal reasoning to explain how I got started.

1. I was cocky, overconfident, unrealistic, and conceited.
2. My knowledge of the markets themselves, their price behavior, and volatility was lacking.
3. These two combined to create a losing attitude.

This is most likely the same set of failures to which most traders fall prey. There are may things that can be done to alleviate item 2: classes in trading, reading, and direct experience can all help. But what about item 1? No amount of direct experience with the markets can change one's attitude toward the market. But self-knowledge can be the key to success. It's one thing to know that you're beating your head against the wall; it's a far greater achievement to know how to stop.

4

Psychoanalytic Theory—Do Childhood Experiences Affect Behavior?

The traditionally oriented psychologist or psychiatrist attributes many behaviors to unconscious motivation. The human mind is divided into three theoretical structures: the id, ego, and superego. These "structures" are responsible for behaviors that ultimately seek expression in waking and sleeping life. A child is born with basic needs related either to the taking in of food or the letting out of wastes. These are the child's greatest needs, and the child comes to see the world in relation to body openings. The mouth and all activities associated with it become centrally important in the reduction of a need state and the production of satisfaction. The fondness for oral satisfaction is then generalized to other oral activities such as biting, licking, and tasting. The world is experienced orally. This stage of development continues during the first year of life. These are *id impulses.*

Id impulses are essentially animal drives. They are the most basic needs of the organism, driving it to aggression, possessiveness, extreme emotions, and unchecked sexual acting out. Fear and greed are id impulses. Id impulses have an irrational or driven quality to them. The individual acting solely on id impulses does not stop to logically or intellectually consider the consequences of his or her behaviors. The process of socialization is one whereby id impulses are held in check in order that they are expressed at the right time and in the right way; right being determined socially.

The next issue of importance in the child's personality development, is sphincter control. During very early childhood, little emphasis is placed on the child's eliminative habits. But as the child grows older, parents begin to place more demands on the child for self-control. This represents the first arena of struggle between child and parent and, therefore, between child and the outer world. It is the first true experience between child and authority.

Freud suggested that activities surrounding elimination also take on a pleasurable tone. The central theme of Freud's theory is the "pleasure principle." The child acts in certain ways because they bring pleasure. Whether this pleasure be one associated with the actual eliminative process or one of control that the child exerts on the parents, it is, nevertheless, a pleasurable activity. If Freud's theories are correct, then many a personality has been shaped in response to toilet training issues.

Following toilet training and the opposition that it brings from the child, interest in the rectal area declines and shifts to the genitals. From what begins as curiosity, the child develops a profound interest in these parts not only as a result of their pleasure-giving ability, but also as a means of differentiating one sex from the other.

The important things to remember about a child's early development are:

1. The child functions on the Pleasure principle and
2. These experiences are not remembered later in life without considerable effort, if at all. The principle of "infantile amnesia" is a central feature of Freudian doctrine. It suggests that we cannot remember important childhood experiences and that, therefore, we do not have a thorough understanding of the forces which comprise or stimulate our current behaviors.
3. Conflicts between parent and child set the stage for later conflicts between the individual and society as a whole and for the individual vis-à-vis other individuals.

Castration Complex/Oedipal Complex

These two concepts are also cornerstones of Freudian theory. According to Freud, the child, at some point in his or her life, fears punishment by parents in the forms of castration. These perceived threats may result from the child's sexual attraction to the opposite-sexed parent. The guilt of such attraction and/or sexual fantasy is transformed into fear of reprisal by the other parent. Fear that a part of the body, particularly the sex organ, will be severed as punishment is called the *castration complex.*

There has always been heated controversy about this aspect of Freudian theory. Although Freud claimed that these experiences were common to all children at some point in their development, many social scientists assert quite arguably that this experience is not common to all children. Some respected psychologists and psychiatrists contend that very few children actually experience castration anxiety.

Still other social scientists have gathered considerable cross-cultural data that strongly suggests that castration anxiety is more of a cultural phenomenon than a universal fact. Freudians argue that since these feelings are buried deep in the unconscious mind, they cannot be remembered and it is impossible, therefore, to prove that they do not exist. The controversy continues today.

Following the very early stages of childhood personality development, the early instinctual life of the child makes a transition into what is called the *latency period.* The latency period is one during which the child develops what Freud called "defense mechanisms." An understanding of the various defense mechanisms is basic to an understanding of psychoanalytic theory. This elaborate system of protective attitudes, mental devices, and actions serves to defend the individual from a plethora of childhood memories and experiences that are either too painful to remember, or too threatening to cope with. There are appropriate and inappropriate defense mechanisms distinguished by the degree to which they remove an individual from the reality of a situation. While some protection from past psychological pain is acceptable, too much protection as well as the "wrong" type of protection are dangerous and exhibit themselves in psychological pathologies known as neuroses and psychoses. Here is a brief listing of the various defense mechanisms posited by Freud. Inasmuch as defense mechanisms are very important in achieving a thorough understanding of trader behavior, they will be more fully explained as my presentation of trader behavior and psychology is developed.

Sublimation. This term describes a process of refining childhood impulses into socially acceptable behavior. Freud and his followers maintained that unacceptable childhood behaviors such as thumb sucking, smearing of feces, withholding of feces, and so on are transformed into acceptable acts in adulthood. Withholding of feces, for example, can be sublimated into stamp collecting, money hoarding, a tenacious personality, or any behavior that can be interpreted as "holding in" or "collecting."

It is an individual's ability or lack thereof to sublimate, or express in a socially acceptable fashion, id impulses that facilitates or retards social development; that either insures success or guarantees failure in life, business, and personal relationships. The difference between a football player and a murderer is the ability to sublimate aggressive needs; one method works well and brings both wealth and fame while another is dysfunctional and results in failure and incarceration.

Repression. This term applies to the "forgetting" process associated with early childhood experiences. It can apply to any traumatic event. There is a tendency for all of us to repress, or push into the unconscious, extremely painful experiences. Repression is not a conscious process. It just seems to happen outside of our awareness.

Suppression. The intentional repression of negative experiences is called suppression. It is the conscious act of pushing events from memory as opposed to the unconscious nature of repression.

Regression. Under stress, some individuals tend to resort to childlike behaviors. Some psychiatric patients will soil themselves and/or urinate. Others will act silly, talking in "baby talk," or they assume any number of childhood behaviors. The elderly often regress to a childlike state, requiring the same supervision and primary care one would give an infant.

Reaction-Formation. Some individuals have an unusually strong dislike for certain situations or behaviors. Psychoanalytic theory tells us that this very strong overreaction derives from the child's having acted in a similar way. The adult does not remember this behavior as a consequence of childhood amnesia (mentioned earlier). Nevertheless, the individual feels very strongly about certain behaviors but tends to act the opposite way.

Intellectualization (Rationalization). In certain instances, individuals resort to the "refined" defense mechanism known as intellectualization. This form of self-protection is based on what seems to be rational and intelligent reasoning. The individual believes that a particular problem can be "explained away" through the use of what appears to be logic and common sense. Someone who is a habitual smoker may reason as follows,

"Not all people who die of lung cancer or heart disease are smokers, and not all smokers die of lung cancer or heart disease . . . smoking is not such a bad habit after all."

There are many ways in which a situation can be intellectualized. This is by far the most common defense used by speculators and investors. Since intellectualization appears to be a rational process, it is often difficult to detect. Virtually every intellectualized defense has some basis in fact which makes it difficult to detect as well as difficult to refute.

These are only a few of the other defenses and coping mechanisms that will be referred to in future chapters.

Psychoanalytic Theory and Psychological Treatment

Freudian theory is treatment oriented. The object of psychoanalytic treatment is to free the individual from his or her appropriate use of defenses through the process of insight. Insight involves verbalizing conflicts and recognizing their development and origin in childhood. Once the conflicts being shielded from consciousness by various defense mechanisms are "ventilated," or brought to the surface, change, the theory states, will occur and emotional difficulties will have been successfully treated.

The manner in which such treatment is given varies according to the particular therapist and branch of psychoanalysis. Primarily, it is the role of the therapist to arouse transference in the patient. Transference is the transfer of emotions, feelings, attitudes, and conflicts that the patient originally felt about his or her father and/or mother to the therapist, who acts as a substitute parent in order that the patient may ventilate feelings in a less threatening environment.

As I've pointed out earlier, the theories of Freud, in particular his theory of psychosexual development, have been strongly criticized by many psychologists and psychiatrists. In today's age of scientific validation, it should come as no surprise that Freud's work, which lacks solid scientific validation, should come under fire. Furthermore, many of Freud's ideas would, by today's standards, be considered sexist. Yet the true test of any theory, validated or not, is its ability to withstand the test of time. The fact is, for whatever the underlying reasons may be, Freud's ideas have persisted. Furthermore, they have been used successfully in a number of clinical treatment modalities.

Variations of the Freudian themes have also been in the forefront of modern psychoanalysis for many years further attesting to the underlying validity of Freud's work. We cannot state with certainty that empirical testing will validate all of the concepts advanced by Freud, however, we do know that one of the most important factors underlying all of Freudian theory is the relationship between therapist and patient. The "transference" relationship allows the patient to interact with the therapist in a fashion that mimics conflicts originally experienced with parents or parental figures. And this facilitates the development of psychological mechanisms that reduce neurotic behaviors inasmuch as the therapist can fully understand the conflict and assist in the process of achieving insight.

Of the many concepts originally proposed by Freud, perhaps the most difficult to understand and accept is his assertion that the male child experiences castration anxiety as a result of guilt arising from his attraction to mother. The source of the anxiety is simple enough to understand. The male child feels attached to the mother with whom, after all, he has had a very close relationship. Fearing that the father will punish him for his attraction to his mother, the male child becomes consciously or unconsciously anxious that his father will retaliate by castrating him. While you may not necessarily accept the theory in its literal form, it is easily understandable figuratively.

There are many men who cannot cope with success inasmuch as success arouses feelings of fear that were originally experienced in relation to father. These originated in very early childhood and have been generalized neurotically to adult life. Hence, the male investor or trader who is successful may fear, unconsciously, as a result of early childhood experiences, that he will lose all he has attained. To many men, the loss of material possessions is emasculating and, hence, is expressed on an unconscious level as castration anxiety. After completing a very profitable trade or investment, some men feel that "something will happen to take it all away." The feeling is often a very specific one. They may fear that the tax man will take it all, that bad luck will befall them, or that they will lose it all if they don't stop trading. These are neurotic fears which, in psychoanalytic terms, are expressions of castration anxiety.

Id, Ego, and Superego

As mentioned earlier, a central feature of psychoanalytic theory is its tripartite division of the mind. Id is the term Freud used to describe the "lowest" of the three aspects. Within id dwells all animalistic, instinctual drives, impulsiveness, childishness, and the pleasure principle. Id seeks only self-satisfaction and avoidance of pain to the total disregard of social control. Ego seeks to apply some control over id impulse and tempers its drive. This controlling mechanism develops during the latency period and reflects authoritarian attitudes. It is in essence an internalized parental voice. Superego, the most highly developed mechanism, rules over all other drives and reflects the social and self-controlling efforts of the individual. Moral and social values come from superego.

The various ways in which id, ego, and superego express themselves in conscious life is the substance of psychoanalytic study and treatment. We can learn a great deal about ourselves if we learn to recognize the source of our drives. The fear and greed so often experienced in speculation reside within id. Id impulses may get us what we want at times, but they tend to ignore the inherent dangers to self that can accompany their fulfillment. This is discussed in detail later.

Dream Interpretation

Freud believed that dreams represent a symbolic acting out of id impulses and conflicts. Frequently, dreams are not understood since they are disguised by the unconscious to protect us from their real, threatening meaning. During the therapeutic process, the analyst uses a patient's associations to dreams as another key in the process of gaining insight.

There are many interpretations of the dream. Neo-Freudians believe that the dream is not nearly as important as Freud believed. Others see dreams as a problem-solving technique. In any event, the dream can tell us a great deal about how we really feel. For some individuals who are not aware of their feelings, impulses, and expectations, an understanding of their dreams can provide valuable insights. This will also be discussed in a later chapter.

These basic aspects of traditional psychoanalytic theory will certainly not qualify you to practice psychoanalysis, but this background will permit you to understand the material that follows. Those who have never been exposed to these ideas may be inspired to do some soul searching and self-evaluation. (See the Bibliography.)

It may be difficult for you to imagine how Freudian principles can be applied to the markets. Before moving on to the next major topic, the basics of learning theory, I'd like to give you an example illustrating one of the key aspects of Freudian analysis.

Forgetting, which is considered as a normal everyday event, is, according to classical psychoanalytic theory, not merely a random event. An individual forgets because he or she does not want to remember. Recall the previous discussions of repression and suppression. These two mechanisms are primarily responsible for the forgetting process. Consider the case of a trader who "forgets" to place orders to liquidate a position in sufficient time to avoid delivery. Has this trader really forgotten? According to the traditional Freudian interpretation, no. A strong case could, in fact, be made for an unconscious desire to take delivery! Since there is no "forgetting" according to analytic theory, the act of "not remembering" is given deep symbolic significance in the therapeutic situation.

While occasional forgetting is not unreasonable, the individual who repeatedly forgets is revealing some highly significant aspects of personality, motivation, desires, and unconscious processes. I remember a trader who was constantly "misplacing" his commodity trades. He kept only mental notes of his positions. All too often he "forgot" about a trade and by the time he was reminded, a large loss had accumulated. To rectify the problem, he initiated a record-keeping system (which he should have had regardless) and entered each trade as it was made. The system seemed to be going well until he "forgot" where his record book was. This soon became a habit and he realized that the new system would not work. It was suggested that he have his broker read the positions to him daily. This technique achieved immediate results, but unfortunately they were short-lived. It seems that our wayward friend found it increasingly difficult to remember his broker's telephone number!

This may sound improbable to many of you. But for the individual who is afflicted with such emotional problems, the anguish is very real. And there are many people who suffer from symptoms that are considerably more destructive. How would such a problem be treated? What does the "forgetting" mean? According to psychoanalytic practice there would most likely be a different answer for each individual, dependent upon his or her history. In this case, the habitual "forgetter" was telling us quite clearly that (1) he was anxious about his trades and hence chose to forget them in order to avoid the fear and/or anxiety, (2) he was unconsciously creating a situation that would eventually bring him a large enough loss to drive him out of the markets entirely. Both results confirm an unconscious desire to fail.

This is a simple yet profound example of how one might explain seemingly innocent behavior using the traditional Freudian approach. Many behaviors that traders exhibit daily can provide useful insights. Through the use of insight, the therapist can help one overcome these and even more serious problems standing in the way of financial success. The three goals of psychoanalytically oriented therapy are to confront problems, interpret their meaning, and restructure in a positive way.

The explanatory material just presented is intended as a brief overview of a highly complex and vast field of study. Chapter 5 also provides an overview of psychological theory and practice that covers yet another aspect of trader behavioral dynamics. The purpose is to establish for you the basis of an initial foray into the mind and behavior of the trader, and to develop a general framework upon which to build an understanding of the chapters that follow.

REVIEW

1. Sigmund Freud is the founder of psychoanalytically oriented psychotherapy.
2. This view of human psychology attributes considerable influence to early childhood experiences and explains present-day personality in relation to such experiences.
3. The "pleasure principle" is a central feature of Freudian theory, as is psychosexual development and the development of defense mechanisms.
4. Development proceeds through various stages, and specific conflicts characterize each stage.
5. After the first few years of life, most early childhood experiences are forgotten.
6. Id, ego, and superego develop as unconscious control mechanisms.
7. The dream is assigned an important role in psychotherapy.
8. The gaining of insight, the ventilation of conflicts and feelings, and transference are all goals in traditionally oriented therapy.
9. There has been considerable controversy regarding the lack of experimental and scientific validation of traditional analytic concepts. It is difficult to test Freud's theories in a scientific and objective manner.

5

Learning Theory: Is All Learning Stimulus-Response?

Gypsies have been reported to train bears to dance to music by a simple conditioning procedure. The bear was chained to a surface under which a fire was built to heat the stone on which the bear stood. The Gypsies played music while the bear moved about to relieve the pain in his feet. The music became a conditioned stimulus. After this experience, the sound of music elicited foot movements that resembled dancing.

L. M. Stolurow, in Wolman, 1973, p. 483.

Basics of Learning Theory

The "technician" of psychology is the behaviorist. Not only does this school of psychological theory find itself at the opposite end of the continuum from psychoanalysis, but it has also aroused considerable controversy. I will attempt to give you an unbiased working knowledge of the principles and issues, but this chapter may reflect my leaning toward the behavioral school.

Behaviorism dates back to the Russian physiologist I. P. Pavlov whose experiments on the salivary reflex of dogs are familiar to most readers. Yet few understand the ramifications of his work. In the 1920s, Pavlov demonstrated that various animal responses could be conditioned to arousal by stimuli that were not originally related to the response itself. His work was deceptively simple. Following a surgical procedure during which a tube was placed within a dog's salivary gland, the dog was stimulated to salivate in response to meat powder. The saliva entered the tube and was measured as it dripped into a cup. A few seconds prior to the presentation of meat powder, a bell or buzzer was sounded. The meat was then presented and the salivary response resulted. After a number of simultaneous buzzer and meat presentations, the meat was no longer given. The animal, however, still responded, or salivated, when the buzzer was sounded as if the meat had been given. The amount of saliva was measured. If meat was totally eliminated, the buzzer continued to elicit a salivary response. With each presentation of buzzer alone, the amount of saliva decreased. This decrease phase was termed "extinction." It is, in many ways, analogous to "forgetting." The process of attaching the buzzer stimulus to the salivary response through the use of meat powder was called "reflexive conditioning." It is possible to condition virtually any reflex to any secondary conditioner in animal and human.

Pavlov's work marked the start of a behavioral revolution in the psychological world. His full theory and experimental procedures are too involved to be discussed fully here. For a good look at his early work, I recommend reading his classic text *Conditioned Reflexes* (1927).

During the same period of time, American psychologist E. L. Thorndike was involved in work on human and animal intelligence. Another American psychologist, John B. Watson, applied principles similar to those of Pavlov in his study of human emotion. His work was important not only for its discoveries about the human learning process, but it also represented a total departure from traditional methods and understandings.

His beliefs were a radical departure from those of his contemporaries. They flew in the face of everything considered right and proper in the study of human learning, perhaps the single most blatant of which was that he made no sharp distinction between man and animal in terms of learning processes. And equally blasphemous, he assigned no power to the unconscious and introspective tenets of traditional psychologists. In 1913, Watson wrote:

Psychology as the behaviorist sees it is a purely objective experimental branch of natural science. Its theoretical goal is the prediction and control of behavior. Introspection forms no essential part of its methods, nor is the scientific value of its data dependent upon the readiness with which they lend themselves to interpretation in terms of consciousness. The behaviorist in his efforts to get a unitary scheme of animal responses recognizes no dividing line between man and brute. . . . The position is taken here that the behavior of man and the behavior of animals must be considered on the same plane; as being equally essential to a general understanding of behavior. (1913, p. 158)

The problem with other theories, Watson felt, was that they were not scientific or objective enough to be used consistently and successfully. Six years later he wrote:

> Psychology as a science of consciousness has no community of data. The reader will find no discussion of consciousness and no reference to such terms as sensation, perception, attention, image, will and the like . . . I frankly do not know what they mean, nor do I believe that anyone can use them consistently. (1919, p. xii)

Watson's position is, in many ways, similar to the position taken by market technicians. Whereas, Watson was concerned with the use of data relative to the prediction of human and animal behavior, the market technician is concerned with the use of data in predicting market price and trend. The market fundamentalist also uses data, but the conclusions and techniques vary considerably due to the many unknowns that are part of fundamental analysis. These unknowns are subject to interpretation and opinion in the same ways that introspection and consciousness are unknowns. The objections Watson had to the use of these concepts are similarly valid in rejecting some basics of fundamental market analysis.

In a classic experiment with Mary Cover Jones, Watson was able to clearly demonstrate the role of conditioning in human beings. Using a baby and its fear response to loud noise, Watson "conditioned" fear of a rabbit. A child was placed in the experimental setting. A loud noise was introduced. The child cried bitterly in response to the noise. A loud noise was then made while a rabbit was shown. After a number of trials or repetitions of this procedure the child would also cry at independent presentation (no noise) of the rabbit. This was termed a "conditioned fear response."

Watson also noticed that the child would cry in response to white furry objects resembling the rabbit. The closer the resemblance, the more certain was the fear response. This was called *stimulus generalization.* The crying response could be stimulated without noise. The child had, in effect, been taught to cry in response to a once neutral or positive object. Here was a true breakthrough indeed. Watson had demonstrated in a definitive scientific fashion the validity of his theory. Many behaviors are learned through stimulus, response, and consequences. This was truly a revolutionary idea, albeit a simple one. It has been more than 50 years since Watson's awesome discovery, yet many American educators still fail to realize the importance of his work.

Watson did considerably more work on the human organism and conditioning. He believed that any human could be conditioned or taught virtually any repertoire of behaviors. He believed that internal or unconscious processes such as those theorized by the Freudians had little or no bearing on the understanding or explanation of human behavior. His extensive and concise experimental work supported his theories, helping them attain considerable credibility. Whereas the Freudians were lacking hard empirical data for their methods and beliefs, Watson and other behaviorists were beginning to accumulate a wealth of experimental and objective data in support of their theories. Watson, however, was only one of many behavioral learning theorists who helped advance the work.

Contemporary behavioral theory owes a considerable amount of its status to the work of B. F. Skinner. Using animal subjects, Skinner developed his behavioral concepts into a unified system of experimental results. His work was not only objective and highly scientific, but it was extensive and innovative as well. Ultimately, Skinner's theories stimulated the development of behavior therapy, a clinical treatment technique based on the principles and experimental findings of behaviorism. Tolman, Guthrie, Hull, Lewin, and Wolpe, all behaviorists, made significant contributions to the field of behaviorism, both in theory as well as in practice.

The Behavior Law of Learning

Simply stated, the behavioral law of learning states the following:

> The outer environment acts on an organism, which then responds to the external stimulus. The organism's response results in any number of consequences. The positive or negative quality of these consequences determines the future history of the response. If the consequences are pleasurable (remember Freud's pleasure principle), then it is more likely the given response will occur again. If negative or painful, then it is likely the frequency of the given response will be decreased.

The model or paradigm of behavioral learning in Figure 5.1 is considered basic to all human learning. By amplifying each of the elements, it is

Environment→Stimulus→Organism→Response(s)→Consequence(s)

Figure 5.1 The learning paradigm.

possible to explain and experimentally validate virtually all learning situations. By using the learning paradigm, it is also possible to teach or shape new behaviors, or eliminate current behaviors by manipulation of the stimulus, response, and consequences elements. The ramifications of this theory are immense and, by virtue of their enormity, controversial.

In his experimental work, Skinner trained pigeons to perform a number of highly complex tasks.

Using similar principles and methods, other behaviorists have been able to train dogs, chimps, and birds to perform highly complex tasks involving everything from assembly-line work to number sequence recognition. The limits of training are bounded only by the physical ability of the organism and the behaviorist's imagination.

Since the 1950s, behavioral therapists and learning theorists have slowly but surely developed clinical treatment techniques based on Skinnerian principles. These therapies have been highly effective, and the results obtained have persisted. It has been possible to successfully treat behavioral and "mental" disturbances previously considered incurable. Specificity of technique and reliability and speed of results have accounted for the increased popularity of behavioral techniques. Virtually all aspects of treatment are derivations of the simple learning model discussed earlier.

Please be certain that you understand both the learning paradigm as well as the basic behavioral learning principles. In discussing behavioral principles and trading in greater detail, I will refer extensively to the underlying concepts.

The Learning Theory Approach

The behavioral approach seems to be the most promising area of market psychology. I indicated earlier that the behavioral theorist considers learning to be the basis of most human behavior. In my experience with different areas of clinical treatment, I have come to know and respect the behavioral approach. In terms of results and ability to explain human behavior, this technique is unexcelled. Furthermore, speculation and investment are so easily understood and explained in terms of behavioral principles, that it appears to be the most effective approach to take.

Moreover, behavioral analysis and therapy are among the most effective, efficient, and lasting techniques known to modern psychological science. There are those who argue, however, that behavioral treatment is shallow, inhumane, ineffective, and mechanistic. They claim that it allows no room for insight and mental processes. I will discuss these criticisms later, after I acquaint you with more details of the behavioral methodology.

Basic Applications of Behavioral Learning Theory

The basic tenet of behavioral learning theory is the reinforcement principle. The rule that any behavior followed by a positive event tends to be repeated is deceptive in its simplicity. There are many ramifications of this learning paradigm.

Let's now plunge into some of the basic applications of the behavioral learning model as it relates to speculation and investing. Remember that I am not doing justice to Skinnerian theory in this general analysis. The field is considerably more complex than I have indicated herein, however, my discussion will help you understand the major methods, issues, and directions. (Those wishing a more thorough understanding should read the texts listed in the Bibliography.)

Let's take our basic learning model and modify it slightly by placing the investor and trader within the sequence of steps (Figure 5.2). Let's trace the sequence of events involved in a typical transaction. I use the word typical in the sense of "ideal," although as you know, many situations in the markets are not ideal. But if we know how a situation should run in its typical state, then we can appreciate the deviations and possibly change them.

If trades or investments were made rationally, on the basis of firm technical or fundamental factors alone, then market indicators, which are a function of prices, would act on the speculator, whose reading of the signal would bring about a given response. This response would take

Stimulus	Organism	Response	Consequences
Markets Signals Indicators	Speculator Trader	Buy or sell Do nothing	Profit/loss
#1	#2	#3	#4

Figure 5.2 The investor and the learning paradigm.

the form of a buy order, a sell order, or no order at all. Time would pass and the result would be either a profit or a loss. If the result was profitable, then the trader would be more likely to follow this signal in the future. Hence if the signal was reliable, more profits would follow. If the net result was a loss, however, then theoretically the same signal would lose its reinforcing ability and the response to it would be diminished or extinguished. Note this sequence of events in Figure 5.2.

A stimulus acts on the organism, in this case the investor, the investor responds, and the consequences are either positive or negative, that is, profit or loss. Based on this model, and assuming it is perfect, most traders should eventually achieve better results if the system they are following has validity.

Given this interpretation, experienced individuals should achieve an admirable record in terms of net results, since bad signals (that is, unprofitable) would lose their reinforcing ability. But alas, such a perfect state is no more of a reality than is the perfection of the market itself. In a sense, however, the model holds up well since the odds of a successful trader continuing as a successful trader are quite good. Losing traders, on the other hand, continue to lose unless they are able to change the stimulus response consequences of their behavior.

Let's take a look at some of the various factors in the learning paradigm that may act as conflicting and/or confounding roadblocks to perfect trading. The first problem arises in section 1 (note that all elements in the learning paradigm, Figure 5.2, have been numbered). The seemingly simple task of following a signal based on market behavior is as simple as it appears to be. There are perhaps as many different interpretations of signals as there are schools of market analysis. The same technical signal may result in totally different behaviors among several investors. Consider the following situation. A trader analyzes the futures markets on the basis of moving averages. Each time the three moving averages he monitors are moving up, or when one average crosses the others, a signal to buy occurs. A buy signal occurs in gold futures. The appropriate response would be to buy. This is the *only response that would lead to effective learning,* regardless of whether its culmination was profitable or not.

Let's assume, however, that the trader has just finished reading *The Wall Street Journal*. The lead article he has just read advances several bearish arguments in gold futures. The trader is plagued with two sets of conflicting information. On the one hand, experts who wrote the article claim that prices will move lower; on the other hand, his signals say that the market will go higher. What should he do? His dilemma is not unlike one experienced by all of us at some time or another.

Here are some possible outcomes. Let's assume that the trader follows his signal to buy gold and that he does so in complete accord with his system. This would be the best action. The net result, if profitable, would be considered a learning experience with positive consequences. The trader has not only been rewarded for following the system, but he has also been rewarded for not being influenced by an extraneous source of information; a source of information that had no bearing whatsoever on the system which was being used. Whether the contradictory information originated in the news media, a broker, a friend, or an advisory service, the mere fact that the trader in my example followed his or her own system was a great achievement. Only several such positive events are necessary for the behavior to be stamped in, or learned.

Unfortunately, however, most traders never pass step one. Their very first trades often are not a result of a system but rather the end product of being influenced by numerous outside influences unrelated to the system. Their system, whether intrinsically good or bad, is never given the opportunity to be tested or to prove itself in real trading. Hence learning is faulty from the start. As time progresses, the faulty learning becomes more entrenched and, hence, difficult, even impossible to unlearn or, to use the behavioral learning term, extinguished.

Let's assume that our trader does not follow his signal, but rather takes advice given by a report he read, a broker, or a friend. And let's assume additionally that his original signal would have been wrong and a loss would have resulted. By avoiding the negative experience of a loss, the trader has been rewarded for a behavior that will not only be difficult to eliminate later, but will also prevent the trading system from being tested in real time because the signal which was followed was *not generated by the system* that was being used. Learning theory (remember the paradigm or please refer to it) indicates that the individual is now more likely to act similarly in the future, than he was prior to this "inappropriate" or non-system-related behavior. Thus, the system may never get tested, and, in fact, it will most likely be abandoned completely before it has even had a chance to prove itself—win, lose, or draw.

Let us assume a third possible outcome. The trader follows his signal and takes a loss. A negative experience results from following the signal. Paradoxically, the negative result will eventually have a positive effect. By repeatedly following a signal our trader will test the system in actual markets and thereby "learn" if the system he is using is a profitable one or not. Without consistent adherence to the precise trading rules of a system, there will be no adaptive learning and, hence, no test of the system. See Table 5.1 for an analysis of the outcomes.

This last point is the quintessential consideration in determining trader discipline. My experience has taught me that the vast majority of traders lose money *NOT* as a function of their system but rather as a function of their discipline. You can't learn anything about a trading system or method, technical or fundamental, unless you follow it. I'm reminded of a joke frequently told by comedian Jackie Mason. In one of his comedy routines, Mason states that he wasn't always as well adjusted as he is today. To improve his emotional stability, Mason visits a psychiatrist who begins his psychological treatment with the following statement to Mason "and now the search for the REAL you will begin," to which Mason replies, "if I'm not the real me then who am I? And if I'm not the real me, then for all I know YOU (the psychiatrist) could be the real me and if you're the real me then why should I pay you, or perhaps I'm the real you and you should pay me . . . I'll ask my friends . . . they know who I am."

It's a joke, of course, but it's particularly relevant to the present discussion. If you want to find the "real you" in terms of trading systems and methods then you have to BE the real you. And you can only be the real you by trading your system as close to ideally as possible. It's that simple and it's that complicated.

Of even greater importance in the situation just described is the concept of partial or random reinforcement. Let's assume that our trader follows some signals and not others; that he selectively trades according to his system. Let's also assume that some of the trades made by this

Table 5.1

Analysis of Outcomes Generated by Various
Responses to Trading Signals

Signal	Response	Outcome	Evaluation
Valid signal from system	Follow signal	Loss	Positive learning
Valid signal from system	Follow signal	Profit	Positive learning
Signal from other source	Signal not followed	Nil	Positive learning
Signal from other source	Follow signal	Loss	Positive learning
Signal from other source	Follow signal	Profit	Faulty learning

individual are recommended by brokers, some by advisory services, and some by fellow traders. Essentially, this individual is on a schedule of reinforcement in which his or her behavior—selecting a trade—is not linked to any one stimulus. This confounds the learning process and leaves the individual not only poorly trained but also in a state of insecurity and confusion.

The second aspect of partial reinforcement relates to the "addictive" nature of speculation and, for that matter, all forms of gambling. There is enough variability in the markets to provide most traders with partial or random rewards. This schedule will result in a strong attachment to the market, making the trading habit difficult to break. Whatever the outcome, the number of random wins will act toward the creation of a very strong bond between trader and market. You, in fact, may fit into this category, along with the thousands of others who have been maintained on a random schedule by the markets.

Losers Outnumber Winners

For every one winning trade there may be ten losers. And yet the game goes on and the losses continue. Now imagine the individual who does not stick to one specific trading plan. The combined effect of partial reinforcement from the market itself and faulty learning resulting from acceptance of signals and trades from other sources can create a confused, frustrated, addicted loser. B. F. Skinner demonstrated unequivocally that a random or partial reinforcement schedule resulted in learning that was the most difficult to extinguish. He proved, beyond a doubt in fact, that behaviors that are learned on a random schedule of reward are actually never forgotten or extinguished and that the organism can slip right back into them even after many years of "perfect" behavior.

What I have just told you is perhaps the single most important thing I will tell you in this entire book. If you understand what I have just said and if you understand its vast implications for your behavior, then most of my task will have been achieved. Faulty learning begets more faulty learning. And more faulty learning will obscure the true path to success. It is best, therefore, never to begin on the road to failure by the inconsistent application of your trading system or rules or you will find it very difficult, nearly impossible, to take a different tack. This is due to the nature of learning as just described. This is why most losers will always be losers and this is why most winners will become even bigger winners.

Please reread this chapter and understand it fully. Internalize it. It is the most important thing I can tell you and, I feel, the most important thing you can ever know about trading and investing.

REVIEW   We have taken a look at the behavioral model of learning as it relates to the trader. We have also looked at the specific stimulus-response chain from the point of market signal to the result of a given trade. The consequences of various decisions and outcomes have been presented. Partial reinforcement can result in strong learning, productive, or loss-producing.

In addition, the following points were made:

1. The principles of behavioral learning can be used to understand and change trader and investor behavior.

2. Human learning can be explained very thoroughly by Skinnerian learning and reinforcement principles.

3. As a result of this learning process, we are affected by the complex interaction of market signals (stimuli) and the many trades (responses) we can make.

4. The result of these responses-whether positive (profits) or negative (losses) will create either a successful trader or a chronic, behaviorally conditioned loser.

5. To derive the full benefit of the learning model, you must avoid confounding signals, following your system rigidly.

6. Each response (trade) should be a result of the trading system. In this way, it will be tested quickly and thoroughly.

7. Any response (trade) to the system that is not "pure," or exclusively part of the system, will act to confound the reinforcing action of results.

8. The study of partial reinforcement in animals can help us understand the importance of complete dedication to a trading system.

6

The Response Sector

A Distant Look at the Response Sector

Now let's take a look at what else can go wrong or right in the behavioral chain. The time elapsed between market signal and trader response usually is very brief, but the intervening process is highly complex and intricate. Looking at the model piece by piece, as we are doing, should lead to some valuable conclusions.

The second phase of our behavioral chain is "response." Let's assume the trader, the organism in our equation, has acted on a signal. Let's also assume that his action was based strictly on his own signal and not on the advice of others. The trader is now prepared to respond. Within the intervening time lapse between stimulus (the signal) and response (the act of following the signal), we can add the perceptual set factor, another variable that will be discussed later. In Figure 6.1, the redrawn learning model, you can see that perception can affect the trader's response.

Let us assume for now that the perceptual factor is not significant. In other words, the information (signal) received by the trader is received exactly as it is sent. There is no misperception of the signal. In reality this will be the case for few individuals, but perception will be considered in a later chapter.

Figure 6.1 Trading paradigm and perceptual filter.

What can the trader do once a clear-cut signal is received? One would expect a clear-cut buy or sell signal to result in a clear-cut buy or sell response. This is not the case, however. Most traders will allow any of several interfering variables to confound the response. What are the available options? There are three possible responses—buy, sell, or do nothing.

Consider the following example of what can occur between the decision to buy or sell and the actual execution of the order. Our trader friend gets the signal to sell cattle short. He reads the indicator properly and calls his broker to place the order. The broker says, "Are you sure you want to sell them? The Cattle on Feed report is coming out today and you might not want to be in the market through the report." "Sounds reasonable," says the trader. And the trade is not made. The same series of events can occur as in our previous discussion. If a loss is avoided, then the trader has been rewarded for listening to something other than his or her own reading of the signals. Again, this will result in faulty learning and the outcome will be long-term negative. The most appropriate action for the serious trader to take would be strict adherence to signals and decisions regardless of input from any other source. Whether the signal indicated a buy or a sell, any deviation from it once again jeopardizes the learning process.

The decision to do nothing, regardless of a clear-cut signal, can also result in maladaptive learning. Indecision is perhaps the greatest enemy of the speculator or trader. He who hesitates is lost, particularly in the markets. There is a very specific syndrome of indecision that will be described later. It relates closely to neurotic behavior in everyday life. The advantage of making no decision at all is that no risk is taken. Hence the consequences are not negative and, in fact, may be anxiety relieving and thus reinforcing. The net result will be no real test of the system and no productive learning on the part of the trader.

Before going on, I want to make certain that you understand the difference between the very first point I made concerning stimulus and the current discussion of response. In the previous situation, our trader made no response to his signal as a function of competing opinions that interfered with his reading of the signal. In the current situation, our trader made the appropriate analysis of his system but failed to carry it to completion. Although there is a very fine distinction between the two situations, our second trader is better off than our first, since he actually attempted to respond in the appropriate way.

In the first situation, the interference came prior to a reading of the signal. In the second, the stimulus resulted in proper intentions, but it did not result in the appropriate behavior because a competing factor appeared after the correct decision. Quantitatively, there would be no difference for the true behaviorist. All he sees is response. Since response was lacking in both cases, they are, for all intents and purposes, similar. However, there is a major difference between the two situations. Our first trader has much more ground to cover along the path to success. Our second trader has already arrived at the decision-making level. He has actually picked up the telephone, made the call, and placed the order, but his ultimate response was incorrect. Qualitatively, his level of achievement is much more advanced and different corrective measures would be taken.

I am giving you this microscopic analysis to help you determine where you are in the behavioral sequence. If you know just where you stand, it will be possible for you to more effectively combat the problem. Some traders I have seen are so totally lost that they haven't the slightest idea of what they're doing wrong. The object of this painstakingly specific analysis is to help you identify the exact problem or problems you might have. If you feel that what I am saying just doesn't apply to you, then skip this chapter. But if you have experienced repeated losses and have a sneaking suspicion that there is nothing wrong with your basic market analysis, then you owe it to yourself to read on.

The first situation is one in which decision making was totally avoided. Several corrective measures will be discussed in Chapter 7. The second situation does not relate to a faulty decision-making process; it does, however, indicate faulty actualization of decisions. I will also discuss treatment methods regarding this problem in Chapter 7.

Each of the situations discussed can be applied to every aspect of the trading situation. The use of stops, placing orders to enter or exit a market, and similar devices, are all subject to the same learning model. Each individual situation should be considered as one response in a larger behavior. The entire process of trading could be broken as shown in Table 6.1. The process involves basically three steps.

Each step has its own specific result and requires a clear-cut action. It is possible to break down each individual step into its component behaviors. Step 1, for example, requires the maintenance of a trading system. Many individual behaviors enter into the use of a system, regardless of type or orientation. If you have a problem that goes back even earlier than

Table 6.1
Inputs, Outputs, and Results of the Trading Process

Step	Inputs	Outputs	Effective Result
1. Maintain trading system	Data	Buy, sell, hold	Trading decision
2. Call broker	Signals	Place order(s)	Market entry or exit
3. Await new signal	Data	Buy, sell, hold	Trading decision

the examples given, it will be necessary to take even more intensive corrective action, as discussed in Chapter 7.

A Closer Look at the Response Sector

Examining the behavioral aspects of any action is a relatively simple task. It is a far greater achievement to put our observations into action. Many of us have been raised and educated without exposure to behavioral concepts. We continue to believe that most external life is an expression of internal forces that are too difficult, too repressed, or too threatening to experience directly. There is much to be said for the traditional viewpoint; the acknowledgment of behavioral psychology as a viable explanation of human action does not necessarily mean that one must reject the teachings of traditionally oriented psychologists. It is possible to effectively synthesize the behavioral and the psychoanalytical.

The significance of response is no less important to the Freudian than it is to the behaviorist. Response is, after all, another term for action. And action is the only means by which we can judge the nature of underlying processes. Although it is not necessary to understand internal concepts in order to observe action, there are those whose perception of response (in themselves and others) can be assisted by an evaluation of underlying causes. French psychologist, Emmanuel Mounier, made the following observations about action:

> The sole proof of a man lies in his deeds. They are the only irrefutable confirmation of the value of his words, and the authenticity of his thoughts. This is because we are thrown into action before we can reflect on action, compelled by urgency before we can deliberate. The study of character culminates in the study of action, the nature of which dominates all other aspects. (1956, p. 122)

It follows that response, or action, is the only objective way of determining the functioning of a trader. In order to evaluate a system, we must focus exclusively on its actions and results. We must therefore be certain that the results are a true reflection of the system itself—not contaminated by influences due to a deficiency on the trader's part. The trader must respond appropriately to the system to obtain a true reading of the system's value. The trader, however, may discard a technique that has validity or continue to employ a system that has no underlying value. The final test of any trading methodology is therefore inextricably tied to the individual who is using the technique.

At this point, you may be prompted to look at computer technology for the answer. But alas, the computer is no better than he who uses it. Should an individual lack self-discipline, should his response chain be defective, there will be no assistance of value from the computer. Borrowing from the psychoanalytic school, we can surmise quite accurately that a trader who has unconscious self-destructive tendencies will find a way to lose, no matter what technology he employs. Whether you adopt the behavioral or psychoanalytic interpretation, the trader is an instrumental factor in either the success or failure of a system. As I have indicated on many previous occasions, the trader is, in fact, more important than the system. It is possible for a disciplined trader (one with the appropriate responses) to profitably use virtually any system.

The value of response is therefore threefold. First and foremost, it is a key item in the real time testing of any and all trading systems. Whereas we can get a computer to test a system objectively, thoroughly, and without error (assuming correct programming), we cannot get a human being to subsequently trade the system in an objective fashion unless that individual is emotionally capable. You may ask this appropriate question, "Why not get a computer to trade the system automatically?" This is well within the realm of present technology. All one need do is acquire the necessary hardware and software—the rest is a matter of mechanics. There are several immediate drawbacks to this system. Cost is perhaps the greatest limitation. Another drawback of the computer system is that it is subject to mechanical failure. If a computer system is automatically set to make trading decisions and implement them by sending orders in the form of a wire, errors are possible. Fail-safe parameters could be built into the system to avoid such problems. The main point here, however, is that any mechanical system will be limited in its functioning by those who design and use it. If those who designed it lack discipline, then the system will reflect this liability.

The second value of response lies in its reinforcing ability. Simply stated, response will always let you know if what you did was right. Without response, there can be no test. Without response, there can be no result. This is why I am personally opposed to the old technique of "paper trading." There are some instructors who tell their students to trade on paper before you get your feet wet in the real market. This is supposed to let you know how well you're doing. Some also reason that people can learn how to place orders, use stops, and gain general expertise by paper trading. It is my opinion that paper trading can only teach one thing—and that's paper trading. Based on a strictly behavioral analysis of the situation, the act of paper trading (or pretend trading, as I prefer to call it) carries no risk whatsoever. Losses are not losses, profits are not profits, and errors have no consequence. Without consequence, there can be no true learning. An astute instructor, using behavioral principles, will know how to generalize paper trading into real trading. But to my knowledge there are no formal courses in market study that even touch on this technique. To trade without risk or reward is to not trade. To learn how to trade by trading without risk or reward is to not learn how to trade. I will discuss how to practice trading in Chapter 8.

The third value of response is its ability to permit objective evaluation of results. Each individual, whether skilled in trading or not, must look at the record objectively. If one has taken pains to implement trading signals precisely as dictated by the system, the feedback of results is an objective test. This test, as previously indicated, will be free of most influence by the trader and his emotion.

Is Perfection Necessary?

In discussing response, I do not want to give the erroneous impression that perfection is a necessity. Human beings can only approach perfection. If we all implemented behavioral learning techniques with strict discipline, there would be no market. Markets function through the imperfect state of man. Speculation is built on the fact that individuals have different responses to similar stimuli. The thrust of what I have been telling you is directed at insight and change. Those who are not aware of their internal limitations should gain the necessary insights and then use these insights in conjunction with behavioral principles to alter their response mode in the direction of perfection.

Fortunately, the markets do not require perfection as a predetermining condition of financial success. In fact, it is possible to be far from perfect and still be a winner in the markets. Were it possible to measure perfection in trading on an objective scale with computer perfection ranking a 10, and abject disorganization ranking a 0, we would find most successful traders in the 7 range. Most losers would be in the 5 range and lower, and the tremendously successful would rank only 8 or higher. This is my estimation of reality based on personal observation. If my analysis is correct, then there is only a very fine line between the response perfection of winners and losers. What I am telling you is simply that a small amount of behavioral change in your response mode can bring a very large change in trading results.

In closing this chapter on response, I will leave you with the words of John B. Watson:

The behaviorist has been criticized for his emphasis on response. Some psychologists seem to have the notion that the behaviorist is interested only in the recording of minute muscular responses. Nothing could be further from the truth. Let me emphasize again that the behaviorist is primarily interested in the behavior of the whole man. From morning to night he watches him perform his daily round of duties . . . in other words, the response the behaviorist is interested in is the commonsense answer to the question "what is he doing and why is he doing it?" (1924, p. 15)

REVIEW

1. Response is the only thing that can lead to consequences.
2. Response and action refer to similar behaviors.
3. Response provides feedback, reality testing, and reinforcement.
4. To improve trading results, the response segment of behavior must be changed.
5. It is not necessary to be perfect to be successful.
6. Responses can be changed through the use of behavioral techniques.
7. "Paper trading" is not a good way to learn.

7

The Consequences of Behavior

The recognition of our own mistakes should not benefit us any more than the study of our successes. But there is a natural tendency to avoid punishment. When you associate certain mistakes with a beating, you do not want for a second dose, and stock market mistakes wound you in two tender spots—your pocketbook and your vanity. But I will tell you something curious:

> A stock speculator sometimes makes mistakes and knows that he is making them. And after he makes them he will ask himself why he made them; and after thinking over it cold-bloodedly a long time after the pain of punishment is over, he may learn how he came to make them, and when, and at what particular point of his trade; but not why. (Lefevre, 1965, p. 117)

The words of Edwin Lefevre (Jesse Livermore) indicate his awareness of behavioral consequences in speculation. It is, in fact, impossible to trade any market without cognizance of the inherent reward and punishment. Whether you call it risk (as brokerage houses do) or losses and profits, which is what it ultimately boils down to, the consequence of trading is perhaps the only observable indicator available to speculators. Eventually the market will let you know how you are doing. In the case of commodity futures, the time elapsed between action and consequence is relatively brief. In stocks and other forms of speculation, it may take many months before the outcome is known. The ultimate result of any trade in any market, at any time, is a profit, a loss, or a breakeven. Given this cold but true fact, we can see why the markets are best understood in behavioral terms. The "why" of behavior is relatively unimportant. There are few individuals who can benefit as much from the knowledge that comes with "why" as they can from the profits that come from "how." Lefevre recognized the importance of consequences, particularly the negative ones, but he also realized the relative unimportance of asking why things happen.

The Why and How of Behavior

In previous chapters, I indicated that the "why" of behavior is left to those psychologists who study underlying causes. The "how" of behavior is the domain of behaviorists. There are some psychologists who have integrated both the "why" and the "how." Dollard and Miller (1950), both trained in psychoanalytic techniques, applied behavioral principles to the basic Freudian concepts in an effort to explain the "how"—of their existence. For our work, it is not necessary to delve into the synthesis of behavioral and psychoanalytic models. Much more relevant is how behavior can be changed, using the most efficient and parsimonious theoretical concepts. In many respects, the simplest approach is the most effective. This, by the way, holds true for trading systems as well.

Reviewing briefly the behavioral learning model, you will recall that the last element in the chain is "consequence." It is consequence that determines whether a given behavior or behavioral chain will be more or less likely to occur in the future. It is impossible to overstate the power of behavioral consequences in shaping and maintaining behavior. Skinner and other behaviorists in their experimental work manipulated consequences in order to bring about, or shape, the behavior(s) they wished to develop. If a given behavior has positive consequences, it is not only likely that the behavior will be repeated, but it is also very possible that the behavior will be repeated in exactly the same fashion. In animal studies, rewarded responses are frequently similar down to the most minute muscular level.

To some individuals, the degree of control potentially attainable through the application of behavioral techniques is both threatening and morally unpalatable. Certainly the possibilities of behavioral engineering are practically without limit, but they can be used for either constructive or destructive purposes. Rather than devoting space to the morality of behavioral change, I will say only that in a world functioning on behavioral principles we are all instrumental in changing each other daily. We dole out social rewards and punishments, we approve of good behavior, disapprove of or punish bad behavior. The market is merely a reflection of life itself.

It is natural to assume that a profit will tend to increase a trader's use of profitable signals, whereas a loss will tend to decrease use of such signals. But this is not always the way it works. Remember that the behavioral definition of the term reinforcement (reward) considers a reinforcer to be anything that increases the frequency of a given behavior or set of behaviors. This makes it possible for an event or circumstance that is seen as negative to act as a reinforcer. For example, a classic study on classroom behavior revealed that children who were scolded by the teacher for "out of seat" behavior tended to exhibit more of this behavior than children who were ignored. In other words, the "punishment" the teachers thought they were administering was actually functioning as positive reinforcement. It was possible to determine that this was happening by measuring the increase or decrease in "out of seat" behavior.

The Role of Punishment and Failure

If you have ever punished children or pets only to find that they are misbehaving even more than before the punishment was started, then you know how "punishment" can act as a reward. In fact, punishment is a form of attention, and to some individuals negative attention acts as a reward. The why of such peculiarity can also be explained in behavioral terms. Suffice it to say, however, that the ultimate value of anything considered a reward must be measured in terms of its effect. If I believe that I am rewarding someone for a given behavior, and if the behavior does not increase in frequency, then I am not truly rewarding it. Another reinforcer must be found. If I believe that I am punishing a given behavior and see it increase in frequency, then indeed I am not punishing it and must look for another punishment.

I am reminded of the individual who called me one day seeking consultation on his trading. Asked to precisely define the problem, he stated, "I just can't make any money in the market. Every trade I make turns into a loss. Every time I put in a stop it's hit. Every time I meet a margin call I get still another. And all my friends think I'm an ass."

"How do you feel when you lose?" I asked.

"Bad," he replied without hesitation.

"How bad?" I probed.

"I feel so bad that I can hardly get home from the office," was the response.

"How do you get home?" I questioned further.

"My friends drive me."

"Do you go straight home?"

"Well, not really. First we stop and have a few stiff belts at the local bar. That helps me forget about my losses. Then we have dinner at a good restaurant."

"What then?" I asked.

"Then I go home and tell my wife about how badly the market's punished me."

"And what does she do?"

"She gets hysterical. She tells me that she's going to get a divorce if I keep losing money in the market. She has tantrums and throws things at me. Then she calls her mother. And her mother gets hysterical too. Sometimes her mother comes over and throws things at me too. It's almost funny to see how upset the two of them get. It's as if they had earned the money."

"And how do you feel when they get upset?" was my next question.

"Well, like I said, it's almost funny, if you know what I mean. I kind of enjoy watching those two shrews frothing at the mouth . . . serves them right."

"What is it about them getting upset that seems funny?"

"Well, all these years I've been working and slaving at my business while the two of them spend my money. I wish she'd honor her threat and divorce me. Then I could do anything I wanted to do. I could stay out late, not come home at all if I don't want to, go fishing when I want to, and trade the market as much as I want. If I didn't have to worry about her big mouth, then I could make money in the market. I feel good when she gets mad. I'll show her who's boss . . . who makes all the money . . . and if I want to lose it in the market, then I'll lose it in the market . . . it's my money!"

"Sounds to me like you really enjoy getting your wife upset," I observed.

"Wouldn't you enjoy it too if your wife was a nagging shrew like mine is? Wouldn't you want to get her mad and make her suffer too?" he pleaded.

"Sounds to me like you enjoy getting your wife upset more than you dread the pain of losing money in the market. In fact, it seems as if you lose in the market with the intention of getting her so upset that she'll eventually divorce you. The market is merely a tool for you. You're using it to get something that's much more important to you than either profits or losses," I noted further.

"That's the biggest bunch of bull I've ever heard," was his parting comment.

Several years later I met him at a commodity seminar. He apologized for his behavior on the telephone and told me that my original observation of his problem was correct. After going through a bankruptcy, a divorce, and several hundred thousand dollars in market losses, he was forced to stop trading. During his involuntary retirement from the market, he realized the stimulus-response consequence of his behavior. He explained it to me as follows.

"The problem with my trading was not really related to my trading at all. When I first started in the market I took some losses the way all traders do. But each time I took a loss I would make a big deal about it. I complained to my friends and business partners. They felt sorry for me. And I wanted them to. Every time I took a loss, they'd try to cheer me up. I enjoyed the attention. Instead of taking the loss, forgetting about it, and moving on to the next trade, I milked it for all the attention I could get. I had a nagging feeling after a while that I might be losing on purpose. But it was hard to accept that possibility. All I know is that every time I took a loss, I got a great deal of attention. Every time I took a profit, I got no special attention. I'd tell my friends about the big profit I took and they'd say, 'That's great, Chuck, old boy, I knew you could do it.' And that was it. Whenever I took a profit they made no special deal about it. Possibly they were jealous. Yet when I was a loser it was somehow an occasion to celebrate. We'd go out and drink under the guise of 'drowning the loss.' I realize now that this was acting as a reward for losing. I should have received absolutely no attention for being a loser. We should have gone out partying when I had made a profit. The money wasn't nearly as important a reward as was the attention.

"And to make things even worse, the losses upset my family. My wife would punish me and actually all that time she didn't realize that I enjoyed her being aggravated. I didn't realize it either. The consequences of my losing were serving some very important purposes in my life. Not only did they get me attention from friends, but they also irritated my wife, and that made me happy. If I had realized the connection between losses and their consequences, I might have been able to change the outcome. I realize it now. Fortunately, it's not too late."

I asked him how his trading was going. "Couldn't be much better," he replied proudly, "I know now that the market is much less important than me. I know that every loss is a lesson and every profit is a reward. Each time I lose I forget about it as soon as I can. I try to see if I made a mistake in reading my trading system. If I made a mistake, then I write it down and keep a record of it. I consult it often to make certain that I don't make the same mistakes repeatedly. When I take a loss it's just between me and my broker. I mention it to no one else. When I take a profit I celebrate. I spend some of the money, put some in the bank, and tell my friends about how smart I am. I pat myself on the back and enjoy all the rewards that the profit should bring."

This true story is worth more than any system, course, theory, or signal. To many it rings a personal bell. Those who cannot relate directly will recognize elements that are part of their own makeup. The essence is, to be sure, behavioral. Recalling once again my words about consequences, you can see how this trader was being maintained by consequences that increased his losing behavior. Too many of us believe that the money made from trading will be sufficiently rewarding to keep us trading well. This is not the case. For those who are in touch with their goals and motivations and for those who have few conflicts in their home life, money can serve as a great consequence. For many traders, the money gained from investing is just not enough to maintain winning behavior.

How Market Results Affect Behavior

Let's look at the various consequences of market results. For each possible outcome there are only three potential consequences—reward, punishment, and break even. I will discuss each combination and its implications. Assume that a trade is made with profit as the result, ideally the profit should be rewarding in and of itself. Since I maintain that for most traders, the profit alone will not suffice, there are several additional consequences that might assure positive reward. If you find your trading is not as profitable as it should be, then examine the consequences accompanying each profit. Most likely you will find that your profits are not bringing you anything more than financial reward. Personally, that's enough for me. With the exception of those who do not find money sufficient, there are many additional rewards that should be used.

Table 7.1 lists positive consequences that could be added to each profit after it is taken. Remember they should not, under any circumstances, be used unless a profit has been taken. In other words, do not reward yourself before a trade has actually been completed. A completed trade is defined as one round turn in the market. This consists of a buy and a sell, or a sell and a subsequent buy. No rewards are in order for open positions,

Table 7.1

Positive Consequences of a Profitable Trade

---

1. Enter winning trade in ledger or record book.
2. Pat yourself on the back. Tell yourself how well you did.
3. Tell others about your trade. Seek out their verbal praise.
4. Celebrate. Have a party; treat yourself to an expensive meal.
5. Buy something. Now's the time to get that new car or tape player.
6. Immediately tell your broker to send you a check for 25 percent of the profit.
7. Put some of the profit in your savings account.
8. Solicit your broker's approval.
9. Gloat over the profit for several days.
10. Don't feel any guilt about being immodest.

---

intended positions, imaginary positions, paper trades, or "I would have" trades. The best time to apply positive consequences is immediately after the profit has been taken. Table 7.1 is a list of possibilities. You may find some of them amusing. I know for a fact they can help.

Profits and Punishment

What about a profit that results in punishment? Is it possible that taking a profit can bring negative results? This can most certainly happen. In fact, it is very common. A brief example will illustrate the point. You take a profit of several thousand dollars and feel rather proud. You tell a "friend" about the great event and he says, "You know, there's a loser for every winner in the market. Don't you feel bad about the poor slob who lost that money? You're taking his money and he might not have enough to feed his family." Another punitive statement comes from the "friend" who reminds you about taxes. "Sure you took a profit of 6000 bucks, but by the time Uncle Sam gets through with you, you'll only have $2000 left—big deal." Another "friend" might say, "Well, that was sure a lucky shot, probably won't happen again." With friends like these, you don't need enemies. If you know that the profit was not a result of your trading system, then avoid any of the frills listed in Table 7.1. But if you're certain that the profit came from strict adherence to your system, shun any and all attempts that make you feel bad. Avoid all negative statements either by yourself or by others. If you find others who are consistently

Table 7.2
Negative Consequences of a Profit (Avoid Them at All Costs)

1. Do not attribute the trade to luck.
2. Do not refuse praise from others.
3. Do not minimize the profit in any way, shape, or form.
4. Do not allow others to minimize your accomplishment.
5. Do not accept any guilt from anyone.
6. Do not feel sorry for the person who lost.
7. Do not worry about the taxes you'll have to pay.
8. Do not allow the profit to cause you anxiety about the next trade.
9. Do not feel ashamed for having been right.
10. Do not allow any negative fantasies to enter your mind.

negative when you take a profit, then avoid them. Even consider terminating your relationship with them. Table 7.2 is a list of things to avoid when a profit has been taken.

Although in the minority, some individuals feel guilt or shame after taking a profit. They feel that another trader has suffered because of their personal gain. Some traders get sheepish and others feel that they must continue to "perform." There is absolutely no place for such feelings in the repertoire of successful traders. Each victory, if based on the trading system, must be fully and totally enjoyed. No attempt whatsoever should be made to minimize the gain. Avoid everyone who seeks to punish or otherwise negate your positive consequences. If such negatives are permitted to enter into the behavioral chain, they will reduce the rewarding power of financial gain and thereby decrease the overall success rate of your trading system.

Break Even

Another possible outcome of trading is the "break even." There are several ways to relate to this event. If, after you deduct commission from the profit, you break even, then you have, in reality, taken a profit. A break even trade is, in effect, a winning trade. It should be treated in the same way as a profit. Breaking even on a trade is merely an indication that your trading system is working. The consequence should therefore be a positive one. Certainly it is not possible to reap any of the financial rewards, but all others that apply to profitable trades should be taken. Any attempt to make a break even trade bring punishment should be avoided as in the previous example.

Consequences of a Loss

What can we say about the consequences of a loss? First and foremost, it is much more difficult to deal appropriately with losses than with profits. If you have taken a loss, then you already feel bad. How much more punishment is appropriate? Here are some guidelines regarding the appropriate consequences of losses. As in the case of a profit being ideally sufficient to maintain behavior, a loss should be sufficient to result in fewer losing trades. For most speculators, this is not the case. In an earlier discussion, I stressed the importance of making certain that your trading signals are entirely a result of your own indicators. Assuming that they are, and assuming further that you take a loss, you can reach either of two conclusions. First, the loss may reflect the intrinsic limitations of your system: all systems take losses. Second, the loss may be caused by your misreading, miscalculation, poor order placement, early exit, or abuse of stop loss. If your loss is a result of some limitation of your system, then you would want to deal with it in a different way than you would with the second possibility.

If you take a loss trading your signals with proper follow through, then nothing else should be done in the way of consequences. Merely accept the loss, enter it in your record book, double check that the loss was justified by the signal, and forget about it. Too much attention to a loss will reward it. Avoid all attempts by yourself or others to soothe the losing experience. Table 7.3 is a list of don'ts that should follow a justifiable loss.

Above all, do not allow anyone to make your loss into something positive. You will note that item 10 mentions over eating, over drinking, and sex. This does not mean that each loss should result in starvation or celibacy. It does mean that you should not respond to the loss by excess in any of these areas. There is no such thing as "drowning a loss in wine" or "eating a loss into oblivion." These behaviors will merely reward you for losing. The time to engage in satisfaction of these primary needs is after profits and not after losses.

How about the loss which results from an error in implementing your trading system?

Table 7.3
Consequences of a Justifiable Loss

---

1. Accept the loss and forget about it.
2. Record it in your ledger and do not "rehash" it.
3. Do not recruit anyone's sympathy or sorrow.
4. Do not feel sorry for yourself.
5. Do not feel as if you have been punished.
6. Do not discuss the loss with anyone.
7. Do not accept ridicule or blame from your broker.
8. Do not punish or hate yourself for losing.
9. Do not blame your trading system.
10. Do not soothe your loss by going overboard on food, drink, or sex.
11. Do not allow yourself to accept any punishment from loved ones.
12. Do not alter your technique, system, or methods.
13. Do not fear making the next trade.
14. Do not respond by allowing your market studies to fall behind.

What should be the consequences of such a blunder? What kinds of errors should be considered? Each loss, if not justifiable, must be a lesson in proper trading. An observation from the writings of Jesse Livermore (Edwin Lefevre) is in order:

> Of course, if a man is both wise and lucky, he will not make the same mistake twice. But he will make any one of the ten thousand brothers or cousins of the original. The Mistake family is so large that there is always one of them around when you want to see what you can do in the fool-play line. (1965, p. 117)

There are indeed hundreds of things one can do wrong in the market, but only a precious few that one can do right. It is possible to blunder at any step in the behavioral chain. For every one correct behavior, there may be more than a hundred possible errors. How can they be avoided? Table 7.4 lists some behaviorally oriented suggestions. If you have taken a loss due to error on your part, then I suggest you adhere to the points outlined in Table 7.3. In addition, exercise the steps listed in Table 7.4 each and every time you blunder. Perhaps the most important role of errors is the educational one. Any trader who makes a mistake and then forgets about it is not getting full benefit from his or her tuition money (loss).

Table 7.4

Consequences of a Nonjustifiable Loss (Market Blunder)

1. Specify the exact error as precisely as you possibly can.
2. Record the error in a "mistake book" kept for this purpose.
3. Place the error in its appropriate category.
4. Review the error or errors to make certain that you were indeed at fault.
5. Relive the situation from start to finish (more on this in Chapter 8).
6. Recruit the help of a broker if the error is one that can be recognized by others.
7. See if you can devise a system to signal the error before you make it.

I recommend a specific procedure for dealing with errors that is designed to make their recurrence less likely. I consider the rectification of errors so very important that Chapter 8 is devoted entirely to its discussion.

REVIEW

1. It is more important to learn how to correct market errors than why the errors were made.
2. The profits that come with good trades and the losses that come with bad trades are not necessarily enough to change behavior.
3. To determine the reinforcing aspects of a behavior it is necessary to thoroughly observe and record its consequences.
4. Many positive and negative social consequences follow profits and losses.
5. It is important to distinguish between market errors and a justifiable loss.
6. The behavioral learning model can be used for effecting positive change as well as for the analysis of efforts.

8

The Discovery Process—
How to Know Yourself

Whether you're a conservative investor or an active speculator, you must know your strengths and weaknesses. Each individual must have the most thorough and extensive self-knowledge possible. Although one might reason that knowing one's self is a rather simple thing to do, paradoxically, it is one of the most elusive and difficult tasks any individual can assume. Our many defense mechanisms make it almost impossible for us to know ourselves thoroughly. Vanity, pride, fear, jealousy, denial, repression, and suppression all prevent self-awareness. There are, however, a number of techniques that can be used to acquire self-knowledge.

Most psychotherapy is designed to bring insight and self-knowledge. Although many people have pushed feelings out of awareness, they have not repressed them beyond retrieval. But if you suffer from defensiveness, you will not find it possible to invest successfully, no matter how hard you try to follow a specific plan. If you cannot change, regardless of effort, you might want to seek professional help. The market may not be your major problem. If your life, marriage, job, and interpersonal relationships are defective, then intensive help is necessary. And in such cases, the techniques and suggestions covered in this book may not suffice.

It is impossible to truly understand yourself and your behavior unless you make a thorough assessment of the factors and stimuli that motivate you and of your responses to various internal and external events. In order to help you on the road to self-discovery, I have prepared a checklist that is based on my experiences as a trader and a psychologist, and on my observation of other traders through the years. While this list is by no means an exhaustive assessment of your repertoire as a trader, it is, I feel, sufficiently detailed to allow a general picture of your trading personality.

I've found that the most efficient, prompt, and economical way to evaluate your own goals and emotions is through the use of a checklist. This requires responses to a series of statements and/or questions. By answering all items honestly, you may be able to obtain a general idea of your overall strengths and weaknesses. The checklist that follows is not a validated or standardized test of trading readiness. It is not a psychological test, rather it is an evaluation technique designed to help you in your trading and investing. Remember that my intention is only to highlight areas that may be causing problems with your trading.

Checklist

Instructions: Respond to each question with a yes or no. Please answer all questions. Evaluation of your responses appears at the end of this checklist. Remember that total honesty is necessary if results are to be meaningful.

	YES	NO
1. I subscribe to more than three advisory services.	——	——
2. I believe that brokers should give advice to their customers. It's a broker's job to know which trades are good and to advise their clients of the best trading opportunities.	——	——
3. My investment strategy is planned well in advance of my actual trades.	——	——
4. Most of my market exits are due to stop losses being hit.	——	——
5. I trade primarily for the long term.	——	——
6. I keep several accounts at different brokerage houses so that I can get a good idea of what the different experts are thinking.	——	——
7. My behavior at home is intolerable when I have lost money in the market.	——	——
8. I like to trade for the challenge of winning.	——	——

	YES	NO
9. I have been a net loser in the market during the last five years.	____	____
10. The market is "fixed." Only insiders make money.	____	____
11. Brokers make you lose money because they make you trade too much.	____	____
12. The market is all luck.	____	____
13. I buy on good news and sell on bad news.	____	____
14. I'm primarily a bull. Most of my trades are from the long side.	____	____
15. I don't like to buy when prices are high or sell when they're too low.	____	____
16. Some of my largest profits have come from trading upside or downside breakouts.	____	____
17. The pit traders always try to "pick" your stops. That's why I never use them.	____	____
18. I tend not to get too frustrated by the market. A loss is a loss.	____	____
19. I often lose sleep over the market.	____	____
20. My average profit is larger than my average loss.	____	____
21. I have a set time for studying the market.	____	____
22. I set specific price objectives for all of my trades.	____	____
23. Before making a trade, I try to get as many opinions from others as possible.	____	____
24. I'd make more profits if I had a better trading system.	____	____
25. I have never read the writings of Livermore, Gann, Baruch, Pugh, or Wyckoff.	____	____
26. The best way to be successful in the market is to isolate yourself from others' opinions.	____	____
27. I never (or hardly ever) change my mind about a trade once it has been made.	____	____

Evaluation of Results

Now that you have responded to these items let's go through and examine what I consider to be the "best" response and my rationale.

Item 1.   Most successful traders do not subscribe to more than a few advisory services. It is the emotionally weak investor who draws advice from too many sources. Perhaps two or three reputable advisory services are all that is required. You are always best off trading either on your own market evaluations or on the basis of advise from only a few sources. A "yes" response to this item is not a positive indication. Score yourself 0 for a "yes" answer and 1 point for a "no."

Item 2.   It is not the job of a broker to give advice. It is the job of a broker to provide good execution of orders, quick response time to an order, and correct fills. With few exceptions, those who depend on brokers for anything more than good service are net losers. Those who expect more from a broker are usually disappointed. If you truly believe that it is the job of a broker to give good advice, then you are most likely not a successful trader. If you answered "yes," give yourself 0. If "no," give yourself a 1.

Item 3.   If you answered "yes" to this item, then add 1 point to your score. It is the mark of a successful trader to plan investing and/or trading strategy well in advance, carrying out plans to their completion. If you answered "no," then score 0.

Item 4.   This is also a mark of successful trading. A disciplined trader places stops and lets them ride until his system indicates. Stops are the key to success for many traders. They tend to limit losses. Notwithstanding the time-tested value of stops, their use is a distinct mark of trading maturity. Stops need not actually be entered, but they must be used! It takes an even more disciplined trader to not enter stops, keeping them in mind and using them when the appropriate price level has been hit. If you answered "yes," then score 1; score 0 for "no."

Item 5.   If you answered "yes," then add 1 point to your score. Another indicator of successful trading is "long-term orientation." Typically, those who trade for the short term (excepting pit brokers, floor traders, and professional traders who have this as their sole occupation) are net losers. The most successful individuals are those who buy and hold, or sell short and hold. If you answered "no" and if you do not trade as a profession, then score 0 for this item.

Item 6.   It is also characteristic of immature traders to keep accounts at several different brokerage houses so they may obtain "good information." Typically, this results in a confused trader, inasmuch as he or she receives so much contradictory information that a profitable decision is unlikely. It is also a sign of insecurity. There is nothing wrong with having several different accounts at several different brokerage houses. It is the rationale in this case that is faulty. One ought not depend on brokers for information. Score 0 for "yes" and 1 for "no."

Item 7.   This is an obvious item. Certainly if you admit that your behavior at home is intolerable when you lose, then you are aware of your shortcoming. This is symptomatic of emotional traders. I hate to punish you for your honesty, but if you answered "yes," then score yourself 0. If you answered "no," then add 1 point to your total score.

Item 8.   This is not a good reason for trading; one might as well go out and climb a mountain. The only acceptable reason for trading the markets is to make profits or to hedge and to avoid losses in cash market operations. Those who trade merely for the challenge are not necessarily effective traders. They are prone to gamble, take chances, and trade for thrills. They will most likely end up net losers. If you answered "yes," then add a 0 to your score. Add 1 point for a "no" answer.

Item 9.   The single best indicator of emotional ability in the market is your net performance over the past five years. Even if you have broken even you are well ahead. But if, after five years, you are still a net loser, then you are most likely in need of some psychological shaping up. Read the rest of this book carefully, and do some deep soul searching. Also add 0 to your score. If you are about even or a small net loser, then you may add 1 to your score. Also add 1 if you are a net winner.

Item 10.   This attitude is typical among those with a losing orientation to the market. It is also common among those who have never been net winners. If you answered "yes," then you have negative attitudes that will most likely lead to further losses. Score 1 if you answered "no" and 0 if you responded "yes."

Item 11.   It is foolish to state that a broker "makes" one do anything. The trader alone is responsible for his or her losses. Those who indicate that their broker "made" them do something or "not do" something are basically immature and have losing attitudes. Score 0 for a "yes" answer and 1 for a "no."

Item 12.   Another losing attitude is embodied in this statement. Those who believe that the market is all "luck" do not believe in themselves to be the instruments of success. Thus they will not be successful traders and most likely have not made too many profitable investments in the past. Score 0 for a "yes" and 1 for a "no."

Item 13.   Unsophisticated investors and traders buy in response to good news and sell in response to bad news. Knowledgeable traders buy in anticipation of such news and sell into the actual event. They buy on expectation and sell on realization. Those who answered "yes" to this question are revealing "public" attitude. They are most likely net losers in the market. It takes emotional maturity to buy into bad news and sell into good news. A "yes" answer should be scored 0. For a "no" answer score 1 point.

Item 14.   This is another representation of "public" attitude. It's a fact that knowledgeable and successful traders play both sides of the market. It is emotionally difficult to sell short. Those capable of doing so have the necessary qualifications for profitable trading. Whereas it is true that large sums of money are made on the long side, it is also true that the fastest money comes from short positions. If you trade from the long side exclusively or primarily, then score 0 for this item. Score a 1 for "no."

Item 15.   The successful trader does not stop to think about whether prices are too high or low. If a signal is flashed, then the signal is followed. Little consideration is or should be given to price. The novice trader, or the investor who is not capable of emotionally following a buy or sell signal, will always be second guessing his system, saying things such as "prices are too high now, I'll wait for a pullback before buying." This is not to say that there never are times when prices are too high or too low. Certainly there comes a time when prices are too high to buy. This time will be so indicated by most reliable trading systems, technical or fundamental. It is when the relative cheapness or expense of a stock or commodity is used as an excuse for not following a signal that it is destructive and indicative of poor discipline. Score 0 for "yes" and 1 for "no."

Item 16.   Trading with the trend is a hard thing to do. It is a fact, however, that trading with the trend, buying on strength and selling on weakness, buying into breakouts and selling into breakdowns is a successful technique. It requires emotional readiness. Those who can do it usually show large profits and emotional discipline as well. Score 1 if you answered "yes" and 0 if you answered "no."

Item 17.   This is an excuse for not using stops. If you use this excuse, then you are most probably a net loser in the market. Score 0 for "yes" and 1 for "no."

Item 18. No investor is perfect. We all have our frustrations, successes, and failures. But for the most part, those who trade profitably tend not to get frustrated by a loss. Their usual response is to forget about the loss as soon as possible. If you dwell on a loss, brood over it for days, or let it affect you by undermining self confidence, then you are not emotionally ready to trade. Score 0 for a "no" answer and 1 for a "yes."

Item 19. This item relates to 18. We all tend to lose sleep now and again. We do so, at times, because of the market. If, however, one loses sleep frequently over positions or trades, then one is too emotionally tied to the market, and a problem exists. This is a prime symptom of insecurity, lack of confidence, and poor skill. Score a 0 if you answered "yes" and a 1 if you answered "no."

Item 20. The size of your average loss, compared to your average profit, is an indicator of trading discipline. Those investors and traders who follow a well planned strategy tend to show smaller average losses, and fewer total losses, on a per trade basis. If you fall into the larger average loss category, then you are probably not trading in accordance with effective psychological principles. You are, perhaps, riding losses too long, contrary to your trading system. Score 0 for "yes" and 1 for "no."

Item 21. This is perhaps the single most important indicator of winning discipline. And winning discipline is possible only through emotional control. Traders and investors who are successful, year after year, have a well-scheduled and planned time for studying the markets. Regardless of orientation, technician or fundamentalist, they spend a specific amount of time on the market, at regular intervals. If you answered "no" to this question, subtract 2 points from your score. If you answered "yes," then add 2 points to your score.

Item 22. This is a further mark of the individual who is following a disciplined trading. As such he or she is a mature investor, capable of sticking to a plan of action. This ability is a prerequisite to profitable trading. If you answered "yes," then add 1 point to your score; if "no," add 0.

Item 23. Those who need to assess the collective opinion of others are highly insecure individuals. Such a need is symptomatic of poor emotional readiness, and is a definite psychological handicap. In fact, it is common knowledge that the consensus of opinion is usually wrong. Only a secure trader can carry out a trade from initiation to completion without the approval or advice of others. Score 1 if you answered "no" and 0 if "yes."

Item 24. Such statements are made by investors who have not as yet realized that they alone are responsible for their profits and losses. The trading system itself is not nearly as important as what is done with it. An idiot driving an expensive automobile is still an idiot, albeit a "classy" one. If you blame your lack of profits on a trading system, then you most probably lack the necessary psychological readiness for trading. Score 0 if "yes," 1 if "no."

Item 25.   The experiences of successful traders and investors have been put into writing so that we may benefit from them. An investor who wishes to improve his or her results will be seeking a better way. Undoubtedly this investor will have turned to the great masters' writings. If you have not done so, then I recommend you explore these sources of knowledge as soon as possible. Score 0 for "yes" and 1 for "no."

Item 26.   The truly successful investor and trader recognizes the importance of isolation. Many of one's best decisions and trades are made in isolation. It is a sign of emotional readiness and ability to block out interfering stimulation. Score 1 for "yes" and 0 for "no."

Item 27.   Firm resolve and follow-through are also characteristic of profitable trading. If you lack the ability to stay with a trade through its prescribed conclusion, then you lack a key element in the formula for profitable trading and investing. Score 0 for "no" and 1 for "yes."

Now add up your score. The highest possible total is 28 points. Use the following guidelines to interpret your score.

If Your Score Was in the 21–28 Range.   You are probably a very successful trader. If you scored this high but do not show large profits, then you may very well be using a poor trading system. I suggest you experiment with different trading methods.

Score of 15–20.   You have the right idea, but still need a little polishing. You are on the way to profitable investing and trading but need to develop more discipline. Many of the exercises in this book can help. Pay particular attention to the items you answered incorrectly.

Score of 10–14.   You have scored 50 percent or less. This is not indicative of pending success in your trading, and is a warning that you need to work on your discipline. I urge you to pay particular attention to the behavioral trading programs outlined in this book.

Score 9 or Less.   Be careful! It is my belief that you are heading for losses if you have not already found them. You must begin to re-educate yourself emotionally at Step 1. I would even go so far as to suggest you stop trading until you have evaluated your specific problems and formulated a comprehensive program to deal with them.

REVIEW   It's one thing for me to tell you that you need help. It's a far greater thing for me to tell you exactly how to go about getting help. Certainly, the many techniques and suggestions in this book can be instrumental in the progress of change. But if you are one of those investors or traders who has been losing money for years, then it may be very difficult to take even the first step toward change. If you lack the self-discipline for profitable trading, then it is natural to assume that you lack the necessary discipline to retrain yourself. In this case I have a number of suggestions I truly believe can help. Remember that my comments are directed primarily at those who score less than 15 on the evaluation scale. Some of the suggested methods will be helpful to all traders regardless of score.

1. **Take time to be away from the market.**   I suggest you start by reading some of the classical texts on investing. I recommend Lefevre's *Reminiscences of a Stock Operator* as an ideal first assignment. At the end of this book, you will find a Bibliography. You may wish to study most of these books prior to trading again. The best way to end a losing situation is to get out of the situation, at least temporarily. This is why I recommend standing aside. If you continue to beat your head against the wall, you will become immune to the pain and won't realize that you are destroying yourself and possibly your family as well.

2. **If you must continue to trade, then form a club or group.** This can help keep checks and balances on your trading. Group pressure and guidance is a very helpful asset for the wayward investor. Investment clubs are easily found or formed. The degree of discipline which the democratic process can instill is truly amazing. It often takes such clubs many days to decide on a specific buy or sell. But the process is thorough, well-researched, and frequently profitable. When you have internalized some of their techniques, you can reevaluate yourself and strike out on your own.

3. **Don't "paper trade"!**   My specific objections to this common technique were stated in Chapter 00. Paper trading will not, in my opinion, teach you a darned thing about the real market world. It will only give you a sense of false confidence and could very well frustrate you to the point of error.

4. **Obtain professional help from a counselor.**   If you are having difficulties in other areas of your life, find a mental health professional. Problems in the home are a good indicator of emotional difficulty, as are extreme mood swings.

9

How to Rectify Trading Errors

All human beings, at one time or another, make mistakes. But some individuals seem to make many more errors than others. Psychologically there exists a relationship between anxiety and accuracy. Up to a given point, a certain amount of pressure and/or anxiety can be beneficial. Some individuals perform very well under pressure. But beyond the point of maximum benefit, stress and anxiety can increase significantly the degree and seriousness of errors. In the market, where anxiety is high, stress typically results in loss. Whether or not the given error or errors are being made with an unconscious desire to lose, it is possible, in my opinion, to structure the trading environment in a way that will minimize not only their frequency but the relative intensity of each error as well. The individual who has at his or her disposal the necessary behavioral tools (as described herein) to alter error behavior, but who does not do so, may require more intensive therapeutic assistance. I do not believe, however, that this is necessary in most cases. One can, in fact, overcome many problems with the behavioral approach. Before attacking the many blunders a trader can make, I would like to acquaint you with some details about the behavioral concepts of shaping and extinction.

You will recall that the term *shaping* applies to the behavioral learning process. A psychologist decides to teach an animal to press a bar. The bar is connected to a switch and pressing it will cause a pellet of food to be delivered into a dish. Food reward will maintain the bar-press behavior. But animals are not born with bar-pressing skill. They must learn it—enter shaping. In order to teach an animal the bar press, we observe its behavior very closely as it walks about. As it approaches the bar, we drop a food pellet into the cage. Before too long our subject is standing close to the bar, since he has been rewarded for proximity to it. Time passes and we continue to give rewards for closeness to the bar. We now place a food pellet on the bar. As the animal touches the pellet, he accidentally applies pressure to the bar, and another pellet drops into the attached dish. After several such repetitions, the animal presses the bar independently. A behavior has been shaped (taught).

Scheduling

We now put our subject on a schedule. We decide to reward him once for every 5 presses of the bar. After he is responding steadily we change the rules and reward him once for every 20 presses of the bar. After some time, we increase the behavioral requirement to 50 presses, and so on. By employing such a reinforcement schedule, it is possible to obtain a great deal of work or behavior from the subject. Assume that after several weeks of training we drop the reward entirely. What happens? You naturally assume that the animal will stop pressing the bar after a while. This is true. But what happens first? The animal's initial response to termination of the reward is an increase in response rate. It is almost as if he is trying harder. The "frustration effect," as I like to call it, is a common element in all behavior once reward has been terminated. As time passes and food is not given, the bar press will be extinguished (forgotten). From time to time, the animal may try the bar press again. But the longer reward remains absent, the bar press will be increasingly rare. Figure 9.1 is a typical learning curve from acquisition to extinction.

Assume now that we put our animal on a random schedule of reward, that is, reward will be given at irregular intervals, whether time-based or response-based.

No matter how many times the bar is pressed, reward could come at any time. The learning curve for this behavior will be somewhat different. Although the behavior will take longer to acquire, it will ultimately be much more resistant to extinction. Some experimental animals maintained on a variety of random schedules seem to go on responding indefinitely, even after reward has been totally terminated for many months. The market, in many respects, is similar to the random reinforcement schedule. Even after rewards have been absent for many months, traders go on trading. There are many parallels to gambling behavior. After a behavior has been present for many months or many repetitions, it becomes so entrenched that it is virtually impossible to avoid. It becomes a

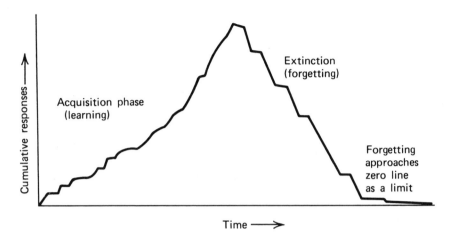

Figure 9.1 Typical learning curve.

habit. Not all habits, as you know, are productive. Many individuals continue with self-destructive habits to the point of death. Smoking and drinking are two obvious examples.

I belabor the point in order to remind you that trading the market is also a habit. It can be a productive habit or a self-destructive addiction. How can inappropriate and/or painful habits be changed? The ultimate answer is simple. Remove the positive consequences, apply negative ones, redirect the behavior to a productive end, and reward it. But that's easier said than done. In the experimental situation, where the psychologist has total control over the subject, it is a relatively mechanical task. But in human beings, such change becomes difficult to implement. It is hard enough for a therapist to help the patient change. It is even more of a challenge for the individual to change without assistance. The precise organizational scheme outlined next is presented in an effort to make change more likely when self-administered.

Record Keeping

There are several tools that must be used in order to initiate the change process. The first is record keeping. I suggest all traders keep an ongoing record of trades. The record should list date, buy or sell, signal for entry, date of exit, amount of profit or loss, and, most important, reason for loss. Reason for loss should be listed by code in one of several categories.

A justifiable loss—one that cannot be directly related to the trader (as discussed earlier)—should, for example, be assigned a given code letter or number. As losses occur, you will become familiar with the reason(s) for their occurrence. Each trader will have his or her own set of weaknesses. Some of the typical reasons are shown in Table 9.1. You may have reasons that do not fit these categories. Your list might include such things as "had hangover and couldn't read chart correctly" or "didn't show up at the office and forgot to put in stop." The reason should be specifically indicated. If and when a new behavior crops up, you must also list it. Generally traders will have only two or three major classifications of mistakes with many subsidiary errors falling under the group headings.

Keep a running tally of which mistakes are most frequent. In addition, it would be a good idea to note any particular rewards or punishments that followed the error(s) and any noteworthy events that preceded them. Figure 9.2 shows how such a record sheet might look.

At the end of each month, review your record sheet. Note any errors that seem to be very frequent. Also make note of any previous conditions that are repetitive. The thing to look for is a pattern or patterns of behavior inherent in your trading. Once isolated, these patterns will become your target behaviors.

Unless you have a clear idea of what you are doing incorrectly, it will not be possible to change. It is therefore impossible for me to overemphasize the importance of record keeping.

Table 9.1
Typical Reasons for Market Losses Attributable to the Trader

1. Not using stops.
2. Listening to broker.
3. Not following signal to liquidate.
4. Not raising stop.
5. Getting out too soon.
6. Getting in too soon (before signal).
7. Taking a tip.
8. Making a trade due to government report (or earnings report) but no signal.
9. Anticipating a sell signal prior to stop getting hit.
10. Nonspecific fear or greed.
11. Margin call forcing liquidation before signal.

Let's take a look at where we stand prior to beginning the important topic of treatment. Here is a brief review of steps taken so far:

1. The behavioral learning model has been discussed with particular emphasis on the stimulus-response-consequences chain.
2. The point was made that behavior is maintained as a function of consequences. If, for example, a behavior continues, we must assume that the consequences of it are rewarding even though they may appear to be negative.
3. By changing the consequences of behavior, we can change behavior itself.
4. In order to change consequences, we must analyze them as specifically as possible.
5. This can be achieved by the use of a trading record. The value of such a record is both educational and therapeutic.
6. Behavior change (treatment), according to the learning model I have presented, must follow an objective, specific, and organized series of steps.

Even if you do not accept the tenets of behavioral psychology, you will most likely agree that the methodology of this approach is highly organized and objective. To accomplish the scientific technique that I believe necessary in behavior change, we must ignore some of the more subjective terms that most of us are accustomed to. This does not mean that feelings and thoughts are useless in my approach. It means, rather, that for the time being we shall not attempt to deal with any entity that is not clearly measurable, observable, and visible.

Changing Behavior

The next step is treatment. Some background into some of the techniques that behavioral psychologists use to implement therapeutic change would be helpful here. As you will recall, the principle of extinction refers to the unlearning or forgetting process. Depending on the type of reward schedule used in the learning process, behavior change will be either a relatively simple task or a rather lengthy one.

It is safe to assume that many counterproductive and pathological behaviors are maintained on random schedules of reinforcement. Certainly this is the case for most market behaviors. Frequently trading rules are

Trade	Date In	Date Out	Profit/Loss	Trading Rule	Reason for Loss–Comment
Bot–Dec 79, corn	6/17/78	6/21/78	–$ 247.50	6, 3	Stop loss hit–rules followed
Sld–Feb 79, hogs	6/23/78	8/11/78	+$1250.50	6, 5	Rules followed–no loss
Bot–100S GM	7/11/78	7/12/78	–$ 245.20	11	"Scared out" too early
Bot–Feb 79, gold	8/12/78	9/12/78	+$1450.00	12, 7	Profitable trade but got out too soon on news report
Sld–Feb 79, hogs	9/15/78	9/23/78	–$1227.60	None	Bot on rumor and took large loss one week later
Bot–200S IBM	9/26/78	9/27/78	+$ 250.00	None	Bot on bullish earnings report –broke trading rules
Sld–Jan 80 OJ	11/12/78	1/14/79	+$2560.00	3, 7, 2	Followed all rules–1st trade after reevaluation of rules
Bot–100S PRD	1/23/79	2/17/79	+$ 980.50	1, 5	Followed rules and made another good trade!!!
Sld–100S PRD	2/17/79	5/25/79	+$1160.50	1, 2, 3 5, 7	All trading rules followed to the letter–profit!!!
Sld–100S XRX	6/11/79	6/15/79	–$ 768.90	5, 4	Followed rules for entry but did not liquidate on stop
Bot–Mar 80, corn	7/01/79	9/11/79	+$ 143.50	3, 4, 5	Entry OK but did not use a stop and gave back big profit

Bot—Mar 80, oats	9/13/79	9/15/79	−$ 265.00	3, 6, 1	Followed rules but still lost—getting frustrated . . .
Bot—Mar 80, oil	9/15/79	9/17/79	−$1220.00	3, 7	No use of stop. Overtrading—very anxious—be careful!
Bot—100S LVO	9/19/79	9/23/79	−$ 550.00	None	System working but I'm not—taking break to evaluate

Trading rules:

1. Buy on penetration of 3-week high—sell on penetration of 3-week low.
2. Buy/sell penetration of 10-day moving average.
3. Buy/sell on 50 percent retracement from breakout.
4. Buy/sell on penetration of triple high or low.
5. Place stop at 75 percent once in excess of $1000 open profit.
6. Buy/sell 3-day pullback to trend change point.
7. Buy/sell on weekend rule (close on high or low of week).
8. Buy/sell on 2-day upside reversal (downside reversal).
9. Buy on penetration of contract high with open interest high.
10. Close out position after key reversal.
11. Buy/sell on new 5-week high or low.
12. Buy/sell new all-time high or low.

Figure 9.2 Trading record—Hypothetical trading rules.

broken and yet a profit results. And there are times that trading rules are disregarded and a loss follows. We never know in advance if our violation of the rules will be profitable. This random type of schedule makes for behaviors which, as previously indicated, are especially resistant to change. Several procedures can be used in changing market behaviors, but before I suggest any, it is important for me to let you know the exact limitations of what can be accomplished through the written word. Since the implementation of my suggestions is not directly under my control, it is impossible to guarantee results. The absence of a therapist to supervise this program places a great burden on you, the individual, should you seek to change your habits. If you can recruit some help, you will most likely be more successful. It is, however, not possible for me to assure you of results, particularly if your market problem goes much deeper than indirect assistance can alleviate.

Stop-Loss Program

For the purpose of our present discussion, I will concentrate on market problem 1 in Table 9.1. Not using stops. Let's assume that the use of stops is preferable in all markets and with most trading systems. In some cases, a "stop reverse" order is used. This type of stop is designed to limit one's loss and at the same time reverse the position. If, for example, one was short the market with stop reverse at a given price, then one would not only get stopped out when the price was hit, but one would also buy at the given price, thereby establishing a net long position. A stop reverse would then be entered on the new position, and so on.

Many moving average systems use stop reverse orders since they want to be in the market at all times. Regardless of the type of stop used, whether it is a close only stop, stop limit, stop reverse, or otherwise, the use of stops, if indicated by a trading system, is a necessity. We can only assume that the individual who does not use stops has been maintained on a random reinforcement schedule. In other words, there were occasions that resulted in a profit even though no stop was used. Although the profit (or avoidance of loss) may have been infrequent, learning nevertheless took place and a bad habit was acquired. This, by the way, is perhaps the most common market problem. Many excuses are given for not using stops. Some are rather artful, but none is valid. The key to successful money management is and always has been limitation of losses. I will not, however, preach to you about the value of stops. I will merely assume that it is in most traders' best interest to use them or another loss-limiting technique.

How can we go about changing this problem with the assistance of behavioral techniques? You will recall the learning model given previously. Let's "plug into" it and take a close look. Figure 9.3 shows how the stimulus-response-consequence chain would look in our treatment approach for the use of stop-loss orders.

The problem with using stops is that their use is not very rewarding. In most cases, a stop will get you out with a less, or a smaller profit than you had. This is how stops work. You can see that there is nothing positive about the use of stops, other than the avoidance of a loss. Each time a stop is hit you feel as if you have been punished. Why should you continue to use stops when all they bring is punishment? If you have a profit and use a stop, you will get stopped out at a profit that is smaller than what you could have had. This also tends to be a negative experience. If you use a stop and the market hits it only to turn around, you also feel bad.

There is virtually nothing intrinsically positive about the consequences of using stops. I might tell you that you will avoid a larger loss if you use stops. But this is also a negative way of looking at things. Stops are necessary preventive measures.

This is what accounts for the hesitation that many traders experience in taking losses. Adhering strictly to behavioral principles, we can see that the use of stops has virtually no immediate positive consequence. In fact, stops are like life insurance—we know we need it but hope we don't have to use it. As a result of the consistently negative experiences associated with stop-loss orders, it's no wonder that many investors do not use them. In Freudian terms, a loss could be compared to castration. This is not intended to be amusing. Some individuals take each loss as if a part of their body had been severed. This is why stops are so difficult to use. This is why stops are resented, hated, abused, ridiculed, and misused. What can be done? We know we need to use stops for money

Figure 9.3 Stimulus-response chain and stop-loss program.

management purposes. How can we find some positive aspect to their use so that we can change the consequences of stops?

Step One

The first step toward changing any behavior must always be to try an approximation of the new behavior, particularly if it is complex or if the individual is totally deficient in this area. Assume that you are an individual who never uses stops. Assume also that you understand the dangers involved in not using stops. Assume further that you have had many losses and wish to change the behavior. I would not expect you to go to sleep one evening a sinner, and wake up the next morning a saint. All you need do is work on the first target behavior toward the goal. And the first behavior is to write your stops down on the record sheet, each and every time you place an order. The simple task of writing the stop will not bring you the loss or negative experience you seek to avoid. But it will help teach you to approximate the ultimate response. If you can recruit the assistance of a friend who has a similar problem, then you will be far better off. You can monitor one another's behavior. Each time you record the stop (on paper), your friend will reward you verbally. He or she will say "Good work, I'm glad you wrote down the stop" or "Keep up the good work" or "I'm impressed with your progress." Any positive statement will do. If you are tempted to make light of this little exercise, then I suggest you "stifle yourself." You may not be functioning at this low level. You may, in fact, be using stops from time to time. If this is the case, you will want to start treatment at a later step. For those individuals who never use stops, for those who are persistent losers, this type of help is a necessity. Remember that we are shaping behavior.

To implement this procedure, you must recruit assistance from others. Not only will you find it difficult to reward yourself for recording a stop, you will be inclined to be dishonest as well. You can be more creative in selecting rewards, and you can tailor the program to suit your specific needs. As you make progress and obtain verbal rewards from those around you, you will find that your goal is getting closer. For those who cannot depend on a friend for assistance, a willing broker might be the answer. You can give him your stops, tell him to record them but not actually enter them, and you can have him keep a record of your progress. He can also reward you accordingly.

Should you be punished for not entering stops during this first phase? I do not believe that punishment will help. If you have even the slightest desire to succeed in the market, this will be sufficient motivation to carry you through the first step. If you cannot get through this step, then I suggest you stop trading. Sad but true, this one bit of advice may save you considerable grief. I am challenging your sincerity by telling you this. If you sincerely want to be successful in the market, then you will implement the program I am discussing. If you do not, then the chances you will ever come out on the profitable side are slim indeed.

Once you have achieved a perfect score in recording stops for a period of three months or 25 trades, whichever comes first, you are ready to start step two. This step consists of giving stops to your broker, but not having them actually entered. You may need to start at this step if you have no one to help you with step one. Or if you have no trouble recording stops, you should begin the "treatment" at step two.

Step Two

In order for effective behavioral change to take place, one must follow an orderly sequence of steps from least to most complex. If your difficulty is very basic, then you must begin with step one. If your problem is less entrenched, you may begin at a later step. This is the manner in which behavioral change occurs. And it is also the manner in which all learning takes place. You must take each step as one small goal toward the final behavior. You must not skip any step. Should you find that you are unsuccessful at any given point, you must retrace, work back, and begin at an even more elementary level.

The second step of our stop-loss program is to begin giving stops to your broker. This step can only be started after you have reached a high level of performance at step one. Essentially the aspects of this step are no different from what was done earlier. The only change is that stop-loss orders are given to your broker in addition to being recorded by yourself and a friend. The broker should be told not to actually enter the orders, but just to keep a record of your stops. If his or her help can be obtained, then it would be helpful for you to be verbally praised each time a stop is placed. Your broker should keep a complete list of all stops. You should keep a list as well. The object is to make stops less difficult to place by removing the negative consequences and fear associated with stops. This is achieved by not having orders actually entered.

As in step one, you should be rewarded verbally by the broker, friends, and any other individual who is working on the program with you. The goal is to achieve 100 percent stop placement rate. This should take no more than several weeks. Once this is accomplished, you are ready to move on to step three, which will entail actual market entry of stops. Prior to this, however, there is another technique you may wish to use in order to attach more value to the use of stops. During the time that step two is in process, keep a record of what your market performance has been, using your current trading strategy (i.e., no use of stops or sporadic use of stops). Keep a record of what your performance would have been had you used the stops you recorded during the program. More often than not you will find your performance without stops much worse than what it would have been with stops. This is a simple exercise, but it can have a dramatic effect on your attitude and behavior. Once you realize the immense difference stops can make, you will be highly motivated to use them. This increase in motivation will, in turn, have a very positive effect on your overall profits.

Step Three

The purpose of any behavioral change program is to "stamp in" behavior. The repeated association of appropriate behavior and positive reinforcement is instrumental in the change process. The more frequently a behavior is rewarded, the more likely it is to occur in the future. The third phase of our stop-loss program consists of on-the-job training, as it were. This step requires the actual use of stops. We will use the same rewards as before—verbal praise by broker, friends, and others—and it wouldn't hurt to praise yourself. A record of stops will be kept, as before. Stops will be placed with the broker. The broker will enter stops accordingly. By the time you reach this phase of the program, your preparation through steps one and two will have been extensive. You will find that stops are being used without fear of consequences. Be certain to continue rewards after you have started this step.

It is always best to strive for 100 percent use of stops. Anything less than 100 percent may cause you to waver from the program and will result in faulty learning. The object is for the behavior to become habitual. It has been my experience that the use of such a program for approximately three months (or 25 trades, whichever comes first) will be sufficient for the formation of a positive habit. Once you have mastered one aspect of the trading sequence you should move on to the next higher level.

Step Four

The next step is to "practice, practice, practice." I indicated earlier the importance of repeated rewards for the behavior we are attempting to change. The only way this can be achieved is through consistent and frequent use of appropriate behaviors. You will find it productive to use your skills correctly so that they may be rewarded. The same holds true for your trading system. The best way it can be tested is to use it. Once you have learned a behavior, you must "use it or lose it."

REVIEW

1. To be successful at trading it is necessary to acquire positive behaviors.
2. Frequently it is also necessary to rid yourself of inappropriate and loss-producing behaviors.
3. Behavioral learning techniques such as shaping, extinction, and reinforcement are instrumental in the formation of new behaviors and the "unlearning" of old ones.
4. Reinforcement schedules can be manipulated to increase, decrease, or stamp in behaviors.
5. Effective and thorough record keeping is an asset to any program and, in fact, is a necessity in the administration of all behavior-change procedures.
6. There are more than ten general categories of market "errors."
7. Treatment, or the process of behavior change, must progress through several steps, the success of each of which is interdependent.
8. Each step in a program must be more complicated than the previous step and all behaviors must be mastered as one moves toward the ultimate goal.
9. Once learned, a behavior must be used in order to be remembered.

10

Further Details on Dealing with Trading Problems

The non-use and misuse of stops are only two of many things a trader can do wrong. There are so very many errors that can lead to losses, it is impossible to cover all of them thoroughly. Fortunately, most of them fit into the general categories described in Table 9.1. The teachings of behavioral psychology provide a basic format around which to structure all programs whose goal is to change counterproductive market behaviors (Table 10.1). By following this sequence of events, it is possible to effectively deal with any, and possibly all, market problems. In order to assist in your independent programming of changes, I will go

Table 10.1

Format for Change

Step Number and Description	Anticipated Result
1. Keep record of behavior.	To isolate target behaviors.
2. Note conditions that precede given behavior.	To isolate stimulus or stimuli.
3. Note consequence of behavior.	To determine what is acting as the reward.
4. Define "new" behavior.	To have clear-cut goal.
5. Change stimulus events.	To help alter trader response.
6. Change consequence events.	To increase frequency of "new" behavior.
7. "Fade out" rewards.	To permit "new" behavior to take over.
8. Monitor "new" behavior.	To be certain it has been stamped in.

through the sequence with another common market problem, liquidating your position too soon.

When initiating a program it is always best to define the target behavior as clearly as possible. Behavioral psychologists refer to this as the "operational definition." The more concise the definition of what is targeted for change, the more successful one is likely to be. The operational definition "liquidating a position too soon" could be stated as follows:

The closing out of any trade-long, short, or spread-before the specific time and/or price objective predetermined in one's trading system.

The next step is to go to our outline (see Table 10.1). Step 1 indicates that we are to keep a record of the target behavior. In other words, we are to use a record-keeping sheet like Figure 9.2. We are also to keep a record of how frequently this behavior occurs during a given period of time, so we may refer to it as an index of how much or how little change has taken place. We should find it possible to state, for example, that 70 percent of our trades are closed out prior to the proper time (or whatever the actual count happens to be).

Step 2 tells us to keep a record of the stimulus conditions that led to the given behavior(s). It is possible, for example, that one specific stimulus may always be the precedent condition for "closing position out too early." In my early days of trading, for example, 90 percent of my positions were closed out too early due to calls from my broker during market hours. These calls shook my confidence. It was therefore possible to change my response by changing the stimulus condition. I simply requested my broker to avoid calling me unless instructed to do so, or unless it was for the purpose of reporting back on order fills. This effectively eliminated my problem and left me free to gain positive rewards by following my system. And in turn it helped build up my self-confidence, which ultimately made it possible for me to "cope" with broker's calls. In many cases, the "cure" for a given problem will be to change the stimulus event or events. Do not overlook this potentially powerful technique. All too often, however, it is not possible to isolate a specific stimulus that can be manipulated. It is therefore necessary to continue with the program.

Step 3 is "Note consequence of behavior." In this case, we should find that to close out the position too early, regardless of how much profit was taken (or how little to be more accurate), tends to relieve the "anxiety" of carrying a position. The relief one feels can be rewarding. Many times one's broker will reward the liquidating act. The broker himself will not be aware that he is rewarding the act as well as being the stimulus for it. It would be well to note the verbal behavior of your broker. After you liquidate a position too early or in response to his call, he may say such things as "Let's be glad we're out of that trade" or "I'm happy you got out, the market's going to keep going down." The following are typical statements that tend to verbally reward this "jumping the gun":

"Well, that's one loss we don't have to worry about anymore."
"At least we got out with a profit."
"Better to take a small profit than any kind of a loss."
"We're lucky the trade was closed out, they'd have 'picked your stop anyway.'"
"We got out in the nick of time—the market went sharply lower right after we got out."

Along with these will be statements designed, subtly of course, to minimize the seriousness of what was done. These can take the following form:

"No harm done, if we're wrong in getting out too soon, we can always jump back in."
"The exception makes the rule."
"Not every trading system is right all the time."
"If we get out now, before the report, all we lose is one commission."

A few more words on the relief of anxiety as a reinforcer are in order. To liquidate a position too early can serve as a reward for some individuals. In some cases, such as liquidating a loss too late, the mere act of liquidating can also act as a reward. The tension of riding a profit or loss may be quite intense for some investors. By liquidating too early, they are relieved of the tension, and, therefore, the mere termination of this situation will have the same result as a positive experience. They will be more likely to behave the same way in future trades. Those who ride losses to unacceptably large amounts also tend to experience the positive effects of relief. Again, the relief can serve to reward an otherwise inappropriate act. It's like the man who, when asked why he kept banging his head against the wall, replied, "because it feels so good when I stop." The investor who cannot face a loss and accept it at the right time may actually learn to take very large losses because of the intense release that comes with the final act of liquidating. In such cases, it is fortunate that money will often run out quickly, thereby forcing awareness. Some behavioral psychologists, such as W. K. Estes, have proposed the validity of termination as a reinforcing event. Hence the situations described here are highly plausible. It is difficult to get back on the right track once a blunder has been made. This is why I stress the importance of an organized, well-planned, and methodical approach to trading and investing, first and foremost as a means of preventing trading errors.

Almost anyone can help stimulate premature trades: It can be friends, advisory services, floor traders, news broadcasts, in-laws, or other relatives. More often than not it is a combination of all these factors in conjunction with the trader's own insecurities. In such an event, the multiplicity of inputs makes it impossible to easily change the stimulus conditions.

Step 4 involves a definition of the "new behavior." More often than not the new behavior (target behavior) will simply be the opposite of the behavior we are attempting to change. It is always best to operationally define the target. It could be defined as follows:

> To liquidate trades if and only if the trading system so dictates, regardless of any other information inputs to the trader.

Step 5 involves changing the stimulus events, provided this is possible. It may not be practical to change the stimuli leading to a given behavior. But we can very often help our program along by eliminating several of the stimuli. For many years, my "life-saving" rule was to avoid, at all costs, discussing, listening, or otherwise exposing myself to others' ideas or opinions about the markets. This is a very difficult thing to do. It requires you to not read trade journals, news reports, advisory services, and brokerage house letters. It also requires you to keep your ears "shut" as much as possible (very often the best way to do this is to keep your mouth shut as well!). This is an example of how I changed the stimulus of a losing behavior.

Step 6, the most important step, is to change the consequences. Here is where your creativity and resourcefulness come into play. You must solicit rewards from others, from yourself, and from the market. The techniques discussed earlier all have merit and there are many variations on the theme. The key is to remember that every time the target behavior is carried through to successful completion, reward must be given immediately.

Step 7 is to "fade out" rewards. This topic has not yet been discussed, but you can get an idea of what's involved by the very name. As time passes and the behavior we are trying to shape increases in frequency, it will be possible to cut down and eventually eliminate the rewards that are being used. Since the behavior will lead to self-satisfaction, and considerably more profit, it will become self-reinforcing.

Step 8 is to monitor the new behavior. This is not difficult since trading results will let you know how your program is working. It is best to continue recording results using the previously mentioned trading record. If there is a change in your overall behavior, it will be evident from the record, if it has not become evident from your overall profits (or lack thereof).

In addition to the typical market problems already discussed, there are many behaviors that must be shaped from the start since they do not tend to come of their own accord. Of these, discipline is the single most important. It is my opinion that if a behavior can be defined, it can be learned. In this chapter I will discuss in detail some of the ways in which you can go about learning self-discipline.

The following key elements in the behavioral sequence should be followed in instituting any program directed at behavioral change. You would do well to remember them in relation to your efforts at improvement.

1. Define all behaviors as specifically as possible.
2. Keep accurate records of all stimulus events.
3. Keep accurate records of all response consequences.
4. Define target behavior as specifically as possible.
5. Rewards should be given immediately after completion of the target behavior.
6. Continue to monitor behavior after the program ends.
7. Fade out rewards when behavior has reached nearly 100 percent.
8. All behaviors are important as part of the overall trading plan.
9. Constantly be on the lookout for symptoms of change in your trading. These will most likely be reflected in increased losses.
10. Obtain as much assistance from friends, relatives, and brokers as you possibly can.

11. Do not minimize the possible benefits of controlling stimulus events.

12. Be organized in your trading. Effective organization makes it possible to keep a good record of all the necessary behaviors, their stimulus-response conditions, frequency, and improvement.

13. Approach your program in a scientific way. Look for behavioral clues, count frequency of behaviors, keep a tally of their occurrence.

14. Avoid introspective reasoning. In other words, do not try to spend too much time understanding why you do something. Take for granted that you are not doing something the proper way, design a program, implement it, and change your behavior.

REVIEW

1. In order to change an old behavior or to shape a new one it is necessary to follow a series of specific behavioral steps.
2. The required steps are outlined in detail.
3. All programs for behavioral change must be highly organized.
4. Help from others should be solicited as frequently as possible.
5. Time should not be spent wondering about "why" a behavior occurs.

11

Scheduling and Self-Discipline

In previous chapters, I have referred to scheduling and its importance. The value of working from a detailed schedule is threefold:

1. A schedule will help you avoid costly errors and omissions.
2. A schedule will help you maintain a disciplined and orderly approach to trading.
3. A schedule will help you develop effective habits and attitudes.

For the learning process to achieve its fullest and most lasting results, the learner must adhere to a well-organized, specific, detailed, comprehensive, and pragmatic schedule. It is absolutely amazing how many things an organized person can accomplish. And it is equally amazing how much free time a well-organized person will have left. Last, and certainly not least, an almost immediate improvement in attitudes and profits can be derived from careful scheduling. Certainly there are many successful traders who do not use schedules and have perhaps never used them. They don't need them. They have already achieved what you are attempting to accomplish. It is therefore not wise to use these people as an example. Once you have arrived at your destination, you can dispense with your schedule, for it will have been internalized. If there is only one thing this book inspires you to do, then let it be the creation of a schedule.

Where to Start

To construct an effective schedule, you must start by listing all the things you wish to include. Since I am talking about a schedule that focuses on your market-related activities, only these goals are included. Should you wish to construct a more comprehensive timetable covering other areas of your life, it will be a simple task once you have made your trading schedule. Some suggested schedule activities include reading market reports, preparing charts and graphs (or fundamental data), making trading decisions, updating your record of trades, reading market-related material, studying trading rules, testing and developing systems, spending time away from the market, and working on a five-year plan.

Once you have decided on what should be included, you can assign each activity, based on its frequency, a particular time slot, as in Table 11.1. Those who trade the market daily will find much more time available. Many individuals are not involved on such an intensive basis. In these cases, it would be preferable to work on the market daily, even if for a brief period of time. This should be done either before or after a daytime job. It is not a good idea to mix one task with another. I do not recommend studying the market while at a full-time job.

It is more effective to work for short periods of time than for longer ones. I would therefore suggest that you focus on most target behaviors daily, but briefly. It is necessary to cover some goals daily, whereas others can be worked with weekly. Figure 11.1 is a typical schedule for someone who has a full-time job, other than the market.

It is also advisable to make a new schedule sheet for each week. By doing this you can check off each activity as it is completed, which will provide you with the necessary feedback concerning your progress.

Table 11.1
Daily Record

Day	Time	Activity
Monday	7–8 PM	Read market reports
Tuesday	7–8 PM	Plan long-term goals
Wednesday	7–8 PM	Analyze performance results
Thursday	7–8 PM	Study trading rules
Friday	7–8 PM	Summarize weekly results
Saturday	2–3 PM	Update charts for week
Sunday	7–8 PM	Plan weekly strategy

Week of _____

Monday 7PM–9PM.   Work on stop-loss program step 3. Evaluate progress made during previous week. Plan steps for current week.

Tuesday 7PM–8PM.   Analyze trades of previous week to determine if all rules have been followed per trading system. Calculate profit to loss ratio.

Wednesday 8PM–9PM.   Discuss progress of stop-loss program with broker to determine if any changes have been noticed. Set next target behavior.

Thursday 8PM–9PM.   Review chain of behavioral consequences to make certain that adequate rewards follow the target behavior(s).

Friday 8PM–9PM.   Define and operationalize next step in trading program. Determine approximate starting date. Evaluate overall progress of current goals and make changes as necessary.

Weekend.   Weekend reserved for work on technical trading system and planning of trades for coming week.

Figure 11.1   Trading program schedule.

How Much Time Is Best?

Too much time spent on the market can be just as destructive as too little time. Ideally the market should not require more than an hour on a daily basis, and even this may be too much. Each trading system has its own time requirement. I recommend no more than 50 percent of your daily allocated time be spent on actual market study and analysis. The remainder should be devoted to analysis of results, self-evaluation, and such things as a five-year plan. As your schedule becomes firmer, you gain experience with it, and you will become more capable of assigning each activity its proper amount of time.

If you have scheduled some of the behavior change programs outlined elsewhere in this book, then you will need to devote more time daily. It is also best to spend about twice as much time over the weekend preparing yourself for the coming week. Generally, you should find that two hours over the weekend is more than enough to prepare your trading for the coming week.

Follow Your Schedule Rigorously

If you want to get results, then it will be necessary to follow your schedule closely. In fact, I suggest you place your daily schedule above all else until it has become part of you. To acquire the discipline necessary for successful trading, it is absolutely necessary to schedule your time appropriately. Shaping the necessary discipline your schedule requires must be the single most important thing you do each day. Without it, you will most likely find it impossible to achieve the kind of trading results you want.

Be Flexible But Firm

The key to developing positive feelings about your schedule is an appropriate combination of flexibility and firmness. If you maintain a negative attitude toward your schedule, consider it boring or hard work, then you will not make it work. Very often flexibility in scheduling will help in the creation of positive affect toward your schedule. If portions of your daily routine are redundant, extremely boring, or otherwise nonproductive, eliminate them and replace them with free time or a more important activity. You may find it more enjoyable to make frequent daily (or weekly) routine changes. Some individuals work better when schedules change from time to time, whereas others work best on a fixed and firm schedule. You must discover which pleases you most since this will bring the best results.

Priorities, Necessities, Free Time

What should ideally be included in your schedule? To a certain extent this is an individual matter. There are, however, some very specific goals I recommend every trader and/or investor cover on a regular basis.

1. Market preparation. If you're a market technician, then you must do work on a regular basis. I prefer to do such work daily. Some investors will find that once a week is sufficient, particularly if their trading or investing decisions are not short term. If you are a fundamentalist, you will want to study the relevant statistics or read the necessary reports frequently. Preparation is the single most important aspect of any total trading system. The most consistent and concerted effort must be applied here. Scheduling this activity should always be foremost in your mind. If you recall my previous mention of market symptoms and negative attitudes, you will remember that failure to keep up with one's market work quickly will lead to losses. You have most likely found that many big moves begin when you have fallen behind in your work. Once your attitude changes and you update the missing material, you will say to yourself, "I never would have missed that move if my charts were up to date." This is precisely what your schedule will help avoid. I strongly recommend you have a set time of the day or week, and a specified length of time for such market work. Even if you choose not to set aside time for any other activity, make certain that you have a set time for your market analysis. I cannot emphasize this point enough. Most market-related problems have an immediate and negative effect on market studies.

2. Trading decisions.   Most investors make their trading decisions as they are updating their charts or doing technical work. I do not recommend you use this procedure. Rather, I advise you to make decisions after all technical and/or fundamental work has been updated. This necessitates scheduling a time slot for decision making. I recommend this separate time slot because of the importance of the decision-making process. Typically a trader's mind will be cluttered with information and data on all markets when he or she is updating work. This tends to interfere with effective and rational decision making. It is possible to be more objective when making decisions after all market studies are complete. Each market then can be viewed in its totality without competing with input from your other work. Decisions should always be made in an unhurried and detached way. I have found that having a special time slot for this process makes the results more reliable.

3. Record keeping.   Equally important is the record-keeping system discussed previously. You must schedule time for this. I believe that a daily review is best for active traders. I would not advise anything less than a weekly review, even for conservative investors. You must know at all times where your investments and performance stand. If you have skipped over the section on record keeping, (Chapter 10) please read now.

4. Behavioral programs.   If you have implemented any of the programs detailed in previous chapters, then allow time for their application.

5. Long-range goals.   Previously, I mentioned the importance of having a long-term financial plan. Time should also be set aside for the formulation and specification of objectives and expectations. It helps considerably to have an established time for working on your five-year plan. When doing so, it is best to put in writing your most ambitious goals, compare previous targets with actual progress, and arrive at an understanding of how promptly you are moving toward these objectives. This all takes time.

Each individual must schedule activities most suitable to his or her trading and lifestyle. For the novice investor or trader, such a schedule can mean the difference between getting started on the right track or falling into a losing rut early in the game. Unless you are ready to make the necessary commitment in the form of a schedule, you are not likely to find success in the marketplace. Any attempt to profit using a disorganized, undisciplined approach is doomed to failure from the very start.

REVIEW

1. To successfully approach the markets, a structured and disciplined program is necessary.
2. Several benefits can accrue from the use of a schedule.
3. Begin constructing your schedule by listing the targets or goals toward which you wish to work.
4. Schedule each activity in a specific time slot.
5. There are a number of market-related goals that should be included in every schedule.

12

The Importance of Trading with the Trend

Experience teaches that following market trends is perhaps the single most profitable trading tool, regardless of the underlying system you are using. Stocks and commodities tend to move in long-term trends. Frequently, these trends will last several years. Those who are capable of selecting investments at the start of a trend will show profits of as much as several hundred percent (if not more). Should they be fortunate enough to exit their positions at the top of the trend, or at the start of a change in trend, they will show even greater gains. Those who speculate and those who trade mainly for the short term can also benefit from knowledge and use of trends. During a given market direction, most short-term profits will be made from trading with the trend. This basic law of market behavior is underscored in the works of all market "masters" and is perhaps most simply expressed in *Reminiscences of a Stock Operator:*

> I began to realize that the big money must necessarily be in the big swing. Whatever might seem to give a big swing its initial impulse, the fact is that its continuance is not the result of manipulations by pools or artifice by financiers, but depends upon basic conditions. And no matter who opposes it, the swing must inevitably run as far and as fast and as long as the impelling forces determine. (Lefevre, 1965, p. 88)

The value of market trend in profitable investing and trading is also recognized by fundamental and technical traders. The investor and market analyst, inclined toward the use of fundamentals, studies such major indicators as earnings, crop conditions, long-term debt, trends in export business, and the like, in order to determine what the long-term price move will be in response to these conditions. The technician who reads chart patterns and looks for such things as "breakouts" or "head and shoulders bottoms" does so in order to determine change in trend. Cycle analysts study economic trends and repetitive patterns in order to isolate the time frame within which trend changes might occur. Moving average systems are time-based and attempt to signal trend changes. Most trading systems, whether fundamentally oriented or technically based, have as their goal the isolation of specific patterns, which have profit potential. Speculators and "scalpers" who trade for the short term are also interested in determining trend. Their work is "fine tuned" and focuses on picking out trends within the shorter term. There are those individuals who trade on over-reactions within the given trend. As a result, they too must be aware of trend in order to know when there has been such an over-reaction.

Despite all the talk about trend, despite all the moving averages, cycles, long-term patterns, signals, trend reversals, key reversals, earnings reports, and market indicators, trading with the trend is perhaps the most difficult thing for an investor to do. Were it not such a formidable task, there would be many wealthier investors and you would most likely not be reading this book. With tongue in cheek, I quote Lefevre once again to illustrate how deceptively simple is the concept of trend:

> Obviously the thing to do was to be bullish in a bull market and bearish in a bear market. Sounds silly, doesn't it? . . . It took me a long time to grasp that general principle firmly before I saw that to put it into practice really meant to anticipate probabilities. (1965, p. 88)

Certainly there must be a limiting factor that makes it difficult to implement trend in the profit-making formula. Most traders would rather be buyers than short sellers. It is my opinion that psychological factors, in and of themselves, are the culprit. It is the "nature of the human beast." And even more frustrating is the fact that trends are so simple to isolate.

What is a trend? Simply stated, a trend is movement in a given direction that remains relatively fixed over an extended period of time. Figure 12.1(a) illustrates the relatively long-term nature of market trends in the corn market. This pattern is no less true in stocks. It is possible to isolate a given trend as I have done in Figure 12.1(a); remove a portion of that trend, examine it more closely as in Figure 12.1(b); study the trend within the trends, remove a portion of this trend as I have done in Figure 12.1(c); study the trends, and so on, until we have moved down to the shortest trend index, tick by tick trades.

Figure 12.1 Long-term corn trend. (Reprinted with permission of Commodity Chart Service.)

As you can well observe, the directional tendency of the market is certainly real. Price movement is not a directionless, up-and-down motion as typified by the oscillations of a random number generator. There are specific, lasting, directional patterns. Studying these patterns, or trends, allows an investor to buy low and sell high. The great majority of trading techniques and market analytical tools seek to accomplish one of two ends: they attempt to determine the underlying trend or they seek to determine when the trend will change. There are all types, breeds, combinations, half-breeds, indices, techniques, and tools for doing this. One of the most successful investors I ever met stated bluntly, "I never use any of that garbage. All I do is look at a price chart. If the price is higher than it was four weeks ago, and if the price is higher than it was four months ago, the trend is up. I then buy stocks when there has been some bad news and prices decline due to public selling. Every now and then I buy close to the top. But there are so very few major tops and bottoms that I'm rarely wrong." And he was right!

Given the fact that determination of trend is a relatively simple task, what makes it so difficult to translate trend into profits? This is best illustrated with a chart and accompanying commentary. Figure 12.2 is a typical daily bar chart of the corn market. In reality, it makes little difference whether we trade soybeans, IBM, or XYZ Corp. Trader reactions and responses are always the most important factors.

Let's assume that the typical investor is watching prices as they decline. He is loathe to sell short, or simply afraid to do so. He waits for prices to "bottom out." Assume also that he is awaiting a specific signal. In this case, he is looking for a "key reversal," a day during which prices trade outside their previous day's high and low, ending higher on the day, after a rather extended move down. It is a very specific signal seen by many traders and investors as a "key" indicator. This reversal is marked on the chart. Technically the investor or trader who is true to his or her system has no choice but to buy (you will recall the earlier discussion on the use of trading signals and systems). The big day arrives. The signal has come. Here is a list of responses most traders make to the situation:

1. "Let's wait for some more confirmation of the reversal."
2. "True, we had the reversal, but the volume wasn't high enough. Let's wait."
3. "If this was indeed a true reversal in trend, then we've got plenty of time to get in because trends run for a long period of time."

Figure 12.2   Daily corn futures chart. (Reprinted with permission of Commodity Chart Service.)

4. "The decline was so severe that I'm afraid to get in, I'd rather wait a few days to make sure the trend has changed."

5. "If I get in now I might get stopped out on a 'test' of the low."

These responses are characteristic of investor reasoning at major market turns. They are afraid to implement their initial trend change signals since they fear a loss. They somehow believe on an unconscious level that it is possible to trade without losses. They fail to realize that losses are a necessary part of profitable trading—that mistakes are part of the game. This unrealistic attitude comes from id impulses. It is a childish fantasy which relates almost directly to the fear of castration. If Freud was indeed correct about castration anxiety and fear of loss as a response to self-assertion or parental opposition, then you can see how it might be carried unconsciously through adulthood.

Despite the fact that some very specific signals accompany major tops and bottoms, there are few traders and investors who have the emotional prerequisites to implement these signals when they arrive. Many hours are spent patiently watching and waiting, and when the big moment comes it quickly passes and no action is taken. The reasons for such behavior (or lack of behavior) include:

1. Unrealistic fear of losses.
2. Lack of self-confidence and positive attitude.
3. Inability to act as a result of negative learning.
4. Lack of appropriate learning with trading system.
5. Acceptance of inputs from contrary sources.

Those who cannot act on major signals (and this applies to most investors) generally have some specific psychological difficulties, which also appear in other areas of their lives. The profile of such individuals is, in my opinion, as follows:

1. Very dominant father, fond of physically punishing the child.
2. Parentally created feelings of dependency that did not permit child to make his or her own decisions.
3. Punitive spouse who is verbally abusive when errors are made.
4. Lack of self-confidence due to negative childhood experiences.

Inability to act on major signals is common. And yet it is very possible to make consistent profits despite such shortcomings if one can make the necessary changes before too much damage has been done. This is, however, an equally difficult task for most of us. Let's assume that our major trend change signal was missed. In most cases, the market tends to "test" the bottom or top once a signal has come. The usual responses to this test, indicated by the number 2 on our chart, are the following:

1. "Let's wait a little longer to see if we can get in cheaper."
2. "The price has come back too far and the low will probably be broken."
3. "Let's wait until it penetrates its recent high (or low) to be sure that the test was passed."

Now that the second opportunity has come and gone without action, investors use a number of defense mechanisms to protect themselves from reality. They usually rationalize or intellectualize the situation by saying, "Now that we know what the trend is, we'll buy into a reaction." They wait for the reaction: it never comes, is never large enough, is never fast enough, is never good enough, or is never reliable enough. Frustration sets in and market errors increase, despite the fact that they know very clearly what the trend is, what the signals are, and what they should do.

One of the most common rationalizations is "we'll buy into a reaction within the uptrend." It's an easy thing to say, but a very difficult thing to do. We, as human beings, take pride in our emotional control, but when the situation is serious, requiring immediate and decisive action, there are hundreds of possible excuses, perhaps millions, that are used to delay action, avoid action, or otherwise sidestep the issue. It is very difficult, psychologically, to buy into a reaction since they are ordinarily quite violent, come on bad news, and are not popular trades. When the reaction we have been waiting for actually arrives, it will usually look as if the trend is changing. Brokers and services will be bearish. Overall opinion will be negative, the news background will be bearish, and frequently our response will not be what it should. These outside influences can and do make it virtually impossible for the average trader to buy on weakness. And one who does is likely to become highly anxious, selling out the position prematurely. The psychological reasons for such behavior relate primarily to the factors discussed earlier.

Richard Russell, a veteran in the stock advisory business, is just one of the many market professionals who recognize the limitations of human ability at major turns in the market. In preparing for a change in the market trend, he wrote the following words of advice to his market newsletter subscribers:

> So, I'm telling subscribers now to steel themselves, to prepare themselves for the possibility of a major bottom somewhere ahead as identified by this indicator . . . it's going to "feel" very hard to buy. . . . Every fiber in your system is going to be telling you that Stocks and Wall Street are finished. At that time you are going to have to go against your emotions. But that will be the ideal time to buy. So start getting yourself ready—emotionally. (Letter #779 Dow Theory Letters)

At any given point in the market trend, there can and will be countless excuses, intellectualizations, and rationalizations for not taking action. None is valid and none brings success. Regardless of the cause for non-action, the result of such behavior rarely is profitable and more often than not is frustrating. It is, in fact, more potentially dangerous to not act than it is to act. To not act will usually bring frustration. Frustration will lead to poor judgment, lack of patience, and a concomitant increase in market blunders.

Back to our market example (Figure 12.2). Assume that the opportunity to buy was missed at points 1 and 2. Assume also that none of the small reactions (3, 4, and 5) was used to establish a position.

Trading with the Market Trend—Why It's So Difficult to Do

Now comes the next, and perhaps greatest blunder. The frustrated trader will rationalize and say to himself, "I'll wait for the next upside breakout. That way I'll be certain to buy with the trend." Comes the breakout (6) and the trader is more paralyzed by fear than ever before. "Prices are too high," he reasons. "Now that the breakout has come and I know it's real, I'll wait for a pullback to the breakout area and buy in." Sometimes this works. Most of the time it does not. Again the typical investor or trader has failed miserably. By now he is very upset, lacks self-conviction, believes that he is a born loser, has a negative attitude, is frustrated, abandons what's left of his trading system, refuses to watch the market, and begins to hate himself. Ordinarily frustration will be greatest when the market is close to a bottom or in its last up leg. When prices begin to run away, the public reasons that the trend has much longer to run, "throws in the towel," and buys. The actual top is usually seen within several days, very often the same day. This is why public bullish consensus is typically at its high when the market is at its top. This is why there are few bulls to be found at major bottoms. Moreover, this is why most traders ignore the top signals when they appear. At such critical times, there is nothing left of self-discipline and there is no system. There is nothing but denial, hope, fear, and frustration. The losing position will frequently be held. Often it will be held until the next major bottom where frustration is again at its greatest.

That's the usual sequence of events. If this sounds familiar to you, or if you can identify with even one or two of the blunders in this chain, then you need help. If you suffer from one or more of these symptoms, then you know the losses they bring. The sooner you change, the better off you will be. Perhaps you will not go broke before help can be obtained. It is a simple matter for me to tell you that discipline is the answer to your woes. I could tell you to go back and read the previous chapters on behavioral change. Aside from the many suggestions I have given previously, I will provide you with an additional list in the traditional orientation.

1. Get in touch with your underlying motivation. By this I mean plain and simple soul-searching. List the goals you have set for yourself. Attempt to understand exactly what it is you are trying to achieve through investing. Perhaps you do not have sufficiently specific goals. If you do not know where you are going, then it will be difficult for you to get there. You must detail your direction, determine whether it is realistic, determine if it can be accomplished best through investing, and measure the commitment you feel toward that goal. In so doing, it will be necessary to be as completely honest with yourself as possible. There are many who invest simply to impress others or to assert their sexuality.

2. Attempt to recall any serious conflicts with your parents. Many internalized attitudes, fears, avoidance responses, and misperceptions come from early childhood. After all, much learning takes place on both a conscious and unconscious level during these years. If you are not aware of how parental treatment may have affected you, then you do not understand enough about your underlying motivation and attitudes.

3. Determine how your marital relationship may be affecting your decision-making ability. (If you are unmarried, examine your relationship with members of the opposite sex to see if they are somehow affecting your outlook and actions.) Very often the married male investor with children will be operating under the weight of heavy responsibility, which may paralyze him. Too frequently we fear negative responses from a spouse. In many cases, there is a lack of common purpose between husband and wife. Shared investment goals will be of immeasurable help in making decisions.

4. Attempt to discipline yourself by following a predetermined set of trading rules as described previously. Should you find it impossible to implement your rules, I recommend that you explore other areas of your life to determine if they are also characterized by a lack of organization and discipline.

5. Recall and relive any traumatic experiences that may be limiting your ability. Very often traumas during early childhood or elementary school days will have an unconscious effect during adult life. If and when you can remember these experiences, it would be wise to "relive" them in your current nonthreatening environment. This type of re-education, or abreaction, as it is called, frequently releases pent-up emotion that can negatively affect market performance.

6. Have a total plan of attack from initiation of investment or trade to completion. Know precisely what it is you wish to achieve, how you intend to do so, what the expected results are, what problems may be anticipated, and how long it may take.

7. Get help from others. It is frequently helpful to work with others. They can point out your shortcomings, and you can help them recognize their limitations. Many investment clubs are successful because of group input and the collective decision-making process. This can be a good place to learn the necessary discipline.

REVIEW

1. The most effective way to make profits in the market is by trading with the trend.
2. Isolating market trends is not a difficult thing to do.
3. Most traders and investors lose money despite the fact that trends and market reversals are relatively simple to spot.
4. Emotional factors are the limiting influences in trend trading. There are many reasons for not following trend signals.
5. It is possible to trade with the trend only a small portion of the time and still make fairly consistent and large profit.
6. In order to remediate lack of trend trading ability a number of suggestions can be implemented. They are designed to overcome the psychological inability to follow trends.

13

The Role of Advisory Services

The problem with most advisory letters lies not in their service but rather with their readership. In earlier chapters, I discussed the importance of maintaining and adhering to a well-planned and thorough trading system. I cannot overemphasize the importance of such consistency. In the same way that an individual can misuse or abuse the advice of a broker, he can also inappropriately employ the advice of a market service. As the publisher of a commodity market service, I am well aware of the strengths, weaknesses, assets, and liabilities that come with your subscription to a market letter. I am also uniquely aware of the many ways in which individuals attempt to pervert the recommendations of their advisors. A well-established market service that has a documented and profitable trading record can be valuable to many speculators. Experience has taught me, however, that no matter how profitable recommendations made by a service may be, there are few who truly benefit to the fullest extent. In fact, there are some individuals who actually lose money following the recommendations of a profitable advisory service. How is this possible? As you have already concluded (most likely from personal experience), the trader who employs (or misemploys) advice is totally responsible for the results or lack thereof.

Before detailing some common difficulties encountered by individuals in their use of advisory services, one must decide whether an advisory service should be used at all. For a majority of traders, the use of an advisory service can be extremely helpful. Most speculators and investors have full-time jobs outside of the market and cannot keep up to date on their investment strategy. A service oriented to one's trading philosophy and/or technique can bring many benefits, but for the individual who is totally immersed in his or her own analytical technique, a service, other than one that provides raw data, charts, and/or fundamental information, is not necessary and can, in fact, be detrimental. To use or not use an advisory service must be an individual decision made exclusively on the basis of one's ability to keep current. Although it is not necessary to follow the market on a tick-by-tick basis, there are many investors and speculators who are too busy even to devote a few hours consistently over a weekend. In such cases, I would recommend an advisory service.

Evaluate Your Needs

In subscribing to any type of service, the trader must be aware of its assets, liabilities, limitations, and potential within his particular market orientation. Even though a service may have an admirable track record, not all individuals will find it possible to benefit. Once again, the inconsistent and undisciplined approach employed by many speculators is at fault. For the individual who has not mastered even the most basic aspects of self-control, an advisory service would be useless. In most cases, such individuals will subscribe to as many services as they can possibly find. The result, to be sure, will be a totally confused trader who is overloaded with recommendations, conflicting opinions, and analyses. It is therefore most advisable to use a market service if and only if one has the necessary self-control to evaluate the many inputs. Opinions are not as important as the factors that will help you determine whether you should use a service. Before doing so, two types of service—informational and advisory—should be differentiated. Informational services provide charts, raw data, moving averages, and fundamental information. They do not make recommendations per se. Their main function is to provide the trader with information that can be used to make trading decisions. Advisory services, on the other hand, are concerned primarily with making recommendations on given stocks and/or commodities. Although they may also provide some informational material, their key function is to make specific trading suggestions.

Information Only Services

There is no danger in using informational services. They can be very helpful to those who are too busy to keep their own charts, gather their own data, or keep on top of fundamental developments. The trader who employs such services will most certainly save considerable time and effort. He will not, however, benefit from the learning that comes with gathering information on his own. There is much to be said in favor of doing your own work. Close contact with the data will give you market "sense" that cannot be obtained by working with information prepared by another. In previous chapters, I underscored the importance of learning. It is the learning that comes with doing one's own work that is very valuable to most traders. One should seriously evaluate these factors before subscribing. The amount of direct experience to be gained from keeping one's own market data is as important as on-the-job training in most other professions. When learning to drive an automobile, for example, classroom instruction can be beneficial up to a certain point, but only actual "hands on" training can complete the educational process. Learning to trade the market by working from charts and data supplied by an outside source is as absurd as having someone else learn how to drive for you. After you have learned the decision-making process you can pass the work on to someone else. If you subscribe to a chart service that is sent out weekly, you may find it difficult and time consuming to re-enter your notes and drawings on each chart weekly. The work you did on your chart last week will not be on the published chart. You will therefore have to spend time rewriting your notes, redrawing trend lines, cycles, and so on. This is perhaps the most significant drawback to the use of informational services.

In summary, there is perhaps only one major objection of psychological importance that should be considered before taking an informational market service. If you have established yourself in terms of market basics and feel that you no longer require hands on experience in acquiring and implementing market information, then you may wish to subscribe. If you find, after several months' use, that the service is truly helping, then by all means continue. Also, if you notice that your feel for the market or overview of trends is suffering, then it would be best to do the work on your own.

Services That Provide Specific Recommendations

The use of an advisory service—one that makes specific recommendations—is an entirely different matter. Those who can successfully use such services tend to be those who have the self-discipline necessary to do so. If you are lacking in self-control, then no amount of advice from others will help. The reason behind the success of most services is their rigid approach. Typically they make recommendations, give specific objectives, stops, follow-up procedures, evaluation of risk, and liquidation orders. In other words, they adhere to a time-tested and successful method of training. The information they provide, then falls into the hands of the weak link in the chain—the trader. Before taking an advisory service, you must decide whether you can follow through on their recommendations thoroughly, honestly, and for an extended period of time.

Another issue of major concern is whether the recommendations made by one's service will influence decisions that may have been made as a result of one's own research. There is an inherent danger in either reading about or soliciting others' opinions of the market. I have found that the degree of trader confusion is directly proportional to the number of advisory services an investor reads. At any given time, each of 10 services may have a different idea about a given stock or commodity. Some will advise holding, others buying, and still others liquidating. The total number of recommended trades may be large, much greater than the typical investor's budget will permit. Hence the average trader is faced with a very difficult decision. Typically the tendency is to make several trades from each service, or to make the trade that most agree would be best. More often than not this results in losses. Again, the culprit called consistency rears its ugly head. Any attempt to use only several of the recommendations made by a given service will not do justice to the trading system employed by that service. The result of such incomplete trading will be a dissatisfied investor who becomes frustrated. There is a tendency among investors, indeed there is a propensity among all human beings, to view only parts of a situation, excluding the whole. You must remember that performance records are based on long-term results. Typically the track records advertised by successful services have taken years to accumulate. They are based on following all recommendations precisely and to the letter. Most investors cannot muster the necessary discipline that brings such success.

There are two specific objections to the use of an advisory service:

1. An advisory service that makes specific recommendations must be rigidly adhered to over an extended period of time for success to follow.

2. An individual investor who does his or her own research may be influenced to abandon original work in favor of a so-called expert opinion.

Generally I find that those individuals who have self-control, discipline, and an awareness of how to trade thoroughly and consistently will benefit considerably. If an individual is lacking in these qualities, he or she will not benefit from the use of a market service, no matter how well it may have done in the past. The focus, as it has been in previous chapters, is clearly on the investor, who alone is responsible for the success or failure of a market service. How can one overcome some of the associated liabilities in order to effectively use advisory information? The following list of suggestions may help:

1. Make certain that the service you employ gives specific recommendations as to buy or sell, stop losses, objectives, entry and exit prices.

2. Your service should not be of the variety that makes too many recommendations each week. It will be difficult to pick and choose. The total number of open positions should be within the constraints of your financial ability.

3. Make every trade recommended using the exact stops, objectives, and so on.

4. Do not attempt to use a service to validate or negate your own signals. Trade your own signals in a separate account. If you use a service that makes recommendations, then you must follow them rather than use them as a verification of your own work.

5. Avoid subscribing to too many services. Two or three are sufficient. The more market advice you get, the less useful it will be.

6. If you have difficulty with self-discipline, then you might be best off avoiding a market service until you have overcome your own limitations.

7. Several friends working with one advisory service can succeed if each keeps an eye on the others. Hence, all the recommended trades have a higher likelihood of being followed exactly as specified.

8. Before subscribing to any type of market service you would do well to plan the precise fashion in which you will implement it. Unless there is a well-devised plan and a clear need, you would do best to avoid any input other than your own. If there is a market advisor whose word you respect, then demonstrate your respect by following his recommended trades exactly, even if you need to open a separate account to do so.

Trading Systems: Thoughts and Caveats

The futures trading world is always on the hunt for new systems, methods and timing indicators. Every month *Futures* magazine and other trade publications are filled with ads touting new systems, methods, and timing indicators. There are so many claims that it's hard for the average trader to sort truth from lies. In fact, some of the claims are so outrageous that common sense tells us they must be lies. Yet hope springs eternal in the human mind. We want to believe the ads that claim we can trade with $100 stops. We want to believe the 400 percent annual rate of return. And we want to believe that we can trade currencies with 85 percent accuracy. The fact of the matter is that many of these claims are misleading, based on very limited data, and/or the result of highly optimized parameters. Without mentioning names, one of the most popular software programs is based on a set of highly optimized variables that are re-optimized frequently. In fact, different buyers of this particular software program often get different signals, since the optimization parameters will have been changed by the time a new user has bought the program.

We're told that the National Futures Association (NFA) was established in order to protect us from this type of misleading advertising. The sad fact is that the NFA is often too busy pursuing and auditing those who are guilty of minor violations, and they're often very busy with on-site detailed audits of CTAs. The NFA does carefully read ads and closely monitor radio and television promotions and they have achieved a lengthy record of enforcement actions, fines, expulsions, and so on. In the meantime, however, those who are not NFA members are free, within reasonable limits, to advertise as they wish. The dichotomy is an interesting and an unfair one; to do business as a trading advisor who manages money or to be a broker, you must be an NFA member, but to simply publish a newsletter or to give advice you need only be a CFTC Commodity Futures Trading Commission (CFTC) member. NFA members live by more stringent rules than those who are registered with the CFTC alone. But while the NFA has gone overboard in regulating its members, those who are not CFTC members have carte blanche by comparison. As an example of how absurd some NFA rules are: NFA regulations prohibit an NFA member from doing business with a non-NFA member. Taken literally, then, I would assume that I cannot hire a plumber to fix my toilet without first ascertaining if he's an NFA member. In the meantime, non-NFA members are free to promote with little supervision. All the while, the public may be incorrectly assuming that its needs are being served by well-run watchdog agencies and, as a result, they assume that the claims they read must be valid. But that's not true at all!

Who's at Fault?

The bottom line, regardless of who's at fault, is that traders are being ripped off by unscrupulous systems developers and marketers. But who's really at fault? Is it the NFA for failure to regulate? Is it the CFTC? Is it the publications that accept these ads? No, it's really none of the above. The real blame falls squarely upon the shoulders of the individual trader. It is the individual trader who makes the decision to buy and to use these systems. No ad, no salesperson, no broker can force you to trade by a given system. The responsibility rests exclusively with you. Unfortunately, too many traders fail to ask the right questions and fail, therefore, to get the information necessary to make an informed decision. They often act on the basis of the claims, assuming erroneously that these claims are correct since they're printed on shiny paper, since (1) they appear in a reliable publication, (2) they were recommended by an honest broker, and (3) they're supported by statistics. But those of us who ask the right questions know that shiny paper is cheap, good magazines take bad ads, honest brokers can be wrong, and statistics can be used to demonstrate virtually anything. Given this state of affairs, I'd like to share some of my ideas with you so that you may make informed decisions.

Some Questions to Consider—Some Questions to Ask

Before you spend your hard-earned money on trading software, I suggest you get answers to or think about the following important questions:

1. What was the length of the historical test?   Many systems are tested on 5 to 10 years of data. By avoiding a lengthy historical test results can appear to be much better than they would be in a long-term test. Since the nature of markets changes, it is important to see how a system would have fared in all types of markets. This can only be achieved by testing the system in many different types of markets.

2. Was there a deduction for slippage and commission?   The standard deduction is $100 per trade. In other words, a system can produce profitable trades which may disappear once reasonable operating charges are deducted from its per trade performance.

3. How did the system handle limit moves?   This is a very important item that's commonly overlooked in system testing. If a buy sign is generated by a locked limit up move then entry might not have been possible, at times, for several days. The reverse would hold true in the case of a sell signal. And stop losses might not be fillable on limit moves against your position. Many systems assume price fills regardless of limit moves. And this falsely inflates the performance of a system. The overstatement of results can be significant.

4. Is the system optimized?   In other words, does the system contain numerous rules that are designed with 20/20 hindsight in order to tailor make a system which fits historical data? Optimized systems reflect the past very well, however, they tend not to work in real time. While the past is often the same as the future, it is never exactly the same. The more rules and variables there are in an optimized system, the less likely the system is to work. It is, therefore, very important to find out the degree of optimization that was used to generate the results.

5. Can the performance results be viewed on a market-by-market basis?   Is the performance reasonably consistent across markets or do several markets contribute excessively to the overall performance? Is performance in each market a function of one or several large profits or do the trades appear fairly consistent in terms of their average profit? I suggest you avoid a system that was successful in back testing as a result of only several trades or markets.

6. What was the maximum number of consecutive losers?   If a system had 10 or more consecutive losing trades, it's doubtful that even the most disciplined trader would have been able to remain faithful to the system. While it is reasonable to expect strings of losses, it is also reasonable to assume that a trader may not stay with a system if the string of losing trades is likely to be excessive.

7. What was the maximum equity drawdown?   This is an equally important figure. If the drawdown was excessive, you must be careful to begin trading the system only when it has experienced a period of significant drawdown. If not, you may be getting in at the top.

8. Do the results represent worst case or best case scenarios? In evaluating a system's performance, you'd want to see the worst case possibilities as opposed to the best case. Yes, you'd also be interested in optimum results but don't be fooled into thinking the test will reflect the reality of the system—this rarely happens.

And finally, don't be afraid to ask probing questions. Before risking your money to buy and trade a system, you need to have confidence that the developers have both a sound theory and a sound system which meets the important requirements I've discussed above. It's hard enough to be successful as a trader with good information, but getting bad information disguised as good makes it even more difficult. When it comes to futures trading systems, caveat emptor!

REVIEW

1. The use of advisory and informational market services is common among those investors who do not have the time to do their own market studies.
2. Such services can be either a help or a hindrance.
3. Charting-type services can save you time, but you will not benefit from the learning that comes with doing your own work.
4. Advisory services, if they are to be used, must be employed consistently, as one would apply any trading system. Lack of thorough use or the use of too many services will lead to losses.
5. Suggested guidelines for the appropriate use of a service are listed.
6. The trader or investor is the key variable in profitable use of a service.

14

Is This You?

"Here goes another losing trade!"

"I'll do my charts tomorrow."

"Let's not follow that buy signal . . . we'll only get stopped out again."

"I'm too much of a loser to make money consistently."

"I hope the market closes soon."

"My trading signals haven't been working, I think I'll just trade on gut feel."

"Let's spread up that position before it turns into another loss."

"I can't make money in the market anymore."

"I'll just close out the account now before there's nothing left."

"I must be having an unlucky streak."

"It must be time for a new trading system."

"It's that damn broker's fault . . . every time I have a good position he talks me out of it."

"I should have had my stops in like I was supposed to."

"I can't do anything right."

"Every trade I make turns into a loss as soon as I touch it."

If you have found yourself making any of these statements, or if you are saying any of them to yourself right now, then you're in the wrong place emotionally. Certainly you cannot always maintain a positive attitude, but this does not mean that your situation should be exacerbated by negative self-statements and attitudes. In order to change your emotional status, there are several steps that must be taken. The current trend in medicine and psychiatry is preventive rather than responsive. It is infinitely more effective to prevent the onset of a disease than it is to respond to the disease after it has become entrenched. The same reasoning holds true for behavioral problems.

123

If you develop a negative attitude, then your trading will invariably suffer. You will start to misread signals, read prices incorrectly, place orders incorrectly, and possibly make trades based on nothing but emotion. This behavior will earn most traders nothing but losses. The ability to recognize the onset of negative attitudes is a skill all traders should develop in their efforts to practice preventive mental health. A losing streak in the markets can be made either better or worse by attitude. Let's take a look at the first step that must be taken: recognition.

Many symptoms will allow you to recognize the onset of a losing or negative attitude. The time to begin your surveillance of attitudes is during a period of successive losses either in the market or in your personal life. Few traders realize that personal life can affect market life and vice versa. All too often we believe that if the market is going well, then all is right with the world. This is a fallacious assumption and you must abandon it entirely. Life is a total experience and influences from all areas will spill over and affect each other. If you have experienced any setback whatsoever—personal, financial, familial, educational—you are a target for negative attitude. Knowing that you are susceptible should put you on guard. The most effective way to signal the possible onset of negative attitudes is to keep a checklist. This will be covered in our review later on.

In addition, there are several behavioral correlates that can assist in the recognition process. First and foremost is a lack of willingness to keep charts, data, or other technical work up to date. You will find your market studies boring, possibly anxiety-provoking, and your level of motivation to keep current will diminish considerably. You may find yourself oversleeping in the morning, late for work, and leaving work early. You will have a "so what" attitude. These will be among the very first indicators of trouble. It is during these times that profitable trades will be missed. And it is during these times that many other traders will have similar attitudes. One day you will awaken to find that big moves have passed you by. You will look at the charts or the fundamentals and you'll say, "That was a perfect signal . . . where was I when that happened?" This will frustrate you even more, thus triggering a series of additional errors.

Another indicator of impending disaster is the negative self-statement. After the proper predisposing conditions (discussed earlier), you may begin to tell yourself and others things that clearly signal danger. Here are some examples.

"Well, there goes another losing trade."
"I can't do anything right."

"There's no use even making the trade because we'll take a loss anyway."

"I feel like quitting the market."

There are hundreds, perhaps thousands, of other statements that fall into the same category. They are among the key indicators of major trouble! Remember also that each individual will have his or her own response pattern. Let me tell you a few details about how I develop negative attitudes and what signals onset in my case.

It takes only four consecutive losses for the process to start. Missing a big move may be the precipitating factor. Every now and then a traffic ticket can set me off. My immediate response will be to miss my daily chart updating. Typically I will leave the office early. Another correlate is consumption of "junk food"—this is the "junk food indicator." The "junk food attack" happens on the same day that my charts are left undone. And on that same day I leave the office early. It is not unusual for these symptoms to last several days.

The next telltale sign comes within a matter of days. I begin to talk about myself in negative terms. Losses become a part of everyday life, and I accept them as if I knew they were coming. Every stop has my name on it and I begin to talk to my brokers in a way that clearly reveals my losing frame of mind. This sequence of events may sound a bit amusing to you. But it happens to be true, and it is also very typical. I stress the point that each individual has his or her own response pattern. In many cases, the trigger is always the same. Become aware of your unique indicator! The more clearly you can define the sequence of events, the more promptly you will spot them. And speed is of the essence. You must think of it as an emotional first aid kit. Each time you fall into the pattern, keep a record of what was said and done.

Not all individuals will react the same way every time. There are those who have well-developed defenses that will prevent them from recognizing the onset of trouble through the indicators mentioned above. In such cases, friends, brokers, and family members can help. In fact, we can always get help from others, since they tend to notice peculiarities earlier than we do. No individual should think that he or she is strong enough to make it alone. Go to those around you, particularly a spouse or loved one, and tell them to let you know when they see changes. Brokers who are in close touch with you can be extremely helpful. Remember that there is no limit to the self-deceptive ability of the human mind. This is a throwback to defense mechanisms developed in

early childhood. We will avoid, repress, suppress, intellectualize, sublimate, and even fantasize problems out of consciousness. As I have told
you many times (and will tell you many more times), our greatest enemy
in the market is us.

Now that you have some specific information on how to recognize the
onset of a destructive attitude, you must learn how it can be treated. First
and foremost, the time to begin treatment is immediately if not sooner.
There will be a tendency to avoid dealing with the problem even though it
has been recognized. You will want to fight yourself every step of the
way and will do everything possible to make the job even more difficult
than it is. This is the natural state of affairs for one who resides in a
negative psychological environment. Believe me, I speak from experience
both as therapist and patient. The essence of treatment is, in my opinion,
brute force. There are "romantic" things I could suggest. I could tell you
to take a cold shower. Or I could say "get in touch with yourself, relax,
say some prayers, free associate, be yourself," or any of the other meaningless things that we are told. But these do not work. A negative cycle
feeds on itself and you must break into the chain. No matter which point
you break into, you must start somewhere.

What do I mean by "brute force"? Very simply, I mean that you must
gather all of your effort and strength, force yourself to work on those
charts, read those crop reports, make those trades, or calculate the signals. This is when you must spend the greatest amount of time working
on your trading system. This is the time to respond in an opposite way
from the manner in which you are inclined to act. The more you want
to leave your office early, the more you must stay. The less you want to
work on your charts, the more work you must do. This also applies to
negative self-statements. The more inclined you feel to put yourself
down, the more positive you should be. This is a very difficult thing to
do. It is especially difficult the first time you do it, but it takes less and
less effort each time you practice.

There are many other things you can do to help yourself. They all fall
under "scheduling," which will be discussed later on. It will become clear
to you after a number of such experiences that the harder you fight yourself, the more likely you are to succeed. Assuming that you are your own
worst enemy, particularly when things go bad, you must learn not to trust
your emotions. You must have a plan of attack available for immediate
use in the event that the time comes for its implementation.

As indicated earlier, the most effective key to improvement is brute
force. Another useful tool is the behavioral checklist. This method of

keeping a positive mental attitude, elementary as it may sound, is extremely effective. I would recommend its use on a daily basis whether or not you are prone to develop negative attitudes. The checklist is such an important tool that an entire chapter is devoted to it.

REVIEW

1. Attitudes have a direct influence on trading results.
2. Negative attitudes can make a losing streak even worse and may, in fact, prevent effective trading by compounding the negativism.
3. Recognition of negative attitude onset is the first step toward a cure.
4. Action should be preventive in nature. This will inhibit improper mental attitude before it can start to affect trading.
5. The onset of such counterproductive attitudes can be recognized by closely observing the symptoms accompanying them.
6. Each individual has his or her own response pattern.
7. Come to know and recognize your unique pattern.
8. Treat the symptoms as soon as they occur. Do not procrastinate even one moment once you have realized the presence of onset symptoms.
9. Use the "brute force" technique to counteract negative impulses seeking to keep you from doing your market work.
10. Keep a behavioral checklist as discussed in a later chapter.
11. Obtain assistance from friends, loved ones, family, and/or broker in spotting your attitudes if you cannot effectively do so on your own.

15

Can a Positive Mental Attitude Facilitate Consistent Success?

The least frequently recognized but perhaps most effective technique for successful trading is the development of positive mental attitude (PMA). Many traders have experienced the losses that can come when they're "in a rut." This feeling is certainly not unique to investors; it is also common in athletes, executives, and politicians. For some seemingly mysterious reason or reasons, when PMA is high, everything appears to go well—profits increase, self-concept is positive, skies are blue. Conversely, when PMA is low, losses rise, more mistakes are made, and outlook for the future is poor. There are those who claim that PMA is a function of external events and not the cause of these events. But believers in self-determination, positive motivation, and PMA would totally disagree. Let's examine some of the aspects of PMA as they relate to trading and how they can improve your results.

During the Middle Ages, many peculiar behavioral cures were developed. In most cases, they were tortures designed to drive out "bad spirits." Their intent was to either force spirits out of the body or to give them an opening through which they might leave. It was reasoned that if the body was an uncomfortable place to inhabit, spirits would leave, out of desperation and discomfort. If the patient survived "treatment," it often seemed to have a beneficial effect. In fact, even magical cures and spells cast by witches seemed to work well. In our age of technological and scientific sophistication, we are inclined to make light of such methods. They are totally unscientific and they do not conform to the laws of physics as we know them. But the fact remains that they obtain results. How do these mystical techniques bring about cures? How does this relate to PMA? How does suggestion enter into the picture?

The essence of all magical cures is suggestion. And suggestion, albeit an age-old technique, is still not totally understood or accepted today. There are many different forms of suggestion. All can produce profound changes in behavior and attitude. Despite our seemingly advanced state of psychological knowledge, scientists still lack a thorough understanding of how suggestion and hypnotism operate. Positive mental attitude is, in a sense, what has been termed "autosuggestion." It is the individual, suggesting to himself that things will go well, that success will come, that his efforts will come to fruition, and that nothing can stand in his way. In so doing, one sets the stage for success.

In the early days of psychiatric treatment, a popular cure based on autosuggestion was introduced by Dr. Emil Coué. The disturbed or troubled patient was to repeat to himself the following curative phrase, "Every day, in every way, I am getting better and better." Strange as it may seem, this technique actually achieved results. The reason behind its effectiveness rests in the power of suggestion.

It is my belief that positive mental attitude is a form of self-suggestion. But PMA is more than just a rote repetition of positive phrases; it is a way of life. The individual who practices PMA seeks out experiences that will provide the necessary rewards. Experiences that are negative are avoided, ignored, or eliminated. If we can view PMA in the context of behavioral learning, it will be much clearer. Essentially the individual who is oriented toward PMA is attempting to control both the stimulus and consequence events of his learning chain. He will not only disallow negative stimulation to enter into his lifestyle, but he will also make certain that positive consequences follow positive experiences. Thus, he will shape winning attitudes. The step-by-step process is more involved than I have indicated here.

In applying PMA, we must remember that in its final state it does not function as a series of mechanical and forced steps, even though it may develop this way. It is not merely sufficient to say to one's self, "I will succeed. I am the greatest. I will have wealth and fame." A complete change of lifestyle is necessary. Virtually every area of the individual's experience must be adapted to accommodate positive experiences. The growth of PMA will not be assured by the mere rote manifestation or assertion of will power. There must be an underlying base of positive, free imagination. There must be an internalization of positively directed will, imagination, and thought. E. Mounier comments on this concept in *The Character of Man:*

> Dr. Court stated the rule that a forced effort of the will was always, without exception, less effective than free imagination. . . . If we wish to succeed in a difficult or dangerous action, it is often good to isolate ourselves (in this way), passively concerned with the thing to be done, rather than concentrating on it tensely: putting oneself in a state of attentive distraction. (1956, p. 154)

One can achieve the maximum benefit from will power and positive mental attitude only after they become internalized. They must become a way of life. Positive mental attitude is, in its totality, a winning way of life.

There have been many texts and courses purporting to teach positive mental attitude. Essentially, courses in PMA, self-improvement, success motivation, and dynamic salesmanship are sessions in group suggestion. Such courses, if reputable, can bring the individual investor many benefits. Unfortunately, most investors and traders are unaware of their generally negative mental attitudes. They cannot recognize the symptoms that characterize such losing self-perceptual sets. In order to change an unsatisfactory state of internal affairs, it is necessary to spot the precedent conditions or symptoms of the attitude we wish to change. I recommend a three-step process in the change from negative to positive mental attitude:

1. Recognition.
2. Initiation of change.
3. Internalization and maintenance.

A "crash course" cannot provide most traders with enough information to effect change. Positive behavior and attitude changes rarely develop overnight. Typically they have a history of growth over many years. The smaller the change, the less time it has been in the formative stage. Those who are trained in the observation of human behavior can detect changes well in advance of their overt expression. And when they are recognized, a program of change can be instituted. The ability to isolate and recognize the early phases of attitude change in the investor is a highly specialized skill. It is an even more specialized achievement for you to recognize it in yourself. Many years of personal experience have resulted in my formulation of an "early warning" list. It is possible for you to exhibit any

Table 15.1
Early Symptoms of Negative Attitude

1. String of market losses.
2. Market studies not updated on schedule.
3. Unwillingness to trade the market or make investments.
4. Persistent misinterpretation of trading signals.
5. Increase in "tip" taking.
6. Increase in negative or self-critical statements.
7. Premature initiation or liquidation of positions contrary to signals.
8. Oversleeping; general physical malaise.
9. Frequent late arrival at work.
10. Feeling best described as "I can't wait until the market closes" (for those who trade daily).
11. Not wanting to know how much of a loss one is riding on an open position.
12. Loss of interest in the markets.

or all of the symptoms outlined in Table 15.1. They can occur in any order, and there are other symptoms not listed.

If, at any time, you begin to observe the symptoms listed in Table 15.1, it is an indication that all is not well. The best time to begin the change process is the instant any one of the listed symptoms appears. Frequently we are not aware of onset and cannot observe symptoms due to the operation of repressive defense mechanisms (defined earlier). In such cases, those close to us, such as family, friends, or broker, can alert us.

Initiation of Change

To remediate a negative mental attitude, and subsequently develop it into a positive one, you must move on to the next step. This involves the initiation of procedures designed to change attitudes. Numerous techniques can be employed in the change process. I will outline a number of these methods below. Note that these are in relative sequential order. Certain steps should be instituted before others. The order indicated is what I recommend.

1. Any attempt to change should begin with a mechanical series of steps.   Previously I mentioned "brute force" as a viable technique. I believe that you will find such methods valuable when first attempting to change a losing or negative behavior. What exactly do I mean by "brute force"? I mean persistence, effort, determination, and good old-fashioned hard work. This can be accomplished through the use of a schedule and a specific behavioral checklist, as discussed earlier. Step 1 will be covered later in greater detail.

2. Each specific symptom of negativism must be counteracted. This will require you to have a list of your precise behaviors, as well as a method of responding or treating each. The following are some examples:

    a. A string of losses, which could easily bring with it negative attitudes, should be countered by reference to your track record. Assuming you have had a good success rate in the past, you should focus on the positive by referring to it in times of crisis. If you have a very poor or brief trading record, then do not refer to it since to do so would be a negative experience. In such cases, use your hypothetical record. This is the record of results achieved by a pretest of your system.

    b. Falling behind in market work can be best countered by use of a schedule.

    c. Negative self-statements should be dealt with in two ways. First, find a way of signaling when you are about to make self-effacing remarks. This will help you stop such verbalizations. Second, solicit the positive comments of others.

3. Associate only with winners, positive people, and successful friends.   We are not only known by the company we keep, but we also tend to behave as they do. If we allow ourselves to associate with those who have negative attitudes and experiences, then we will be weighted down by their mere presence. Since we cannot block out all incoming stimuli, it is difficult to filter out the bad, allowing only the good, or productive, to enter. If we eliminate as much of the negative as we can, there will be no need to guard against it. And there will be a preponderance of positive input. Put yourself in positive situations.

4. Terminate negative relationships if you cannot repair them. Often the best way to repair a bad relationship is to end it. This is, to be sure, easier said than done. You will find, as I have, that doing so will also be helpful in other areas of your life.

5. Institute a systematic check and balance procedure for trading signals.   This will help you double-check your work. In so doing, you will remain close to your signals, thereby benefiting from the overall positive results. Review our previous discussion of scheduling if necessary.

6. Attempt to deal only with a broker who is positive. You'll be surprised how much of an effect brokers can have on your attitude (if you don't already know this). At the very minimum, your broker should be neutral. It's difficult to stick to a trading plan. Negative comments from a broker don't help.

7. Set specific objectives and goals. In working toward goals, you will be moving in a positive direction. Keep goals in mind at all times. If goals are forgotten or overlooked negative thinking can become dominant.

8. Set ambitious objectives. Your goals should be attainable and realistic but ambitious as well. Don't allow yourself to settle for a small part of the pie. Attempt to set your goals above and beyond your ability but within reach. This will help your positive attitude by giving you a rewarding target for which to aim.

9. The "five-year plan" is a technique I use to maintain positive direction and attitude. Set yourself a month-by-month or year-by-year plan. Review your specific goals and progress monthly or semiannually. In determining your target, be as specific as possible. State in precise terms how much money you plan to accumulate, where you will put it, and how you will use it to make more money. Set personal goals as well. Indicate how you plan to improve your trading, education, home life, and working relationships.

10. Keep a list of your trading rules and read them once weekly. I have found that this constant reminder keeps me on a positive track. When things appear to be heading in a negative direction, you can help improve them by reading your list. This will remind you to be positive when the desire to fail is greatest. Ordinarily 10 to 15 brief trading rules are more than sufficient.

There are many other techniques and tools that will help initiate and internalize the process of change from negative to positive attitude. After you have had some experience in shaping such attitudes, you will easily recognize those that work for you.

Internalization

To maintain a consistently positive attitude toward yourself and others, it is necessary to practice the foregoing procedures. Only after one has spent considerable time shaping PMA, using it, and profiting by it can it become an internal or automatic process. I therefore suggest you employ PMA in all areas of your life. Those individuals who do so tend to have successful relationships, marriages, businesses, and trading. As with most behaviors, you must "use them or lose them." Organization and positive attitude work together to produce successful market results. In order to be as organized as possible the use of a schedule is highly recommended (see Chapter 10).

REVIEW

1. Positive mental attitude (PMA) can be instrumental in the success or failure of a trading system.
2. PMA is a form of self-suggestion.
3. In order to acquire positive attitudes it is necessary to follow a three-step process.
4. Recognition of negative attitudes is important. Common symptoms of negative attitudes are listed.
5. The change process must be initiated if you wish to develop PMA. There is a very specific technique for doing so.
6. Positive attitudes must be internalized. They must be used over and over until they have become an inseparable part of the individual.
7. PMA must become a way of life in order for it to achieve its full results.

16

The Broker-Client Relationship

The relationship between client and broker can help maximize either profits or losses. More often than not, neither individual involved in this relationship is aware of the subtleties that transpire daily. Too frequently, the client is likely to blame losses on the broker, and brokers tend to misread the needs of their clients. In most cases, both parties working together can achieve results neither could accomplish alone. There are many directions the relationship can take. In the pages that follow I will attempt to:

1. Define types of broker-client relationships.
2. Define ideal broker-client relationship.
3. Discuss ways in which improvement can be made.
4. Discuss additional aspects of broker-client interaction.

At the source of most broker-client difficulty is misunderstanding. All too often traders fail to be aware of the role, functions, limitations, assets, and liabilities of their broker. There is a tendency among traders to think of brokers as infallible, in the know, and always available. None of the foregoing is necessarily true. The insecure individual thinks of his or her broker as fully informed by virtue of physical proximity to the market. This is, to be sure, not an accurate picture at all. A broker who is close to the "action" may in fact be less accurate in trading recommendations than one who is removed from the market madness. Brokers are expected to serve a trader without error, while at the same time providing good advice, watching the market, listening to relevant news, keeping up to date on charts, and answering telephones. It is not possible to achieve such unrealistic goals.

In order to understand the relationship between broker and client, let's take a look at what a broker's job should ideally consist of, and what a client's expectations and role should be. Every broker should be responsible for carrying out the following functions:

1. Take and execute all orders promptly and accurately.
2. Report back promptly and accurately on all order fills.
3. Keep client informed of news if the client so desires.
4. Maintain and report account balances, margins, and other details.
5. Be available and on call each and every time the client wishes to place an order.
6. Keep abreast of important changes in costs, commissions, legal details, margins, and the like, and inform the client as necessary.
7. Obtain market information for the client upon request.

These tasks are difficult to achieve, and a broker should not ideally be expected or required to do anything more. The self-reliant trader knows how valuable it is to have a broker who performs these duties thoroughly, promptly, and without effort. Brokers are, however, in a peculiar position. The individuals they serve are frequently insecure, unsure of their trading, and unfamiliar with the market. Naturally they assume that the broker is in a position to know precisely what the market will do. This is perhaps the most common misunderstanding among clients. They do not realize that the broker wishes to please them by providing as much information as they feel they need. If asked to express opinions, the broker will comply.

There are many brokers who do good technical and fundamental work. Their opinions are certainly valid and can result in profitable trades. But there are not too many brokers I have met, particularly in the commodities market, who can achieve all that is expected of them in the way of order filling while doing their market research as well.

The problem arises not from the advice and recommendations most brokers cannot help but give, but from the unwillingness of clients to follow the broker's advice to the letter, each and every time. Clients are prone to complain about brokers. As a result, many brokers have become defendants in lawsuits or have been objects of censure by government agencies. All too often these actions are due not to any wrongdoing on the broker's part but to misunderstanding by clients and their unrealistic expectations. The broker is, after all, in the strange position of wanting his client to trade frequently in order to generate commission. He does not want his client to "overtrade" since this not only looks bad but often "burns out" an account quickly. If there is a lack of trading, there is a lack of commission. If there is a lack of commission, the broker does not do well. Most brokers must maintain a delicate balance of recommendations to the client. If the broker makes recommendations to the client, then he must "hold the client's hand" as it were. The broker's job can be likened to the work of a supportive therapist. In recommending positions, yet in not having control over the account, he is open to considerable liability. Here is an example:

> One friend to another, "My broker got me into some wheat today."
> Second trader, "Think it'll work?"
> "Don't know. He gets out of trades too early."
> "What do you mean by 'too early'?"
> "Well, sometimes he gets me out with a little bit of profit when I could have had a lot more."
> "Why don't you let him get you in, and then you can get out on your own?"
> "Not a bad idea, I think I'll do that from now on."

This is typical of what can happen to a broker's recommendation. In fact, this is how most good recommendations, whether from brokers, advisory services, or friends get transformed into losing trades. As soon as an individual who is following the recommendations of his or her broker attempts to alter the trade in any way, the basics of using a trading system are violated. The results will be similar to those encountered by a trader who uses only some of the signals from his own trading system. In other words, the signals will not get an adequate or thorough test. This is where most broker-client relationships run into serious trouble. As you can see, we are right back to the trader. If you will recall, I indicated much earlier that the trader was more important than any other aspect of the trading situation. Here we see how full responsibility falls squarely on his shoulders. Another typical example of broker-client interaction further illustrates the point:

> "I think we should buy some December Cattle with a 200-point stop," says the broker to his client.

"What's the objective?" inquires the client.

"I'm looking for a 400-point profit potential. That's a two to one risk ratio," answers the broker.

"Well, OK, let's put on the trade, but let's do it now. Why wait until the price comes down? We might miss the opportunity."

"We can't do it now," explains the broker, "the price is too high and we'd expose ourselves to too much risk."

"I don't think we should wait. Let's do it now," orders the client with urgency in his voice.

"Please be patient," pleads the broker, "I don't want to jump the gun."

"Patience, shmacience," cries the customer, "what's a lousy 50 points, it's only 200 bucks!"

The broker reluctantly puts on the position. He suggests to the client that a stop loss be entered. "Stop loss," shouts the customer in surprise, "forget it! All they have to do is see my stop and they'll pick it. Don't put in a stop. You're close to the market. Just keep your eye on the trade and call me if we get near the danger point."

"That's not too good an idea," explains the broker, "I might be busy and not see the stop price get hit. And I might not be able to get in touch with you."

"Don't worry about it," the client assures him.

Time passes and the trade goes contrary to expectations. The broker calls his customer and explains the situation. After some agony the client refuses his broker's pleas. The trade has not been closed out. The broker cannot do so without permission. The client has his head in the sand (or worse) and will not admit to the loss. The broker's hands are tied. In agony the client chides his broker, "You should have made me get out earlier!"

"But you wouldn't listen to me," explains the broker in his own defense.

"That's what you're there for," retorts his client. "You should have made me do it no matter what I said. You're just another crooked broker!"

That's how the story goes. Many is the broker who has been in similar situations almost daily. The essence here is lack of control over the trader and all trades but full responsibility for bad trades.

How can such a situation be rectified? The following suggestions can result in a much more productive outcome:

1. Ideally a broker should not be expected to fulfill any functions other than those shown earlier, unless he is the legally specified account manager.

2. If you decide to take a broker's trading advice, make certain you know his track record. Even though this cannot be verified, it will give you some indication of his accuracy.

3. If you decide to take a broker's trading suggestions, then take all of them. If you do not follow his recommendations fully, to completion of each trade, then you are not doing justice to him or to your account.

4. Never put your broker on the spot. If you vary from his recommendations, then do not hold him responsible for the result(s).

5. Never chide your broker for anything other than errors in order execution.

6. Never depend on your broker to trade for you unless you are prepared to hold him harmless from blame or responsibility.

7. Never demand advice from a broker unless you have made certain beforehand that he feels comfortable giving it. Never ask a broker to rectify an error you made on your own.

8. Do not expect a broker to advise you if he has other work to do. You cannot be the only client in your broker's life.

9. Do not leave your broker "holding the bag." If he gets you into a trade, then let him get you out.

Some traders simply want their broker to be a "yes man." They put on trades and to alleviate their own insecurity want a broker who will agree with them. If they do not get the kind of support they want, they move on to the next broker. The value of a broker, for them, is not how well he or she executes orders, but rather how much support the broker can give. This type of "broker collector" will often have a number of accounts at different houses in order to get as much support as possible. Wherever he gets the support is where he will trade. If you are in this category, or if you are a broker who has this type of client, then I suggest caution. There is no one individual who can help your trade be right simply by agreeing with you. This problem must be dealt with behaviorally, according to the guidelines previously provided. If you are a broker, you can discourage such behavior by not pacifying any client.

The Broker-Therapist

Another type of broker-client relationship, similarly nonproductive and potentially hazardous, is the "broker-therapist" situation. In this case, the customer expects consolation from his broker. When a trade goes bad, he wants to be told that everything will turn out well. When a trade goes well, he worries that the profit will disappear and wants reassurance. His level of anxiety is very high. He calls about five times each hour to "get prices." But in reality he is calling for support and consolation. When a big loss is taken, he complains bitterly and seeks advice as to how the money can be made back.

All in all, this type of individual is not in need of a broker but rather in need of a therapist. We can look at the situation in Freudian terms in order to understand it better. You will recall the transference relationship between Freudian therapist and patient. This is one in which the patient looks upon the therapist as a parent substitute and seeks to resolve problems within the surrogate relationship. The therapist is seen as an authoritarian. The patient acts in compliance and defiance, and long-standing problems are worked out in this fashion. There are many correlates in the broker-client relationship. The client considers his broker as the authority. The subsequent "acting out" of problems and need for reassurance is pathological. The end result can only be losses.

The Headhunter

Some traders are headhunters. They play the "I'll get that broker" game. These individuals seek to make others—particularly brokers—the scapegoats for losses they have had as a result of their own shortcomings. Consequently they go from broker to broker in an attempt to "get him." They look for errors, possible legal violations, or any other behaviors that will bring about conflict. This is counterproductive. The conflict stems from unwillingness to accept total responsibility for your own behavior. The individual who falls into this category is in need of professional help.

Brokers' Problems

What about brokers? Can certain types of brokers be readily identified? For the most part, brokers have fewer problems than clients. Brokers do their work for a living. Most customers, on the other hand, do not trade for a living. If a broker has emotional problems, or if he does not do his job well, he won't be around very long. Most customers did not make the majority of their money in the market. They have other jobs and come to the market to lose their money. As such they can have many market-related problems, and as long as their money lasts, they can stay in the market. This is why I would be hard-pressed to isolate any specific type of broker in terms of behavior. As a lot, they are much healthier emotionally than are their customers.

The Broker-Client Contract

What can we learn from this? To begin with, we must realize that for a majority of traders, the relationship with a broker can either add to or detract from net results. The broker must realize what he or she is up against and how to deal with it. Both individuals must realize that working together is necessary for profit and survival. I have several suggestions for broker and client that will assist in their overall productivity. Before listing these, I would like to say just a few words in support of the broker-client "contract." The skills and limitations of a broker are well known to the trader who has made the market his profession, sits at a desk all day, trades his account, and/or manages others' money. He rarely relies on brokers for advice, follows his own trading for better or for worse, and is therefore not susceptible to the problems outlined in this chapter. The average trader, however, should establish a clear understanding or contract with his broker in which each party loosely outlines expectations of the other. This will help avoid many difficulties, both legal and otherwise. The contract, although not a legal document, and possibly not even a written one, would be entered into prior to the opening of an account or shortly thereafter. If, for example, a client wished no trading advice, he would so specify. If a broker wished to give no trading advice, then it would so be indicated and agreed. The agreement would be made in order to avoid any difficulties that arise from misunderstanding, unrealistic expectations, or misconceptions. I believe the following specific suggestions will benefit both customer and broker:

1. Brokers and clients should establish a clear understanding or "contract" prior to the start of trading.

2. Customers should strive to be independent of brokers' advice, using only their own trading system.

3. Brokers should avoid advice-seeking traders unless they make virtually all trades as advised, following them through to completion.

4. Brokers should avoid involvement with overly dependent traders who seek handholding and consolation rather than good brokerage.

5. Brokers should encourage their clients to trade on the clients' own signals, since this will more often than not produce a successful, lasting account.

Some readers may find it difficult to imagine the many ways in which trading losses may arise from a disturbed broker-client relationship. Certainly, the situations I have described and the behaviors I have mentioned are extreme. Remember, however, that it is the nature of emotional difficulties to be extreme and peculiar. In many cases, the individual who is suffering from serious psychological shortcomings is neither aware of these problems nor willing to admit that a problem might exist. This is characteristic of the denial that accompanies emotional disorders. My purpose in outlining some of the possibilities is to inform you of what can occur if the early warning signs are ignored. Few if any behaviors have a sudden onset. They may seem to have developed overnight, yet close study of their precedent events will reveal a progression that in many cases can only be identified by a skilled professional. The essence of success in the investment game is anticipation. Trades must be made on anticipation of positive results, and losses must be limited on anticipation of more seriously negative results. The psychology of trading or investing is equally amenable to anticipation. In the broker-client relationship, it is therefore necessary to practice preventive techniques. This is best done by following some of the suggestions I have outlined in this chapter. It is not necessary to implement all the recommended items. I would strongly suggest that you keep them in mind with prevention as the objective.

REVIEW

1. Broker-client relationships can be productive or destructive.
2. Relationships that are counterproductive should be avoided.

3. Behavioral techniques can be applied to the solution of problems between broker and client.

4. Various types of relationships can be defined.

5. Broker and client should strive to be completely independent in terms of the individual functions of each and this will bring good results to both.

17

Putting It All Together— Where You Fit

It's one thing to talk theory. It's a far greater accomplishment to obtain results. Although I have attempted to give you some real life examples of how to use psychological principles in solving investing and trading problems, there are still those who may find it impossible to implement my suggestions. How can we, without professional help, find our own way to success? Certainly the most simple, nonspecific answer is be persistent. It is difficult to reach one's goal, or overcome one's difficulty, lacking the necessary experience to do so. How might a relatively inexperienced trader gain the ability to correct his or her mistakes? My intent is to provide not a "cookbook" method to self-awareness or success, but rather a checklist of guidelines that might be used in the improvement process.

By now you have realized that my bias in behavior change is primarily learning-theory oriented. I have serious doubts about the ability of traditional techniques to affect change within a brief period of time. I believe that psychoanalysis can help, but I do not believe that it can help quickly enough. Trading problems need prompt relief, as do emotional difficulties. The most effective technique I know is the behavioral method, a portion of which has been described earlier. I believe it is possible for the average trader to use behavioral principles in the overall improvement of his or her investing success, but change must proceed in an orderly fashion.

Do You Really Have a Problem?

Many investors believe that they have market-related problems when indeed they do not. The results of your evaluation, or *Investors Quotient,* as

I have called it (see Chapter 8), may be a good indicator. Another good indicator is your overall profit picture. I will assume that you are following an organized trading system. (If you are not, then reread my previous discussions on this matter.) Examine your profits and losses. Consider the five relevant questions asked in this chapter.

1. When liquidating a position do you get out within 30 percent of a top or bottom, or do you generally give back more than 50 percent of your open profits?   This is more of a technical problem than a psychological one. The answer will be found in the stop-loss or follow-up method you are using. It is often difficult to distinguish between a market or system problem and an emotional involvement. If you show overall profits from your trading and investing, then it is unlikely you have a psychological difficulty. Check your system first!

2. Are losses taken at or near the stop loss point?   If the answer was "yes," then you are following your trading system and should examine it for possible shortcomings. A small adjustment in stop-loss procedure can make all the difference. A net losing system can become a winner. If most of your stops are being executed quite a distance from your original market exit point, chances are that you are tampering with them. This is a psychological problem and should be treated according to my suggested methodology.

3. Are your market entries based on your technical work or advisory service? Are they executed at the indicated price, too early, or too late?   As in the case of stops, your entries should be close to the intended price. Failure of such order execution is more than just the result of "bad fills," particularly if orders are consistently being placed well outside the acceptable range. This is an emotionally related problem and not the fault of your broker, friends, or advisor. Entry at the indicated price level suggests that you are following the rules. If so, any lack of profits should or could be traced back to the trading system or advisor.

4. How do you act when you take a profit or loss? Does your behavior spill over into other areas of your life? Does your home life affect your trading?   Some of these issues are touched on in the trader evaluation provided earlier. To answer these questions honestly, it will be necessary to ask those around you for an objective evaluation of your behavior. It is normal to react in a positive or negative way to market experiences. It is, however, a warning sign to react too violently in one direction or another. If this is the case, then you are indeed suffering from a psychological or emotional difficulty.

Perhaps the most common difficulty among traders is their inability to separate system-related defects from personality-related difficulties. By failing to draw a clear-cut distinction between system failings and personal limitations, the investor may assume responsibility for a loss that is not due to the investor's own inability. This will undermine his or her self-confidence, resulting in an unwillingness to use the system. There are occasions when an emotional problem will be taken to be system related. Failure to enter a stop at the appropriate time may be blamed on the system, when in reality, it is the fault of the trader. The single best way to overcome the potential confusion is to draw a very clear-cut line between technique and implementation. The most effective way to accomplish this goal is by strict adherence to specified system rules. I suggest you keep a sheet which indicates system signals and trader action.

Table 17.1 is a sample from a fictitious trading system. Note that each and every signal generated by the trading system has a specific follow-up procedure to be implemented by the trader. This is the only way in which errors of judgment versus system errors can be identified. If your trading system is not presently operationalized as indicated in the table, then I suggest you do this immediately. You may be pleasantly surprised at the results.

You've Decided That You Have a Problem . . . What Now?

The severity of any emotional problem is always determined by the degree to which it limits or inhibits effective functioning in society. An individual who is so totally psychotic that he or she cannot function will be hospitalized for treatment. The market, at times, arouses severe symptoms in investors. This is more true in the case of active traders than long-term oriented investors. The decision must be made as to how intense your difficulty really is. Several questions are in order:

1. Have you lost more money in the market than you can afford? Have you done this more than once? Are you in the habit of borrowing

Table 17.1

Signal-Action

System Signals
 1. Closing penetration of three-week high.
 2. Signal 1.
 3. Advance of 20 percent from signal 1.
 4. Additional advance of 10 percent from signal 3.
 5. Advance of additional 10 percent from signal 4.
 6. Position stopped out.
 7. New entry signal indicated by signal 1.
 8. Closing penetration of 10-day moving average.
 9. Signal 8.
10. Ten percent rise from buy price.

Trader Action
 1. Buy next day on open at market.
 2. Place stop loss at 2 percent under three-week high.
 3. Raise stop to 50 percent profit point. Use close only stop.
 4. Raise stop to 78 percent profit point. Use straight stop only.
 5. Raise stop by increments for every 10 percent advance. Maintain at 83 percent profit point and use straight stop.
 6. Make no additional trades for three market days.
 7. Follow 1–6.
 8. Buy opening two days later.
 9. Place stop close only 1 percent under low of last three trading days.
10. Take profit of 10 percent increase from buy price by placing open order MIT as soon as trade is entered.
11. Two successive days of down closes. Place stop close only under low point in 10-day moving average.

---

money to trade? Do you sacrifice some of life's necessities in order to obtain trading capital? If the answer to any of these questions is "yes," then you are a gambler and not a trader. Cruel as this may sound, I suggest you immediately stop trading and consult either a professional therapist or Gamblers Anonymous for help. This is a serious problem. It is perhaps the single most serious psychological difficulty connected with the markets. Help is needed at once!

2. Does the market cause you anxiety?   Do you suffer from hypertension (high blood pressure)? Is it aggravated by your trading? Do you have other psycho physiological dysfunctions such as ulcers or colitis? Do they "flare up" when you trade? It is not uncommon for such symptoms to afflict many traders, particularly those active in the markets. Typically their symptoms are irritated by trading. This does not mean that trading should be stopped. It does, however, mean that treatment is necessary in order for the symptoms to be minimized. Those who do not get treatment for such problems may, in fact, die of the attendant complications. Psycho physiological disorders are highly responsive to treatment. Traditionally, psychotherapy and/or counseling as well as drugs are used. Excellent results can be obtained from behavioral treatment. Biofeedback, reciprocal inhibition, and counterconditioning should be investigated with an appropriate therapist.

3. Are you immobilized or incapacitated by the markets?   Following a loss, do you withdraw, become reclusive, depressed, morose, and unable to work at your full-time job? If so, then you are also suffering from a serious problem. Trading, as you can see, has become more than mere "trading." It has taken on psychological importance above and beyond the mere call of the market. A loss is not merely a loss, but rather a painful emotional experience, which most likely relates back to your childhood or adolescent days. In such a case, more in-depth psychotherapy is necessary. I suggest you consult a professional for assistance.

4. Do you become outraged, violent, or aggressive following a market loss?   Do you "take out" your aggressions and frustrations on others either verbally or physically? Are you impossible to live with following a loss? If the answer is "yes," then you also need professional help. The market is not for you in your present condition. The best course of action is to stop trading and enter treatment with an appropriately disciplined therapist. Such reactions to market losses are also deep-rooted personality disorders and must be treated before they become even more serious.

5. Are your ups and downs closely related to market ups and downs?   Is your daily life a reflection of the market? There is nothing wrong with an individual simply because the market causes him or her to act in a certain way. As long as the behaviors do not inhibit his functioning, then such people are not in need of treatment. It is only natural to be affected by events around us. It would be absurd, and even pathological, to not be happy or ecstatic when we've taken a large profit. The thing to watch carefully is the degree to which such profits and/or losses affect your overall functioning. If there is too much of a carryover, then you may be heading for trouble and should start on a program or programs to improve the situation.

Market Problems Are Symptomatic of Other Difficulties

The single most important thing I can tell you about market problems that are *not* related to your trading system is that they frequently indicate the presence of other difficulties. We do not live our lives in unrelated segments. Life and experiences are part of a larger flow of events. The teachings of most psychologists underscore the fact that we cannot separate any one human experience or failing from the totality of an individual's environment. Difficulties in one sphere of life will make their presence known in another. Problems with a spouse may interfere with trading. And problems with trading may then have a reverse effect, in turn causing marital difficulties. An anxious individual may take it upon himself to trade the market actively. His anxiety may have been the result of early childhood experiences. This anxiety will result in poor trading discipline. The resultant losses will make him more anxious. In turn he will function poorly at his full-time job, or he may relate negatively to his family. An increase in anxiety will follow, and with it more losses.

This is the manner in which problems feed on each other. One aspect of life has its effect on another. The interaction of behaviors and their consequences form the total picture we call "personality." The point is: Any market problem is more than a market problem. Any home problem is more than a home problem. Any sexual problem is more than a sexual problem. It is not unusual, for example, for men with sexual dysfunctions to compensate by extreme aggressiveness in the market. In so doing, their lack of objectivity may lead to losses, hence their efforts bring only more pain.

I advise you to consider your relationship with the market very seriously. Make certain that you are not using the market to achieve an end that is best achieved in other aspects of your life. Make certain that your trading decisions are not merely a reflection of difficulties in the home. If you should find that your trading is causing you considerable pain, loss, and frustration, you must begin to look for the answer at home. Start by looking within yourself for the problem as well as the solution. Take care of yourself first, market successes will follow.

REVIEW

1. Some of the theoretical considerations previously discussed were put into a real life framework.
2. Several indicators of trading problems were mentioned.
3. Actions for beginning treatment of problems were suggested.
4. The correlation between market problems and difficulties in home life and interpersonal relationships was pointed out.

18

Social Psychology and the Markets

The net effect of a person's perceptual, behavioral, and psychosexual development is overt action as it is shaped by the interaction of these factors. The individual does not live in a vacuum. Each action has a reaction, which in turn influences continued behavior. Interaction with others shapes attitudes, opinions, perceptions, and ultimately behavior. The perceptual filter to which I referred earlier could, in fact, be renamed "social filter." As such it is necessary, indeed potentially profitable, to examine the social psychology of investing.

As psychology expanded its experimental base, theorists recognized the importance of studying man within his social element. Results obtained in strict laboratory settings often proved insufficient in describing the total picture. Theories frequently lacked predictive validity in true life situations. The interaction of individuals within the social structure is the raw material of social psychology. Any act that requires frequent and intensive dealings with other human beings is fair subject matter for the social psychologist. Few areas of life are immune from the effects of society. A behavior as complex as investing or trading involves the interaction of many humans. The seemingly simple act of picking up a telephone to place an order with one's broker can lead to literally hundreds of reactions, by thousands of investors. Hence, an understanding of the social forces affecting our psyches can bring insights that may be valuable in the total investment picture. A strict textbook definition of what is studied by the social psychologist might read as follows:

The behavior of an individual in the presence of another person is at once a response and a stimulus to that other person. Because the other person (O) reacts to the behavior of an individual (S), the behavior of S is likely to be tempered by the presence of O. S may consciously or unconsciously

151

behave so as to elicit a particular response from O. His subsequent behavior depends upon his success or failure in eliciting certain behaviors from O. (Secord and Backman, 1964, p. 1)

This brief definition of a social interaction represents only a small portion of possible variables operative in the social process. Inasmuch as the marketplace is an institution that functions on human interaction and emotion, a number of especially relevant topics should be mentioned.

Interpersonal Relationships and Your Investing

Like it or not, we are all influenced by those around us. The most significant consequence of social interaction is that it does, on many occasions, prevent us from implementing investment decisions with the total rationality and discipline required of the successful individual. Since we are all subject to emotional ups and downs, which frequently find their origin in interpersonal relationships, it is helpful to become familiar with several aspects of relationships. Typically, difficulties that arise from an interpersonal basis operate on an unconscious or subconscious level. Before discussing this issue, we would do well to understand what is meant by the term "interpersonal relationship." For the purpose of this discussion, I define the term as follows:

> Any social interaction between individuals closely related by family, marriage, or frequency of contact.

This is by no means a fixed definition. We must examine the role of "significant others" in our overall investment decisions—your immediate family, then friends and business associates. Then you must scrutinize the role of those not as closely involved, but nevertheless significant, such as brokers, advisors, and market experts. Here are some of the questions this discussion seeks to answer:

1. What are the specific interpersonal relationships that can affect an investor?
2. What are some of the symptoms that signal a possible negative effect?
3. How can such situations be rectified?
4. How can interpersonal relationships help you benefit?

Family relationships are perhaps the most significant and influential. These include relationships between parent and child, siblings, and husband and wife. Since almost all investors spent their formative years in a family-type situation, it is not unusual for them to be influenced by their family well beyond the actual move away from home. Psychoanalytic teachings have shown us that the guilt, anxiety, envy, fear, and identification that arise between child and parent of the same sex can have a lasting effect on adult personality. Following the processes of childhood amnesia (discussed earlier), these feelings are rarely remembered when people recall their youthful days. Nevertheless, many long-term fears originate and develop between birth and age 11.

The behavioral psychologist may not agree with much of the analytic terminology but would agree that the process of learning begins as soon as a child is born (possibly sooner). As a result, many of the response styles, attitudes, fears, and opinions acquired during early childhood tend to continue into adulthood. Most individuals do not know how, when, or where they acquired many of their behavioral traits. There are, for example, many investors known as "eternal bears" or "eternal bulls." Such response sets are acquired in childhood and persist into later life. In this case (as in most), parents are the culprits.

Typically, parental attitudes are acquired by children. There is an old saying in the mental health profession that "crazy parents make crazy children." The same holds true for dyed-in-the-wool bears and bulls. For those who have been so trained in early childhood, the consequences in adult life may be disastrous. An investor may find himself constantly bullish or bearish to the point of financial ruin. He does not know where these persistent attitudes had their origin. This tends to act as an aggravating factor increasing frustration, thereby resulting in even greater losses. There are several types of parental attitudes and child-rearing methods that help shape specific investor personalities. An investor's behaviors will, in most cases, merely be a reflection of his or her overall personality. We can acquire considerable insight about an individual by observing his or her investment behavior. Likewise one can formulate a fairly accurate representation of an individual's investment behaviors by studying his personality and its development.

The Eternal Bear

The eternal bear often reflects negative parental attitudes. His or her parents may have been well along in years when their "bearish child" was born. Typically they had grown somewhat cold and/or cynical in their old age. Many of the romantic feelings they had as a younger couple have fallen by the wayside, left perhaps in the trials and tribulations of raising a family. They have become pragmatic, fixed in their ways, resistant to change, and generally rigid. Such attitudes are passed on to their child. If there are additional siblings, the effect is somewhat muted. If, however, other children have grown and moved from the home, or should there be no siblings, the consequences can be profound. Even as an infant this individual may assume "adult" attitudes. There will be a general lack of fantasy life, and a serious, down-to-earth orientation to the world. Insights can be derived by observing such a child at play. His style reflects a rigid, negativistic, and fatalistic underlying attitude. Creativity is generally lacking. In addition, parental attitudes may be negative about virtually all new concepts, products, books, entertainment, and politicians.

This readily translates into bearish market attitudes. Note that I am not passing judgment as to the relative desirability of one position or another. I am, however, indicating that any one orientation, if carried to excess, is indicative of neither potential success nor mental stability. If you are an individual who is constantly bearish, or if you find yourself trading from the short side, despite losses and system signals to the contrary, you are most likely the product of such an environment. Certainly this is not the only situation that can create such attitudes. A teacher at school during adolescence, a surrogate parent, or an extremely influential relative can have the same effect. Children raised by their grandparents can develop a bearish predisposition. Infants whose parents are frequently away from home, leaving an elderly baby-sitter in charge, can develop an "eternal bear" personality.

Marriage may either temper or exacerbate the situation. An individual who is prone to bearish attitudes may, in marrying another who is similarly inclined, develop into a "superbear." The attitudes of one's spouse tend to reinforce what the individual already believes to be true. And this may, in fact, be detrimental to the overall investment result. On the other hand, a marriage partner who is inclined either in a neutral or opposite direction may temper or dampen the attitudes and behaviors that comprise eternal bear syndrome. This may arouse anxiety and protest in the investor so afflicted. And this could, in fact, create marital discord of serious consequence.

As you can see, the extreme position taken by one who is eternally bearish can have many negative consequences, above and beyond mere market misperception and resultant losses. The investor restricted to such an extreme role has difficulties untold. Not only will his persistent market attitude lose him money, but it will also frustrate him, thereby bringing further losses. The vicious cycle of bearish attitude, loss of money, increased frustration, and poor judgment will also deteriorate the home environment.

The symptoms of such an affliction are rather obvious, and perhaps the most simple to recognize. If your trading is more than 90 percent to the bear side over a period of several years and, if your results do not justify the continuation of such a point of view, then you are a sufferer. Most likely you alone will not see the situation as it really is. Others will tell you what is happening. You may not believe them, even though example after example is cited. Such denial is common in neurotic or preneurotic states. The more entrenched the problem, the greater resistance and denial will be. If you know such an individual, you are aware of what I am saying.

The eternal bear is a vanishing breed. The unusually violent bull moves we've witnessed in most markets during the 1970s have all but extinguished the species. Yet there seems to be a new crop every year, and it is advisable to brush up on how they may be "cured." Here are a few suggestions:

1. Threats by family, friends, and associates will not help. They may create more problems than they solve. It is best to maintain a positive attitude rather than a negative one. Why fight negativism with negativism?

2. If you are the one who suffers from this condition, then I suggest you attempt to recall the many childhood experiences that shaped the problem. By relaxing and letting your mind wander through the past, you can relive some of the key situations that influenced your attitudes and actions. This can best be achieved in a classic therapy situation.

3. Through the utilization of a behavioral training technique, as outlined in an earlier chapter, you can "unlearn" the syndrome, retraining yourself in a more realistic direction. In so doing, another's help may be necessary.

4. Discipline can be a great help as well. For those who can recruit the assistance of others, I would suggest the following treatment sequence:

a. Re-evaluate your trading system to make certain that it's hypothetical or intended results are worthy of your efforts.

b. Compare actual trading results with hypothetical results, noting any divergence.

c. If there is more than 10 percent variance between the two, a change in your behavior is in order.

d. Obtain the assistance of a neutral or more disciplined individual. See earlier chapters for further details.

5. Attempt to improve self-awareness. This can be accomplished through the systematic application of gestalt therapy, sensitivity groups, self-awareness courses, and the like.

The Eternal Bull

The market optimist, or eternal bull, is much happier than the eternal bear, but no more fortunate. His overall losses may be smaller, but in the long run, his misery is just as intense. Typically such individuals are reared in families that preached and practiced optimism. Like Dr. Pangloss of Voltaire's Candide, their motto, as expressed in behavior, is "all is for the best, in the best of all possible worlds." Parental behavior shapes their point of view. Failures are taken lightly. There is often no serious consequence of poor performance. In fact, parents tend to gloss over failing marks at school, looking always to the future. This may seem rather unrealistic. And it most certainly is!

The child reared in such an environment will frequently acquire similar opinions and behaviors. When he or she becomes an investor, the response style that has been assumed, although a positive one, will not permit full recognition of a negative situation. This type of investor has so thoroughly adopted an eternally bullish outlook that he will not accept a loss. Rather than admit something has gone awry, the typical response of such an investor will be to deny or rationalize the poor trade. Any number of excuses will be found. Certainly the market will not heed the explanation offered. And in the long run, some very large losses may be taken.

There is a distinct difference between the individual who fears the short side of a market and an eternal bull. Whereas one investor may not find short selling palatable, he can, under the proper circumstances, either sell short or close out a long position that has gone against him. The eternal bull will not only retain long positions, but he will add to them on the way down. This is distinctly different from an unwillingness to sell short. It is not necessary to trade both sides of a market. Many individuals do not comprehend the concept of selling short. As such they do not want to assume this side of a trade since they feel that their risk is virtually unlimited, whereas potential profit is very clearly defined.

As in the case of eternal bearishness, the undying bull will find reasons to support his position. This is a prime example of how the defense mechanism termed "intellectualization" operates. In both cases, there will be a tendency to ignore fundamentals or technical patterns when their signals are not in agreement with the investor's feelings. This typifies misperception and its implications. The topic has been previously discussed.

How can one change such behaviors? Many of the suggestions given for treatment of the eternal bear are also applicable in this case. In addition I would suggest the following techniques and steps:

1. List the possible consequences of taking a loss as you perceive them.
2. Analyze each and every possible consequence, real or imagined. Determine how threatening each may actually be. Attempt to put each possible result in its proper perspective.
3. Study your parents' attitudes and opinions. You may realize that they have helped you internalize an overly positive and optimistic response set.
4. Examine the functioning of your trading system in bear markets. During major bull moves, you may do very well, only to give all the profits (and more) back during downtrends. If this is the case, then your system may actually be biased to the bull side. As such, it is a reflection of your bullish orientation and will not serve you well in all markets. A reevaluation and/or reformulation may be necessary.
5. If all else fails, then professional help might be necessary.

Relationships with Friends

Interpersonal relationships, particularly among friends, play a significant role in determining our social perceptions and actions. Most things we do are intended not to benefit us directly but to bring social benefits. Pressures from within our families and our social circles frequently lead us to choose actions that will eventually prove contrary to our final goals. The unfortunate thing about such a situation is that it often occurs unconsciously. Since social motivation begins at a very early age, we are imbued with values and goals that derive from parental attitudes and expectations. After we have engaged in the fulfillment of these goals for so n.any years, the process becomes automatic. During early childhood and adolescent days, we are quite conscious of what we are doing. In fact, much of the rebelliousness displayed by children is a result of their realization that what is expected of them is not what they really want to do. On the one hand, the process is a necessary one since it provides social skills required for effective functioning. On the other hand, the process has its limitations, since it teaches us to do things that we need not, in reality, do.

When a child matures, the effect of such learning and conditioning can be marked. The conflict that follows can result in emotional and behavioral disturbance. In the market, such difficulties very often express themselves in the form of losses and poor discipline. Thus it is to our advantage if we acquire insight into the process by which we decide to act. Social factors are highly influential in financial situations. If a friend takes a large position in a given stock, we may feel pressured to do the same, particularly if we respect him. If a friend makes a large sum of money in the market, we may begin to feel competitive. The feelings may be translated into market action that is not consistent with good trading. We are subject to similar pressures in the home. This discussion will, however, be limited to the role of immediate friends and acquaintances, and their potential effect on your investing.

Human behavior is determined by needs. Certain psychological theories base their principles on needs and the manner in which they are fulfilled. The following discussion of relationships with friends, and their effect on the market, is based on an analysis of the needs that motivate such actions.

The Need to Compete

As children, we are taught to compete with friends and siblings. After years of experience in this area, it is only natural that, as adults, we continue to seek satisfaction of these needs. The desire to compete is a healthy and, most often, productive need. It inspires us to achieve things we might not otherwise be motivated to attempt. On the other hand, it tends to make us take chances that should not be taken. If the need to compete is intense, we may speculate beyond the point of reason. What is it that can stimulate such speculative action? The need to be victorious is often more important vis-à-vis society than it is to us individually. Many investors are not involved in their program with the intention of making themselves happy. These needs are sufficient to make an investor ignore the basics of his or her trading program. The end result will more often than not be losses. The individual who acts irrationally in response to the competitive impulse typically is suffering from deep-seated feelings of insecurity or inadequacy. It is the need to compensate for these feelings that stimulates unwarranted action in response to achievements by others. There is an emotional aspect to the competitive need, and it is the social need that precipitates the inappropriate act.

Friends, acquaintances, and at times relatives, are key persons who can arouse the competitive instinct. The need is greatest where there has been a long-standing relationship of rivalry. And when the need is greatest, the errors that follow are likely to be the most disastrous. There are several ways in which the need to compete can be channeled in a positive direction. After all, the need is a primary factor in motivation, and we would want to take advantage of the energy it stimulates. There are a number of ways in which this can be done:

1. If you know that this is one of your weak areas, spend some time thinking about exactly who is the target of your need, and precisely why you feel the need. Insights may spring from such deliberations to help you direct competitive energy in the proper direction.

2. It is better to anticipate than to respond. One way to limit the irrational aspect of competition is to be first rather than second. If you need to compete, make certain that you set the pace by taking action before your competitor does. It is much easier to be a leader than a follower.

3. Attempt to make the rules rather than play by them. There are many types of games competitors play. Don't put yourself in the position of playing another person's game. As an example, your brother-in-law, with whom you are competing, is an expert in stock options; you do not have experience with this technique. Instead of attempting to beat him at his own game, stick to what you do best. In the long run, only the money that comes from trading determines who comes out on top. And this should be your primary consideration.

4. Those who can learn to ignore the need to compete are pursuing the best course of action. Some of the relaxation techniques I will describe may alleviate the anxiety that often accompanies the need to compete. For example, when you receive a telephone call informing you that your chief rival has just made a killing in the market, instead of reacting with orders to your broker, use relaxation techniques.

The Need to Please

This is another need stemming from childhood. Since we seek to please our parents (more often than not out of fear), we will also do so in adult life. This is especially true in relation to figures of authority. The result of such actions typically detracts from profitable trading. How might such a situation arise in the marketplace? Many brokers and market advisors accept accounts from friends and relatives. If and when they begin to lose money for these people, the pressure becomes intense and incorrect decisions are made. The need to please is so intense that any disapproval is seen as threatening to internal emotional stability. The punishment that frequently accompanied failure in childhood elevates the need to perform until it is paramount, perhaps causing us to ignore other needs. Typically, the need is greatest among those who have had traumatic childhood experiences in this area. Those who were severely punished for poor school performance are prime victims. How can one successfully contend with these feelings? I have several suggestions:

1. Do not put yourself in the position of accepting accounts, making recommendations, or otherwise influencing decisions made by friends or relatives. This will immediately release you from the need to please. This is a policy I believe every investor should adhere to.
2. If you are aware of the errors in judgment that come from the need to please, then you ought to think twice before handling any investments for others, even clients.
3. Attempt to turn over the decision-making end of things to one who will follow through without concern for the "need to please" factor.
4. As always, strict discipline is necessary to avoid the pitfalls that can result from this situation.

The Need for Approval

We all need approval. Whether we succeed may well be much less important than whether we have done things in a way that gains approval from others. The need for approval is not necessarily similar to the need to please. Typically, one who needs to please, tends to be highly negative when it comes to self-appraisal. The individual who merely needs approval can do well on his own only up to a point. He does not need to please others, he is merely looking for a nod in the positive direction. There are many needs which, if carried to an extreme, will most definitely result in poor trading. An investor who trades only for the joy of others' approval is a sure loser. There are several ways in which this problem can be rectified:

1. Make your own approval. Institute any of the programs discussed in this book.
2. Determine whose approval is important to you and for what reason. Once you have discovered who your "significant others" are, you can study your relationships with them in an effort to limit your need for their approval.

The Need to Be Punished

You may have laughed when reading this. Believe it or not, many individuals actually want to be punished. Just as some relationships function on approval and the need to please, other relationships function on the need for one individual to be punished. Typically, the one who punishes is operating from a need to be the punisher. In everyday circumstances, there are few situations one can detect as clearly pathological in this sense. However, some relationships between friends are maintained on this masochist-sadist basis. Certainly it takes two to tango. Let me illustrate by way of a brief story.

A friend of mine was in the habit of trading without stops. As in most cases, the lack of a stop resulted in consistently poor performance. Several accounts he was trading also did poorly. These were accounts that had been opened for friends who believed in this individual's ability. After each loss, one of his so-called friends would telephone to complain. This went on for several years! In spite of the fact that loss after loss was taken, the friend kept sending money, and the money "manager" kept losing it. He made no effort to avoid the verbal punishment by either terminating the business end of this relationship or using a different trading strategy. The only logical conclusion one could reach was that this relationship was getting both parties precisely what they wanted. They were, most likely, not even aware of the situation on a conscious level.

As peculiar as this may sound to those who are not sufferers, there are many subtle ways in which the punishment factor may affect all of us. Pathology tends to build very slowly in relationships. What begins as a seemingly harmless game can end as a very serious problem. During the very slow process by which this type of learning (and many other forms of learning) occurs, one is not aware of what is happening. Any relationship that is divided along punisher-punishee lines is suspect. If you suddenly realize that most of your time is spent in being punished by a friend or mate, or if you are spending a great deal of time as the one who doles out punishment, then you are most likely engaged in this pathological situation. The end result can only be one that causes considerable pain. Typically, husbands and wives engage in such interactions. The difficulty is by no means limited to close relationships. The relationship between broker and client can work in the same way. Take the case of a broker, or friend, who is jealous about your investment success. Each and every time you take a loss, he will be pleased. He will further aggravate your pain by ridiculing you in subtle ways. You may not even be aware of what is developing. If you continue to accept the punishment, albeit subtle, then you may actually be aggravating your attitude toward the market, which, in the long run, will make things considerably worse.

The need to be punished is much more common than most of us believe. Those who are fortunate enough to realize what is going on can take steps to correct it. It is my opinion that a very specific program to detect and correct this situation can be implemented. Here is how I would proceed:

1. Recognize the problem. Start by taking an accounting of your relationships. If you are involved in a situation that brings you pain, and if you have been coping with the pain of punishment for more than two months, then you are most likely in need of help. If you are not aware of which relationship is causing you the difficulty, then make a written list and keep a tally of the frequency with which you experience conflict with each of the individuals. The relationships causing the greatest number of negative conflicts are those that need to be repaired.

2. Stop the conflict by knowing ahead of time who is punishing you. If you do not respond to the game, then it will soon end. You can expect an initial increase in negative feedback from the person who is attempting to punish you. If you consistently fail to respond, however, you will emerge victorious.

3. Replace the negative interaction with positive experiences. This will quickly put the relationship back on the right track. Do it even if you must force yourself at first, since it will eventually bring the desired result.

4. Do not substitute another negative interaction for the one that you have just repaired. It is easy to fall into the same pattern with another person.

As you can see, there are many different directions relationships with friends can take. My best advice is to keep business and friendship separate. This will help you avoid many problems. Human relationships are extremely complex. We do things for many reasons. We cannot always explain why we have acted in a certain way. The best way to avoid the pitfalls of interpersonal relationships and their effect on investing is to stay with your program. This is just one more of the many reasons for following a disciplined trading system. The human element needs constant attention, close supervision, and the strictest of programs.

REVIEW

1. The role of social psychology and interpersonal relationships was examined in light of the market.
2. Several investor personality types were discussed.
3. The role of relationships with friends was mentioned as a significant factor in overall investment success.
4. There are a number of important needs whose roles can affect investment success.

19

Some Psychological Trading Rules

To those who have been in the market for many years, the time-tested and oft-repeated trading rules are well known. In fact, they're so well known that few of us attend to them. Now that we have examined these maxims in the light of psychological theory, you may be more willing to use them, especially after they are restated in this chapter in a manner that makes their use very clear. In addition, I include here a number of new rules based on much of what has been covered in previous chapters. The brief description of exactly what is meant, in behavioral terms, may also help you. I have found it very useful to keep a list of these rules where I can refer to them often. I find that they help keep me on the right track.

1. Plan your trades specifically and in advance. Keep them available. If you are specific, organized, and act on plans, you will avoid costly efforts often caused by spontaneous decisions. A concise trading plan will help you avoid the losses that can arise from acting on the opinions of others. Regardless of the trading system you are using, such a plan is necessary. In short, plan your trades and trade your plans.

2. You alone are responsible for the success or failure of your trading. You must assume total responsibility for results, good or bad. You alone are the vehicle to profits and losses. By assuming total responsibility and not blaming brokers, friends, or market letters for errors, you will realize the seriousness of trading. This will help you avoid emotional decisions. You will learn that the situation is entirely under your own control. This will make you consistent and truthful to your trading system. And consistency is the single most valuable key to success.

3. Never hope that a position will go your way; never fear that a position will not go your way.   Both these attitudes lead to unrealistic expectations, emotional decisions, and negative attitudes. A position, once established, will result in whatever market action prevails. Once the trade has been made, its fate is sealed and no amount of hope or fear will make things different. Hope and fear are two of the greatest enemies of the speculator, fostering only false perceptions. You must avoid these feelings at all costs. The more rigid you can become in your execution of trades, the more profitable will be your results.

4. Monitor your performance-feedback of results is important. One of the most important things a trader can know about his or her system is whether it is working. The only way to know this is by keeping a thorough record of results. This will also provide the feedback necessary to reward you for good trading. At any time you must know how well or how poorly you are doing. You must also know if poor results are caused by your inability or that of your trading system.

5. Attitude is your greatest asset.   A good trading system is perhaps only 20 percent of the total picture. A positive attitude may very well comprise the balance of successful trading. You must constantly remain aware that the enemies of profitable investing and speculation are never absent. The only way to combat the negative effects of losses, interference from others, and poor trading signals is by the maintenance of a positive attitude regardless of how bad things may seem.

6. Cultivate effective and positive relationships.   We are known by the company we keep. Moreover, we are influenced by those around us. If we surround ourselves with losers, loafers, pretenders, or depressives, we will learn no positive skills. If we associate with those who are highly motivated, who seek to achieve, who have ambitious goals, and who are willing to forge ahead regardless of obstacles, then we will acquire similar drives. Personal relationships as well as business associations should be cultivated along these general guidelines.

7. Don't take the market home with you.   If you trade for a living, you must take great care to leave the market when you leave the office. If you are only a casual investor and do not have a full-time market-related job, then you must also avoid spending too much time or thought on the markets. When things go well, you may allow the market too much influence in satisfying other areas of your life. This is not advisable, since it will cause you to delay solving other problems. If the market is not going well for you and you allow it to affect the rest of your life, this will also be destructive. The market must be seen as a means to an end. It should not become a way of life, and it should not dictate your every move. Make certain you take vacations. Take time each year to close out positions (if necessary) and "get away from it all." By being too close to the situation, you may not see it for what it really is.

8. Enjoy the fruits of your labor—spend some profits, save some profits.   Make it a regular practice to remove profits from the market. Spend some of them and save some of them. You must directly experience the positive feeling of using profits to acquire some of the things you have always wanted to buy. I suggest you do this regularly, perhaps monthly. You will not be motivated to make profits if you do not experience firsthand the enjoyment that can come from spending large sums of money.

9. Avoid overconfidence—it could be your greatest enemy. There are good times in the market and there are bad times. Just as you should not allow the bad times to bring you down, you must not allow the good times to get you up too high. If you are on either of these emotional extremes, your judgment can be impaired and you will not be rational enough to deal with what lies before you. You will be either too brave or too meek. The best course is to even out the peaks and valleys. Each loss should be a negative experience, but not a totally destructive defeat. Similarly, each profit should be taken in stride. Overconfidence may, in fact, be even more potentially destructive than lack of confidence, since it will make you take chances that could destroy you.

10. Your next goal should always be in sight.   Once you have attained an objective, make certain that your next challenge is set. A well-known commodity trader made several million dollars in the market one year. He lost it and almost went bankrupt the next year. I asked him how this could have happened. "Simple," he replied. "When you climb a mountain and you're sitting on top of the world, it gets lonely. There's no place left to go but down." If, however, you have another mountain to climb once you get to the top, you won't be tempted to go down in order to have a new challenge.

There are, to be sure, many other rules that apply. Those just discussed will not be universally useful. You may benefit immensely from a formulation of your own trading rules because you alone are the best judge of what you need. But you can only formulate your rules after you have become totally aware of your needs, assets, liabilities, skills, and goals. One of the best ways to accomplish this is through the use of a self-evaluation technique. You may be one of those rare individuals who can determine personal problems and needs by simple thought. But most likely you will need to use a specific checklist or assessment tool to evaluate your situation. The finer details of this method are discussed in Chapter 20.

REVIEW

1. There are a number of market psychology rules that have time-tested validity.
2. Each trader should seek to internalize these rules, referring to them as frequently as possible.
3. Ten rules are outlined, explained, and discussed.
4. Self-evaluation is introduced as a means of determining one's own trading rules.

20

The Perceptual Factor

Two investors are anxiously awaiting an earnings report on company XYZ. One is long and has brought on anticipation of a bullish report; the other is short and expects a negative result. The report is released, and even though earnings for the year are clearly lower when compared to the same period a year earlier, each investor believes that the report supports his position. "It's bearish," says the trader who is short. "Earnings are much lower than last year. If projected at this rate of decline for the balance of the year, earnings will be down over 37 percent from last year, and 63 percent from two years ago. The stock can't possibly move up."

"Not so," argues the investor who has bought. "This is a bullish report in bear's clothing. It's designed to get as many people short as possible. Although earnings are lower than last year's similar period, they're not down as much as the economy in general. With the slowdown we've seen in overall consumer spending, a 37 percent decline for the first quarter is not bad at all. In fact, the decline is less than other firms involved in the same business. Remember also that last year the company showed record sales and earnings. A small decline is healthy and not bearish at all."

"But wouldn't you rather have seen higher earnings?" inquires the bear.

"It really doesn't matter to me," responds the bullish investor in support of his position. "All I know is that the stock's going up regardless of earnings. Earnings reports are not important anyway."

"Well, they certainly were important to you last year when earnings were sharply higher," points out the bearish investor.

"That was last year! Since then I've learned all about earnings reports and how unimportant they really are. The only thing that's important is the price action of the stock. It's a waste of time to even discuss it until we see what the stock does tomorrow," replies our bullish friend.

The next day XYZ stock falls 3 points by the final bell. Certainly the investor who sold short feels that this is a victory, as well he should. The bull is still not convinced. He defends his position, "You can't really tell how a stock is going to act based on one day's worth of price behavior. The bulls are holding back and letting the bears get short before squeezing them out. I've seen this happen many times before." Within a matter of several weeks, the stock is more than 15 points lower than where the buyer had put on his original position. By now he must certainly be out or, at the very minimum, demoralized. But alas, he still holds the stock. He reasons, "It's just a matter of time before the investing community realizes how bullish this stock really is. It's difficult to be the lonely bull. But I'm brave and have what it takes to weather the storm. In fact, I'm so very bullish, that the only right thing to do is to buy more of the stock. I'll average my cost down and really make a bundle when the stock turns back up."

By now, the next earnings report has come out. The eternal bull buys more of the stock and our bearish friend, who evidently has the facts on his side, stays short. And again the report is clearly bearish. Disappointed, but not ready to give up, the optimistic bull reasons that once the year has ended there will be an improvement in the situation. Even though the report appears to be bearish, it is, under the surface, quite bullish, he notes. And so continues his misinterpretation of market reality. Despite the losses and continued down move of the stock, he holds on for the anticipated victory that does not come. And when the move finally begins, our bull will no longer be long on the stock. He will have sold out in the panic-type bottom that inevitably heralds a bull market.

What has gone wrong? How has the bullish trader been led astray? Is he suffering from delusion of grandeur? Does he feel that his mere buying of a stock signals a bull move? Where did he go wrong? What can be done about this situation? If you have ever been in a similar position, then you can fully appreciate the scenario just discussed. You may have known individuals who persist in their market attitudes regardless of fact, regardless of reason, regardless of losses, and regardless of any attempt to convince them that they are wrong. This can be the result of a perceptual problem that is very common and especially dangerous. Such misinterpretations of reality are certainly not limited to the markets. They are a part of everyday life. Each individual, as a function of life experiences, is set, or primed psychologically, to interpret a given situation in his or her own way. We are all subject to such influences. And they can be either a hindrance or a help. In the preceding vignette, the persistently bullish perception of one investor was a hindrance to his desired goal. Let us examine the perceptual factor and see if we can learn a few things about our own misconceptions and what, if anything, can be done to reverse their negative consequences.

Consider the following situation: a woman is walking her large dog. The dog spots a cat and, in his effort to chase it, tangles his leash around his mistress' leg causing her to fall. The dog falls to his side as well and begins to bark in his frustrated effort to get loose. A male passer-by observes the situation and rushes to the woman's rescue. The dog, already in a state of uproar, begins to bark at the man who is attempting to assist the woman. Meantime, a passing male motorist spies the situation and assumes that the woman is being attacked by the man, who is actually attempting to assist her. He stops his auto, rushes out, and begins to assault the other man. Despite the pleadings of our first helper, the beating continues. A police officer happens on the scene and cannot understand precisely what has transpired. He is not certain which man is "attacking" the woman. He begins to strike both men with his club in an effort to terminate the melee. Three people and a dog have been hurt, and not a single one is guilty of wrongdoing.

Each of the three men had his own perceptual set. Certainly, in our society, it is natural to assume that a woman might be attacked in the street. It is an all too frequent event. And yet, in this case, the supposition, or perception, of the situation was incorrect. As you certainly know, reality is not what it seems to be, but rather what we have learned to expect it to be. If I expect a given situation to occur I will be set, or primed, to react to my expectations. And in doing so, I can be fooled. Here exists a dilemma. Certainly it is important to have particular perceptions of reality. Many of them serve us well, and others do not. In time, the individual will learn what serves him well and what leads to pain, but in new situations there is no good basis for judgment. This is where many mistakes are made. By exploring some of the underlying principles of psychological set, or perception, we should gain some understanding of the developmental process involved in the creation of faulty perception. We can then apply our findings to the market.

What Is Perception?

Virtually all information that comes to our brain enters via the senses. Notwithstanding the role of so-called extrasensory or clairvoyant perceptions, the major inputs are related to overt environmental stimuli. Touch, taste, smell, sight, and hearing are the primary perceptual receptors. From the moment of conception we are constantly bombarded by a huge variety of environmental stimuli, which, combined with developmental experiences, shape our perception of the world around us. The field of psychology has long debated the relative roles of genetic and environmental factors. The net result has been a synthesis of findings, all of which have relevance to the investor and his on-going efforts. In order to completely appreciate the differing points of view, it will be helpful to review some basic findings and concepts.

Many studies have documented the existence of differential response patterns in the newborn (see Wolman, 1973, pp. 875–877). Countless investigations of response and early childhood perception have documented the fact that no two infants are alike from the moment of birth or earlier. Each child is born with a specific response pattern. Stress, for example, arouses distinctly different patterns of physiological reactions in different neonates: their tendency to experience different results from similar situations is clear immediately. Two adults may therefore respond to a similar situation in different ways. Response sets, present from the moment of birth, are with us throughout life and have a market effect on our response or perception of a similar event.

There are many other examples of how individuals differ markedly from the moment of birth. It is a known fact, for example, that children born with congenital cataracts suffer visual-perceptual problems later in life even though the cataracts are treated surgically shortly after birth. It is argued that even a short period of environmental or perceptual deprivation in early childhood can lead to serious perceptual difficulties in adult life. It has been found that there are critical periods among various organisms during which certain skills develop. Chimps whose hands are taped during childhood suffer irreversible damage to sensory and motor ability, even though bandages are removed after several months. There have been many such findings, particularly among mammals.

What it all points to is a complex interplay of genetics and environment in the development of perceptual abilities. Sensory deprivation experiments have demonstrated that dogs reared in low-stimulation environments, devoid of human contact during early childhood, appeared to seek out pain, were dull, and seemed unresponsive to normal types of learning experience. If extrapolated to the human condition, these findings have immense implications.

The point I am making is simply this: For various reasons, we all "see" or "perceive" things somewhat differently. What may appear dangerous to one individual may be enjoyable to the next. What may seem like a challenge to one man may be nothing but an exercise in dullness to another. One of the major symptoms of psychological disorders, according to Alfred Adler, relates to perception.

Adler was one of the first psychologists to break away from the teachings of Sigmund Freud. He stressed the importance of interpersonal experience and situational determinants of human behavior, dealing extensively with insecurity, feelings of inferiority, sibling rivalry, and the unity of the person. He did so in terms more easily understood and applied by the public than were Freud's theories. He was an associate of Sigmund Freud and a leader of the Vienna Psychoanalytic Society. Some Adlerian terms will further illustrate my view of perception.

Adler presented a specific set of manifestations associated with maladaptive or disturbed behavior. Among these were "perception" and "thought." Of perceptual characteristics, he noted two key features associated with mental disorders:

> Perceptual selectivity. In the development of "private view of the world," the neurotic does not recognize events as others do, does not respond to events which would be antithetical to his view, and selects out those parts of events that fit with his prior conceptions.
>
> Perceptual sensitivity. . . . He is overly ready to make certain interpretations precautions, whether or not they are appropriate.
>
> Thought. Rigidity. The neurotic's thought sequences are in general more rigid and consequently less alterable than those of normal persons. (Ford and Urban, 1965, p. 341)

Let's stop for a moment and review:

1. The way we see things can develop as a function of genetic predisposition and environment.
2. Those who suffer from emotional disturbance tend to see things not as they really are.
3. Those who suffer emotional disturbances tend to interpret or perceive reality in a fashion that supports their pathology.
4. Neurotic thinking is characterized by rigidity of thought and perception, with little tendency to change.

Now let's go back to our learning model (see page 51). Note that I have included a so-called perceptual filter in the stimulus-organism response sequence. I will now bring the filter into play as perhaps the single most important element of the learning chain.

Assume that one's perception of a situation is faulty. Take as an example the situation related earlier in this chapter; the persistent bull has misperceived the bearishness of an earnings report. He has demonstrated his rigid thought and perception. This is certainly nothing surprising. Many individuals will defend their position with misperceived facts. They will fight to the finish for what they wish to believe, rather than for what may be real. In other words, we are all familiar with rigidity of thought, defense of an obviously losing position, and clear misinterpretation of reality formulated to defend an untenable position. These are everyday events. But as common as they may be in daily life, they have no constructive value. In fact, they tend to be destructive in the long run. In the market, they are catastrophic. The fact that investors tend to misperceive reality accounts for perhaps 50 percent of their losses. That's why it is important, in my opinion, to understand the development and remediation of what I call "losing perception."

Furthermore, I consider losing perception a learned behavior that may have elements of genetic predisposition. Regardless of the genetic factor, whose existence I cannot either prove or disprove, the behavioral aspects are so overwhelmingly obvious that I believe any predisposition can be overcome by learning. Let's review how losing perception can develop in a behavioral way from early childhood. There are two very distinct ways in which such faulty perception can become habitual. Remember that we are all guilty of misperception from time to time. As long as we are not constantly misperceiving situations and relationships at critical times, we will not suffer too many losses, either personal or financial. It is habitual maladaptive perception I am discussing.

Parents tend to respond to their children in a fashion predetermined by their own personalities. Let's assume that a child is experiencing anxiety in connection with a given situation. His parents could respond in one of several ways. They could tell him to ignore the anxiety, explaining logically that there is no reason for anxiety given the facts. They may then reward him verbally, or in a stronger fashion, for feeling better. After many repetitions of this stimulus-response chain, the child has learned, in a sense, to ignore or reduce anxiety associated with certain stimulus events. Often the anxiety relates to school, examinations, and peer group relationships. Although the interaction is certainly more complex, this is the general way in which perceptions and responses to perception can develop and change. A child returns from school, crying and obviously upset, his parents attempt to console him. "Why are you crying?" they ask. "I'm afraid of the test," replies the youth. "Why are you afraid of the test," asks father. "Because the teacher said that all kids who fail the test will have to stay late after school every day for two weeks." "Well, now I understand why you're scared," responds the parent. "But if you're scared, then you may be so scared that you'll fail the test just because you're afraid," points out the mother. "Sometimes, if we're really afraid of something, it's hard to do that something the right way. And even though we know how to do that thing, we won't be able to do it right because we're upset," she continues. "All people have things that they're afraid of, but if you ignore the fear and study hard for the test, then you'll pass it," points out the father. Although the interchange here is quite simple, the parents have attempted to alter the child's response to a perceived threat. They will reward the child for altering his perception of the situation. Although he may still consider the test situation a threat, he will respond in a fashion that is not affected by his perception. Over time, his perception may change in accordance with the positive consequences experienced in repetitions of the situation. The praise provided by his parents further stamps in the change in perceptual response.

Parental responses are also instrumental in shaping "losing perception." Very often they will teach a child to behave anxiously, or perceive a situation to be something other than it really is. Here is a simple example, one which was very common in the 1950s:

Child: I have a test next week.
Parent: You had better get a good grade or else!
Child: Or else what?
Parent: Or else I'll beat you black and blue.
Child: Why will you beat me?
Parent: For your own good!! Children who fail tests in school become shoemakers or street cleaners. They're poor all their lives, and live out of other people's garbage cans.
Child: Really?!
Parent: Oh, yes, that's what tests are for. Teachers give them to their students in order to find out which are smart enough to become doctors or lawyers and which will become trash collectors or bums.
Child: You mean that if I don't pass the test next week I'll become a bum?
Parent: Oh, no, you have to fail many tests to become a bum. But each time you fail one or get a bad mark in school, the teacher writes it in her book. At the end of the year, she sends the marks to your next

teacher and so on until you're done with school. And if you get too many bad marks they kick you out of school and turn you over to a shoemaker. And you become his helper and stay poor all your life.

As foolish and contrived as this may sound, it happens to represent an attitude that was once very common among parents. By instilling fear in the child, they have altered his innocent perceptual response to the situation of perceived threat. The consequences of one test have been blown out of proportion. The child is now predisposed to feel fear and anxiety. If and when the test is failed, he is punished by his parents and hence suffers double pain. After repeated exposure to such fantasies, in many situations, we have a child who develops an irrational set of perceptions. Despite the fact that he may intellectually recognize the fallacy in his thinking, the perceived threat remains. In fact, the threat may be so subtle that once our conditioned child becomes an adult, he no longer knows why he perceives certain situations in certain ways.

The role of parental attitudes in shaping, maintaining, and reshaping perceptions is significant. In most cases, the perceptions we carry through adulthood are reflections of what has been taught in the home. This is why we are so unaware of their presence and this is why they are so difficult to change. Parents typically teach their children to either feel too much pain, too little pain, ignore too much, or attend to too many stimuli. Very little time is spent teaching a child "middle of the road" perceptions. In summary, then, parents can teach a child to (1) ignore possibly negative perceptions, (2) attend to and amplify the negative perceptions of a situation, or (3) shape new perceptions of a given situation or situations. Through the learning process, such perceptions will become translated into adult behavior. Through the process of generalization, they will be applied to other situations.

Now let's apply such a shaped perception to the market. Take the case of our friend, the eternal bull. He has made a given purchase in company XYZ stock in expectation of a move up. The key word here is expectation. His expectation fails to materialize. He does not perceive the situation for what it really is—a loss. No doubt, his failure to interpret the loss for what it really is relates to his losing perception. It is fairly safe to assume that this investor's perception is at fault. More likely than not, his inability to realize, or perceive, the bearish news as bearish in fact is due to perceptual problems that developed during childhood. This faulty judgment, or misinterpretation of reality, is possibly reflected in other areas of his life. Those observing the situation are inclined to say that the investor is merely hanging on to his stock, fully aware of the fact that he is wrong, but refusing to admit to the defeat. It is true that some investors fall into this category. But there are perhaps just as many who are not aware of the fact that their perception is at fault.

Frequently such difficulties are part of a more pervasive syndrome. It is typical of neurotics to act in such ways either as a means of adapting the world to fit their personal reality or as a defensive technique. In either case, the role played by learning is instrumental. If you recall the behavioral learning model, you can see that the more frequently rewards are given, the more permanent behavior will become. You might then ask why perception does not change as a result of the losses that follow misperception. Simply, the misperception does not always result in a loss. There are times when, perchance, a profit results. Thus the investor is maintained on a random schedule of reinforcement for his maladaptive perception. And this, as you remember, is one of the reward schedules that helps create strong habits.

The upshot of what I have told you is simply that misperception is maintained on a very effective reinforcement schedule. It is a difficult quality to change and accounts for considerable losses. There are, moreover, many different facets of misperception as it relates to the market. Not only can one misperceive earnings reports and their meaning, but potential risk, underlying value of a stock or commodity, technical trading signals, brokerage house opinion, and many other important factors can be misperceived. Any information that comes to us through sensory channels is a potential victim of misperceived meaning.

Another aspect of faulty perception is what B. F. Skinner has called "conditioned seeing." His discussion of the subject is a clear statement of how the behaviorist explains and interprets the nature of perception and its tendency to develop behaviorally. Since this concept is central to investment psychology, I quote from Skinner's *Science and Human Behavior:*

> A man may see or hear "stimuli which are not present" on the pattern of the conditioned reflex: he may see X, not only when X is present, but when any stimulus which has frequently accompanied X is present. The dinner bell not only makes our mouth water, it makes us see food. . . .
> In more general terms, conditioned seeing explains why one tends to see the world according to one's previous history. Certain properties of the world are responded to so commonly that "laws of perception" have been drawn up to describe the behavior thus conditioned . . . we generally see completed circles, squares and other figures." (1953, pp. 266–267)

You will recall my earlier discussion of Pavlov and his canine salivators. Note that the experimental animals were conditioned to respond to a bell as they did to meat powder because the bell and meat powder had been paired. In effect, the animal seemed to respond to one situation as if it were another. Although it is not scientifically acceptable to generalize from dog to human, I will take a bit of license in this case. It seems as if the animal is salivating on expectation of meat powder because of its previous pairing with the bell. Let's take a big step from dog to investor. (Actually, the analogy may not be as far-fetched as you may think. The term "dogs and cats" has long been applied to certain types of stocks; why not apply it to investors as well?) Based on this extrapolation, it may be possible for paired presentation of two stimuli to acquire equal response strength. In other words, it could very well be that "a stimulus function has been assumed by a different stimulus" (Skinner, 1953, p. 266).

Frequently, we see investors buy or sell stocks for what appear to be absurd reasons. These reasons may, in fact, be stimuli that were originally related to profit-making stimuli. Such behaviors fall more appropriately into what Skinner has termed "operant seeing." In this respect, I would also include the Skinnerian term "superstitious behavior." If, for example, an investor calls his broker, places an order to buy, and a profit results, the precise behaviors that led to the profitable call may be repeated in their exact fashion at a later point in time. If the investor placed the call from a red telephone, for example, he may begin to "superstitiously" associate the red telephone with profits. If, perchance, several profitable trades are made using the red phone, there will most likely develop a superstitious attachment to red telephones as a sign of profits. Thus the trader may perceive the red phone as somehow magically related to investing profits. He will be prone to generalize this response or affinity to red. It is amazing how quickly such behaviors, or perceptions, can generalize into all sorts of peculiar manifestations. Red may become the investor's favorite, or "lucky," color. He may become enamored of stocks containing "red" in their name. His investments may be made in obscure stocks. His list of holdings (fictitious, of course) might include "Red's Drive-In's" or "Red Devil Manufacturing," and even "F. R. Edwards Co." Preposterous? Not really. Take a good look at your own habits and you may find examples of what I just described.

How about another example? You call you broker and he reports that there are rumors of Soviet wheat buying. "What do we do?" you inquire. "Let's buy some wheat quickly before the news hits the floor!" he shouts. "OK, buy it but get out as soon as we have a few cents profit," you respond. The wheat is bought. Within several moments after your purchase, the rumor hits and wheat moves up sharply. Observing your instructions, the broker liquidates the position. Within a matter of minutes you've made several thousand dollars. What could be more reinforcing? You have responded to a rumor and the result has been a large profit. Under the surface there are several other possibilities that may lead to superstitious behavior, or as I call it, inappropriate perceptions of reality:

1. If repeated in the future at a given time of the day, you may unconsciously begin to perceive a given time of the day as best for trading. Time of day has become conditioned as a positive event by association with profits.
2. Should you trade profitably once again, while calling from the same location, you may begin to view the location as a key variable in the profit picture.
3. Activity prior to profitable trade, regardless of what it may have been, can acquire superstitious or misperceived attachment to the profit.

There are many other examples of how investors perceive certain situations as predictive of profits or losses. When groups of investors or traders all respond to the same stimulus in the same way, then their collective response will, in effect, result in an affirmation of the perceived stimulus as instrumental in the change process. Such self-fulfilling prophecies are typical in the marketplace. If many individuals believe that a certain trading signal will be profitable, then it will, in fact, become profitable. Although the profit may last only briefly, the majority of investors will persist in their response. The ultimate winners will be those who anticipate the response, buy early (or sell), and close out their position while the majority is pushing prices in the desired direction. Certainly you have seen this happen on many occasions. The threat of a war may drive stock prices sharply lower, since a majority of traders view this as bearish. They perceive war as a threat to the market, and their collective response has been generalized. Even the rumor or threat of war is reason to respond. And, as in most cases, the perception is proven incorrect, a loss results, and those who were quick enough to act in advance of the rumor profit handsomely.

Perceptions and misperceptions are not limited exclusively to the interpretation of outer environment stimuli. Traders are also subject to misperception of internal stimuli. They believe, for example, that certain visceral feelings or physiological responses are lucky. "I feel like this is my lucky day," one is inclined to say. "I don't know why, but I feel as if I'll make it big today." This feeling is, in most cases, a conditioned perception to profits previously made when similar feelings were present. The paired association of the two has resulted in a secondary conditioning of the internal feeling or its perception.

A great deal more can be said both in favor of and in opposition to my behavioral view of learned perception. As long as the facts can be demonstrated in the marketplace, my analysis should be considered plausible. What can be done to rectify faulty perception? How can the investor go about discovering defective perceptual traits in his or her market studies? How can we capitalize on the misperceptions of others? I believe the answers to these questions lie in adherence to a predetermined and systematic investment scheme. The best defense against faulty perception is a strong offense in investment strategy. The best way to avoid losses due to poor perceptual development is by making your trading plans in a structured fashion and carrying them out accordingly. This will help minimize the possible negative effect of extraneous inputs. By not allowing them to enter into the investment scheme, we eliminate their negative consequences.

REVIEW

1. All individuals react to reality in different ways.
2. A combination of genetic predispositions and environmental forces results in different responses by different investors.
3. There is strong evidence that perception can be a learned behavior.
4. B. F. Skinner discussed "conditioned and operant seeing" as examples of learned perceptions.
5. Perception and misperception are important to the investor since they can limit or enhance overall profitable trading.
6. The best way to avoid the development and negative consequences of losing perception is by adherence to a strict trading plan as described elsewhere in this book.

21

Subliminal Perception— Response without Awareness

I t is difficult, if not impossible, to thoroughly understand and specify the internal processes of intellectual activity. The stimulus must necessarily undergo a number of intrapsychic, or unconscious, transformations prior to its expression as response. Psychologists have, for many years, attempted to discover the intervening variables from moment of recognition to moment of expression. They have been interested primarily in attempting to help rectify some of the dysfunctions to which the human mind is subject. Their attempts have been inspired by a need to help relieve the suffering of those who exhibit disturbed or deranged thought processes. The ultimate goal of many psychologists is to harness the immense power of the human brain.

As mentioned earlier, there are essentially two schools of thought in the modern psychological world. At one extreme, the so-called classical psychologist theorizes about internal processes, using experimental methods, observation, and hypotheses to determine the validity of theories. The humanistic psychologist favors a less authoritarian approach but is still concerned about the "stuff" or "matter" of human thought and consciousness. And at the other end of the continuum, we find the behavioral psychologist. In its purest form, the behaviorist's attitude can best be expressed as follows:

> The process by which behavior occurs is not nearly as important as the inputs that result in behavior. We must think of the human organism as a series of inputs and outputs.
> By studying what goes in, and comparing it to what is produced at the output terminal (behavior), we can formulate a series of "laws," which,

if correct, will permit us to predict and control. Hence, it is unnecessary to dwell on the intermediate step. Since we cannot actually "see" what goes on inside the human mind, it is much more productive to avoid dealing with it. This is not to underemphasize or minimize the uniqueness or humanness of each individual. It is, however, necessary to maintain a purely scientific, pragmatic, and empirical point-of-view, even in the analysis of human thought and behavior.

I believe there are many lessons that can be learned from an evaluation of the underlying processes of behavior. Although we may not find it possible to change our behavior purely as a function of insight, the ideas that may be stimulated in the process of discovery can lead to the initiation of change. By discovering that we may be acting in a nonproductive or self-destructive way, we can be motivated to change.

As discussed in the preceding chapter, perceptual factors tend to act as intermediaries between pure stimulus and response. More often than not we are totally unaware of the internal processes that lead us to the decision-making response. Any light that can be shed on the intermediate steps can help us rectify trading errors.

Perhaps the most baffling phenomenon to investors is their tendency to become irrational at crucial times. The history of stocks and commodities is rich with examples of public panics at major bottoms and buying hysteria at major tops. The Cuban missile panic, the Kennedy assassination panic, the many Vietnam war "peace rumors," and the very frequent prime interest rate reactions are among them. In fact, there are numerous technical market indicators whose underlying rationale rests on human emotional response to given economic and political factors. We are well aware of the fact that any one development does not shape the course of market events. Typically the precipitating event will be last in a long progression. War does not break out without warning, nor does peace come overnight. News, as many successful investors and traders have pointed out, tends to be the enemy of most traders since they do not know how to use it.

The importance of news as it relates to the market is not the news per se, but rather the manner in which news is interpreted. In other words, the investing community responds to news once it has perceived it in a given fashion. What should, in many cases, be bullish news turns out to have a bearish effect. What most investors have long waited for turns out to be very disappointing. Perceptions of what is bullish and what is bearish change from day to day, from moment to moment, and from trade to trade. The human element stands as the intervening variable between stimulus and response. Economic fact must inevitably pass through the perceptual filter called the human brain. People will act on what has been perceived, whether the interpretation is or is not correct. Ultimately economic law will take hold, but it is all too often a long, hard journey from fact to reality. It is the time spent between economic fact and market realization of truth that accounts for more than 90 percent of all price activity. Were it not for the fact that people must act on their perceptions of situations, price response would be virtually immediate and almost always correct. There is no great discovery in what I have told you. There is no mystical truth in the fact that human weakness rests at the base of most stock, commodity, and real estate price moves.

Market Indicators

There are several market indicators whose intent, whether actual or implied, is to capitalize on the human condition. In other words, it is possible to quantify human reaction by examining some key price patterns, most of which are well known to the investing community. Let's examine just a few of these indicators.

The Climax Top—The Climax Bottom

As prices continue their trend in a given direction, they tend to pick up momentum. As more and more news stimulates the price move, there is a concomitant acceleration in price (up or down). It is generally believed that the first portion of any price move, called accumulation, occurs as a result of professional buying. The public begins buying next, and as prices begin their greatest acceleration up or down, the public is making its greatest play, whether buying or selling. Finally, at the top or bottom, the professional community is, for the most part, out of its positions since it has slowly but surely distributed them to the public.

The public perceives nothing but confirmation from the news, no matter what its actual import may be. Prices shoot up or down dramatically (depending on whether the trend has been up or down), and there is no end in sight. In a bullish market climate, most news is interpreted as bullish. When bearish news comes, it is seen as an opportunity to buy on the decline. When bullish news comes, it is seen as a confirmation of the trend. And on the day of reckoning, in a bull market, for example, the typical "buying climax" will come after the following scenario:

1. Very bullish news—possibly the most bullish in months.
2. Record high trading volume for the past few months or years.
3. Record high prices for the past few months or years.
4. Highly bullish public opinion.

The configuration of prices for this time period is also quite specific. Figure 21.1 shows several of these patterns. Note that prices move higher for a lengthy period of time. For several days in a row, they close rather strong. And then on a given day, they make a new high for the move and close lower than the previous day's low on very high trading volume. This is a classic "buying climax" and is created entirely by emotional overreaction of the public. Thereafter there are several attempts to recover. They typically fail and the market trend changes. The high turnover of volume and the reversal in price on the climax top day results almost exclusively from investor perception of news. Whereas there had been a bias to view all news as bullish until this day, a major shift in attitude and sentiment has occurred. Selling has overcome buying and a top has been made. The professional community has used public misperception of the facts to liquidate massive quantities of their holdings at premium prices. The opposite holds true at selling climaxes. Note that perception, attitude, emotion, and panic are the key elements in this type of technical formation. They are all psychological factors, and they are all intricately related to perception of world events and economic facts.

Bullish and Bearish Consensus

Bullish and bearish consensus are also indicators of perceptual factors. At most key tops, bullish consensus is very high, whereas it is often very low at key bottoms. The odd lot short sales ratio is a prime technical indicator of public bearishness and typically shows public selling at a high when prices hit major lows. Figure 21.2 shows how the bullish and bearish consensus figures are used in the commodity future market as an indicator of public sentiment.

In addition to these indicators, there are numerous market services that determine professional market sentiment, large trader buying or selling, insider transactions, the volatility of low-priced stocks, and similar

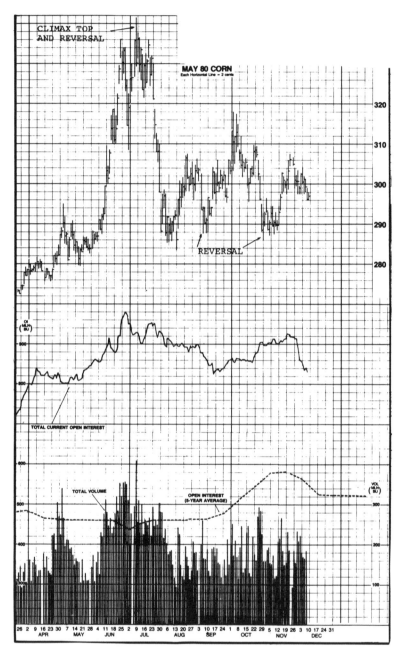

Figure 21.1 Typical bull market. (Reprinted with permission of Commodity Chart Service.)

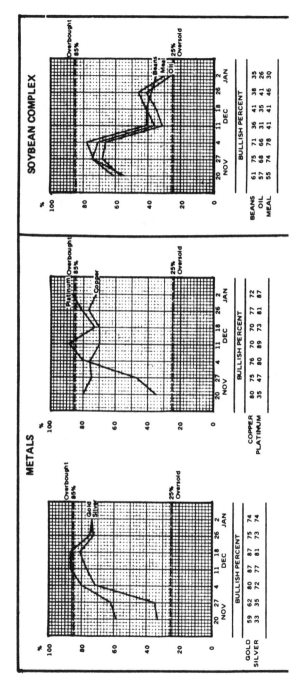

Figure 21.2 Market Sentiment Index—a graphic illustration of bullish consensus of opinions. The Market Sentiment Index reflects the opinions of professional advisors and brokers market letters as observed and recorded by Commodity Outlook, Inc., Portland, Oregon, and graphically depicted by Consensus, Inc. The Index is intended as a guide only. The "theory of contrary opinion" holds that when 85% of these analysts are bullish, it can be assumed that the market is *overbought* and a turn is coming. Conversely, if 75% are bearish (25% bullish on the Index) the market is likely to become *oversold* and a rally will develop soon. (Reprinted with permission of Consensus, 30 W. Pershing Rd., Kansas City, MO 64108.)

(continued)

185

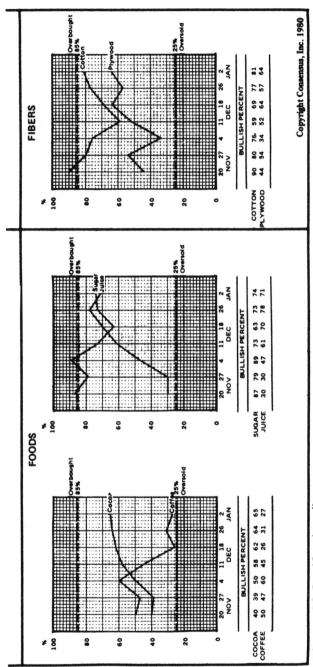

Figure 21.2 (Continued)

factors. All are indicators of investor sentiment, and investor sentiment is a function of investor perception.

A very good example of how perceptions can lead one astray is the response of gold futures to the legalization of gold ownership by U.S. citizens. For many years the ownership of gold other than coins or jewelry was not legal in the United States. When gold became active in the early 1970s, there was an increased public outcry in favor of gold ownership by U.S. citizens. As gold prices climbed steadily from the $40 per ounce level, the demand for legalization of ownership increased. Figure 21.3

Figure 21.3 The gold market following legalization of gold ownership. (Reprinted with permission of Commodity Chart Service.)

shows precisely what transpired after gold ownership was actually legalized. To the surprise of many, the long-awaited move failed to bring the buying investors expected. The anticipation of this buying is what led professionals to buy. When the expectation became reality, they sold, or distributed, their holdings to U.S. investors who expected the move to bring higher prices. Investor perception of the facts was incorrect.

This scenario has been played out on many occasions, in many markets, for many years. It is a market truth that buying on realization of a given fact is not sound market strategy. In other words, things in the market often are not what they appear to be. Why is this so? What is it that causes most investors to act irrationally, or to misperceive reality? Is it possible to respond to a given perception without actually realizing what is stimulating us to act? Enter "subliminal stimulation." I urge you to pay especially close attention to what I am about to say. It is perhaps the single most important psychological fact covered in this book. It may very well be responsible for many market losses.

Subliminal Stimulation

During the 1950s, Vance Packard published his classic work *The Hidden Persuaders* (1957). The essence of this detailed examination of the advertising world was to make Americans aware of the fact that their buying habits were being manipulated with the help of some very subtle psychological techniques. Considerable concern was expressed about the ethics of using such methods as "subthreshold effects" and hypnosis.

> The *London Sunday Times* front-paged a report in mid-1956 that certain United States advertisers were experimenting with "subthreshold effects" in seeking to insinuate sales messages to people past their conscious guard. It cited the case of a cinema in New Jersey that it said was flashing ice-cream ads onto the screen during regular showings of film. These flashes of message were split-second, too short for people in the audience to recognize them consciously but still long enough to be absorbed unconsciously.
>
> A result, it reported, was a clear and otherwise unaccountable boost in ice-cream sales. "Subthreshold effects, both in vision and sound, have been known for some years to experimental psychologists," the paper explained. It speculated that political indoctrination might be possible without the subject being conscious of any influence being brought to bear on him. (Packard, 1957)

The relevance of this assertion, if accurate, is certainly in accord with our major topic. Is it possible for investors to be influenced by subliminal, or subthreshold stimulation? Is there any basis in psychological fact to this possibility? I believe that the experimental evidence supports a general conclusion in this direction. Here are some of the facts. For the purpose of this discussion I will use the terms "subliminal," and "subthreshold," and "responding without awareness" interchangeably. The use of a more specific definition and the discussion of perceptual defense factors would further complicate the issue, but those interested in the overall topic can find considerable material in the current psychological literature.

Several physiological indicators are used by psychologists to determine whether human subjects have received or responded to a stimulus. The most common is Galvanic Skin Response (GSR), a measure of skin conductivity. It is known that changes in emotional state stimulate changes in GSR reading. GSR is one of the primary components of the lie detector or polygraph test. If a human subject is exposed to a given visual or auditory stimulus that arouses an emotional response, there will be a corresponding change in GSR reading. A number of studies (McCleary and Lazarus, 1949; Goldberg and Fiss, 1959; Wiener and Schiller, 1960; Eriksen, 1958, 1960) using GSR and verbal reports substantiate the existence of subthreshold perceptions. In other words, subjects who receive visual and/or auditory inputs that are below their level of hearing or visually presented too quickly to permit complete reading do, in fact, tend to retain some information. Secord and Backman conclude, "Experiments have suggested that, although a person does not consciously perceive a stimulus, he may nevertheless be able to respond as if he had perceived it. This is the phenomenon of subliminal perception" (1964, p. 47).

Considerably more research on the topic was carried out in the 1960s. In a detailed summary, Plotzl (1960) reported on a study cited by Freud regarding the effects of visual stimulation on dream content. Apparently, visual exposure to landscape scenes shown at the speed of 0.01 second influenced subjects' dreams. The scenes often recurred as part of dream content. These findings were later confirmed by other researchers. The existence of such effects tends to lend support to many of Freud's theoretical concepts. Lest we jump to any unwarranted conclusions, let me say also that many studies refute these findings. Although the effects of subliminal stimulation are well documented, it is not known precisely how, if, or when they stimulate behavior. There are many theories about the exact interaction between such stimulation and its ultimate translation into action.

Let us assume, for a moment, that responding without awareness is indeed a reality. The body of evidence, in my opinion, tends to support this as a warranted conclusion. Studies on prejudice, discrimination, attitude and opinion change, and suggestion tend to validate my opinion. What are the implications for the investment community? They are many and significant. First, the concept of subliminal response helps explain many of the seemingly unmotivated actions taken by investors in their decision-making process. In addition, it helps us understand the immense influence opinions and attitudes, particularly of those regarded as respect worthy or expert have on our ultimate trading decisions.

In a previous chapter, I mentioned the potential harm of too much information input. Advisory services and brokerage house newsletters were specifically mentioned. If an investor places himself in the position of reading the given opinions, then he may very well be influenced to act on the information, even though he is not aware of the role it has on his behavior. Note that in this case the information is certainly within the visual threshold of the reader, but it may stimulate him to action after it has been forgotten. It is therefore even more likely that unwanted influences on trader behavior will result. The same holds true for auditory inputs. Listening to the opinions of others can, and most likely does, have an unwanted competitive effect on the independent investment response of the individual. This is the basis of my suggestion that you isolate yourself from all outside opinion, both verbal and written. Many additional factors come to us daily in a subliminal fashion and can have similar influences.

A host of social and sociopsychological variables also mediate and either accentuate or attenuate the magnitude of a given response. These concepts fall more within the field of social psychology and are covered briefly in the next chapter.

Extrasensory Perception

A final and much more elusive concept in this area is that of extrasensory perception (ESP). The psychological literature is becoming increasingly keyed to ESP research. A number of colleges and universities have recognized the study of ESP as an accepted field of specialization. At this time, there are insufficient hard scientific data to substantiate ESP as a viable entity. We have all, at some time or another, experienced extrasensory perception. It is believed that many successful traders who act on "gut feel" are, in effect, being motivated by extrasensory or, at the very minimum, subliminal inputs. An experience recounted in *Reminiscences of a Stock Operator* is relevant as an example of how ESP tends to affect some traders:

I stared at the last price on the board until I couldn't see any figures or any board or anything else, for that matter. All I knew was that I wanted to sell Union Pacific and I couldn't find out why I wanted to.

I must have looked queer, for my friend, who was standing alongside me, suddenly nudged me and asked, "Hey, what's the matter?"

"I don't know," I answered.

"Going to sleep?" he said.

"No," I said. "I am not going to sleep. What I am going to do is to sell that stock." I had always made money following my hunches.

I walked over to a table where there were some blank order pads. My friend followed me. I wrote out an order to sell a thousand Union Pacific at the market and handed it to the manager. He was smiling when I wrote it and when I gave it to him, he read the order and stopped smiling and looked at me.

"Is this right?" he asked me. But I just looked at him and he rushed it over to the operator.

"What are you doing?" asked by friend.

"I'm selling it!" I told him.

"Selling what?" he yelled at me. If he was a bull how could I be a bear? Something was wrong.

"A thousand UP," I said.

"Why?" he asked me in great excitement.

I shook my head, meaning I had no reason. . . .

He knew it was my habit to know why I traded. I had sold a thousand shares of Union Pacific. I must have a very good reason to sell that much stock in the face of the strong market.

"I don't know," I repeated. "I just feel that something is going to happen."

"What's going to happen?"

"I don't know. I can't give you any reason. All I know is that I want to sell that stock. And I'm going to let 'em have another thousand."

"I don't know why I want to sell it. I only know I do want to," I said. "I want to, like everything." The urge was so strong that I sold another thousand. . . .

I have told some of these stories to friends, and some of them tell me it isn't a hunch but the subconscious mind, which is the creative mind, at work. That is the mind which makes artists do things without their knowing how they came to do them. Perhaps with me it was the cumulative effect of a lot of little things individually insignificant but collectively powerful. Possibly my friend's unintelligent bullishness aroused a spirit of contradiction and I picked on UP because it had been touted so much. I can't tell you what the cause or motive for hunches may be. All I know is that I went out of the Atlantic City branch office of Harding Brothers short three thousand Union Pacific in a rising market, and I wasn't worried a bit. . . .

The next day we got the news of the San Francisco earthquake. It was an awful disaster. . . . On the following day, when fuller reports came in, the market began to slide off . . . I doubled up and sold five thousand shares . . . I pushed my luck for all it was worth. I doubled up again and sold ten thousand shares more. . . .

Well, the next day I cleaned up. I made two hundred and fifty thousand dollars. It was my biggest winnings up to that time. It was all made in a few days. . . . (Lefevre, 1965, pp. 69-74)

Much more remains to be learned about subliminal and extrasensory processes. Several conclusions are warranted based on the limited amount of data we have available at this time. They are stated in the review that follows.

REVIEW

1. The process that mediates stimulus and response is difficult to specify clearly.
2. It is possible to state some parameters of the perceptual filter that stands between pure stimulus and resulting response.
3. The role of subliminal response is examined and experimental data are cited in its support.
4. The role of "response without awareness" is further examined in relation to the investor decision-making process.
5. Various "technical market indicators" are examined as they relate to investor perception. Specific examples are given.

6. Galvanic skin response (GSR) is introduced as a measure of response strength.

7. The role of limited informational input as a potential benefit to the investor is reexamined.

8. Several conclusions are reached in relation to the subliminal perception concept:

   a. It is possible for a trader to act without being aware of the reason for his action.

   b. Typically such actions are irrational and produce losses.

   c. The opinions of others, whether verbal or written, can and do have a subliminal and suggestive effect on the investor and may cause him to act without awareness.

   d. The more limited such information input can be, the more successful may be one's overall investment strategy.

9. The role of extrasensory perception is examined through an example.

22

Minimize Stress— Maximize Health and Profits

All individuals react differently to extreme pressure and stress. Whereas some will develop peculiar behavioral mannerisms such as tics, others will turn the pressure inward, developing psychophysiological symptoms instead. Regardless of its ultimate expression, stress is a key factor in the investment picture. In varying degrees, all traders, speculators, and investors are subject to the consequences of such tensions. Inasmuch as we are all potential victims of stress, it behooves us to understand how stress develops, how it expresses itself in behavior and physiology, and, above all, what we can do to effectively minimize its consequences. It has been repeatedly demonstrated that anxiety and stress tend to cause performance to deteriorate. It is certainly true that an individual in a high state of arousal will respond more rapidly to most situations. It is the relative quality of response that suffers. Overreaction and ineffective response are typical symptoms of stress. In the marketplace, this can and often does lead to unwarranted losses, inappropriate decisions, and poor discipline. Moreover, the long-term physiological sequelae of continued or intensive stress are particularly significant. To the investor who has substantial funds placed in the market, ongoing effects of stress and anxiety can be cumulative. In the long run, all the financial gains of trading and/or investing may be overshadowed by the deterioration in personal health.

Fortunately, there has been a growing interest in stress and its correlates. Psychologists, particularly Hans Selye, have studied virtually every aspect of tension and stress in animal and man. Selye's findings support the conclusion that stress and tension have a systemic effect on human and animal physiology. A few of the physical consequences include increases in various hormone levels; increases in blood pressure; increase in heart rate and pulse; increased gastric acid production; increased symptoms such as headache, muscle aches, back of neck pain, backaches, tiredness, insomnia; mood swings of increased intensity and frequency; increased aggression and frustration; and sexual dysfunctions. In addition, there is a host of more specific effects that are part and parcel of stress.

One can also identify a number of psychiatric disturbances correlated with stress. Some researchers claim to have discovered a close connection between certain psychotic disturbances and increases in particular hormone levels due to stress. Typically, industrialized societies show increases in psychophysiological disorders such as gastric and peptic ulcers, ulcerative colitis, high blood pressure, and migraine headaches. Considerable psychological research has been done in this area, and there are many highly effective techniques for preventing tension build-up and treating it once it has occurred. The purpose of this chapter is to delineate the possible side effects of stress on the investor and on investment success.

Effects of Stress on Trading Decisions

In previous chapters, I characterized the successful investment process as one based on specificity, structure, sound methodology, rationality, and organization. The most profitable programs are those that remove, or minimize, negative human elements from the decision-making process. We have all, at one time or another, experienced the poor decisions that result from impulsive or anxiety provoked actions. This so called "fight-flight" response is reserved primarily for situations that are life-threatening. The state of arousal resulting from such a case is a natural mechanism for self-defense and preservation. It is used successfully in all forms of animal life. Humans, however, have been blessed with higher mental capabilities that do not necessitate the use of survival responses in many cases. The application of calm and well-reasoned logic can, in most situations, yield far greater results than the panic response.

To deal intelligently with stress, it is necessary to be aware of one's tendency in the overreactive direction. Psychologically, the best technique for stimulating awareness is the use of a signaling mechanism. In other words, the ability to prevent overreaction depends on the ability to realize that this response is welling up and seeking expression. The mechanism that acts as a signal is different for each individual. The oft-quoted maxim "count to ten" represents one such method. In counting to ten before responding, it is believed that the individual who has become aroused to a temperamental or aggressive response will retain his composure, thereby signaling to his intellect that he is about to explode. It is hoped that the higher processes of logic and control will have sufficient time to short-circuit the fight-flight response. As overused as it may seem, there is time-tested value in this technique. To those who see themselves as more suave and sophisticated, the "count to ten" method may not suffice. The same underlying concept applies to the many methods we use daily without being aware of what we are doing. Such behavioral responses as drumming one's fingers, tapping one's foot, and doodling on a pad of paper are all attempts to deal with tension. When we are anxious or tense, and understand that an impulsive response may not be the best thing, we resort to our internal mechanisms or coping styles for assistance.

The impulsive, or tension-provoked, response in investing should be treated in a similar fashion. Take the following situation as an example. An investor has just purchased a large block of stock. His broker telephones several minutes after the purchase and reports that the company has just announced a termination of its dividend. The stock begins to fall. Naturally, one's response might be the typical "fight-flight" reaction. If responding in flight, the investor would exit the stock immediately. This would be a violation of the trading system we outlined earlier and will most likely lead to losses and regrets. In exercising the fight response, the investor would become angry, his blood pressure or ulcers might act up, and he may actually fight back by buying more of the stock. Ultimately, the act of buying more might prove beneficial. In any event, it was also a violation of the inherent trading system since the purchase was not planned. By using a signal to cue his possible overreaction the investor would be saved from emotional response. His signal might very well be a warning from the broker. "Be careful not to overreact," the broker could say. In fact, the intelligent investor could incorporate such a technique into his trading system. He might decide, for example, that he will not attend to any news, bullish or bearish, that might be released during the same day or week of his stock purchase. This would act as a preventive measure to overreaction caused by anxiety and stress.

The same basic response occurs in virtually all unexpected or otherwise unplanned situations. The net result of action taken in response to anxiety, perceived threat, stress, and/or tension is not only costly, but it also takes its physical toll. Frustration typically leads to aggression. Aggression leads to action and overreaction. Reaction and overreaction lead to losses, conflict, and more anxiety. As such, it is necessary to break into the vicious cycle. Whereas, it is a beneficial decision to avoid panic- and anxiety-inspired responses, it does not help heal the possible physical damage that can result. A number of the previously discussed treatment methods are effective in limiting losses due to anxiety and stress. It is much better, however, to prevent the emotional response in order to limit the chances of financial ruin. The ideal situation is to limit the potential physical and psychological damage that accompanies stress.

Techniques for Coping with Stress

The best defense is a strong offense. And the best way to cope with stress is to prevent it before it requires treatment. This is, to be sure, not always possible. Assuming that many investors, and in particular active traders (speculators), are already in stressful situations, I will begin by outlining some common methods that are useful in coping with tension. I will also evaluate their potential value.

Ventilation of Feelings

This technique was popularized by Sigmund Freud. Its intended use in the psychoanalytic situation was simply that indicated by its name. By talking about the stressful, or anxiety-producing, situation the patient would "ventilate" or clear his unconscious mind of the tension and pain the situation had caused. The old adage "don't keep the feelings inside you or they'll eat you from within" is, in effect, true. By employing this method, Freud was able to help many patients experience almost immediate relief.

There are many ways in which feelings can be ventilated. One form of ventilation is *abreaction*. During World War II and the Korean War, many soldiers experienced mental breakdowns as a result of their continued tension in combat situations. It was found that although the tension did, in fact, help them remain alert, some men could not cope indefinitely. Gradually their behavior deteriorated, they became withdrawn, often exhibiting psychotic or pre-psychotic symptoms. A technique using hypnosis was employed in treating those who "cracked" under the pressure. Frequently the mental breakdown would follow a precipitating event such as seeing a friend killed in action, being trapped in an ambush, or sustaining an injury. The patient was hypnotized and then asked to recall and relive the precipitating event. In so doing, all of the accompanying anguish, tension, fear, and stress were ventilated in a safe environment. Following treatment, the patient would often make an almost miraculous recovery. The key to this technique is ventilation of feelings. In ventilating feelings, many of the internalized pressures and tensions will be relieved. Implications for the investor are obvious. Before pressures can build up to the boiling point, they can be released in a socially acceptable way. This will lead to fewer losses, less physical damage, and less interpersonal conflict. What are the ways in which an average investor can ventilate feelings? We will discuss several of these next.

Free Association.   I prefer to call this technique "talking to one's self." I recommend doing just that each and every day after the market has closed. This is advised for the very active trader. Rather than go to the nearest drinking establishment and attempt to relieve tension with alcohol, take some time to sit down in a quiet room by yourself and talk about the day's events. Pay particular attention to those that caused the greatest amount of anxiety, pain, frustration, or aggravation. If you wish, the talking could be done into a recorder. At a later time, you can replay the tape. This could be of value in tracking your progress. For those who are less active in the market, I would suggest a weekly session. This method, by the way, can be used to relieve all types of stress, not just market-induced pressure.

Daily Dairy.   Albeit simple, keeping a daily diary is another method that will accomplish about the same result as free association. Simply jot down the ideas and tensions rather than talking about them. In both cases, it is best to let ideas come to you freely. Too much structure will be inhibiting.

Physical Exercise.   In addition to having healthful fringe benefits, all forms of exercise tend to be tension releasing. The recent increase in jogging, racquetball, tennis, and handball is an expression of tension-relieving exercises. Any exercise—swimming, walking, roller-skating—has potential value. The rationale for physical exercise is well founded. During the course of exercise, many of the harmful hormones that build up due to stress are released. Once out of the body, their effects cannot be expressed in physiological disorders.

Techniques for Relaxation

There are many methods that help promote relaxation. Among these are yoga, transcendental meditation, self-hypnosis, biofeedback, Jacobson's muscle relaxation, and reciprocal inhibition. They all seek to accomplish the same end—the relaxation of tense muscles throughout the body. Information on all of them can be found in most bookstores. In particular, I recommend Jacobson's systematic muscle relaxation method as helpful, especially for those who suffer from high blood pressure. Recent advances in biofeedback have made this the preferred method for controlling high blood pressure, and it should also be investigated by those who are sufferers. In fact, it is my belief that by 2000 there will be biofeedback techniques to cope with many diseases and psychiatric conditions.

Diet, Schedule, and Sleep

Since I am not an expert in nutrition I will not spend much time on this topic. I can only cite from personal experience and observation that these factors are also critical in relieving and inhibiting stress. I have found, for example, that a diet high in red meat increases my level of stress. This makes sense, since many of the animal hormones found in meat increase heart rate. It is a known fact, for example, that those who maintain vegetarian diets have significantly lower pulse rate and blood pressures than those who do not. Furthermore, the effects of alcohol do not, in my opinion, help release tension. Since alcohol is primarily a depressant, it may act to lock stress deep within the unconscious.

There are many physical consequences associated with the effects of nicotine and caffeine. Both can increase stress. Coffee, in particular, contains enough caffeine to stimulate neurotic anxiety in most individuals. Given the amount of coffee that most individuals consume, increases in physical tension can be dramatic. Diet is therefore another factor that can act to either increase or decrease the amount of stress acting on an individual. The more closely involved you are with the market, the more important your diet may be.

Schedule and sleep are also contributing factors. If your day is planned without any consideration or time for adequate rest, then tension and stress will be magnified. Those in executive positions are especially prone to develop symptoms, and should pay particular attention to their schedule. It has been clearly demonstrated in psychological research that those in executive or decision-making positions are prone to ulcers and high blood pressure as a result of the stress associated with their work. Last and certainly not least is sleep. I cannot tell you how important it is to give the body and mind sufficient sleep. Drug-induced sleep has been shown ineffective in providing the proper type of rest. Sleep must allow the unconscious mind to ventilate as it rests the body. During the sleep state, dreams are stimulated by the conflicts that have been locked inside. Considerable research has shown very clearly that dreams are tension-relieving mechanisms. Many neo-Freudian psychiatrists believe that dreams are actually problem-solving mechanisms. Subjects deprived of dreams in a laboratory situation developed personality defects, hallucinatory experiences, extreme tiredness, and poor judgment. All this, despite the fact that sleep was sufficient. Dreams are necessary, and normally induced sleep is what helps stimulate dreams.

Working Conditions

All too often we do not realize the importance of our working conditions. For the active trader who sits behind a desk watching prices all day, working conditions are very important in keeping stress at a minimum. The chair and desk you sit at—the lighting, temperature and humidity, wallpaper and paint—all can either limit or intensify the effects of stress. The ringing of telephone bells, the shouting of orders, and the flashing of prices and news are all important considerations. You might want to keep noise at a minimum, comfort at a maximum, and lighting at a high level. Telephone bells might be replaced with chimes, or the loudness may be switched to a lower level.

It is also important to change the working environment from time to time. The so-called Hawthorne effect has clearly demonstrated the importance of environment on work production. Although not specifically related to stress, it has been shown (Hawthorne effect) that a change in such things as room color, lighting, temperature, and humidity can increase the level of production.

Vacations

My last bit of advice regarding stress relates to "time away from the market." There are those who trade daily and hence build up considerable pressures. Brokers, pit traders, stock specialists, and account managers are all subject to intense degrees of stress. In order to help relieve some of the pressure, it is suggested that time be spent away from the market. The rationale is obvious and need not be explained in any further detail.

Some Final Words about Preventing Stress

The suggestions I have made may not be applicable to all investors. Yet they are, in certain ways, important for all individuals, man or woman, active trader or sometime investor. Stress arises from many varying sources. Fortunately, contemporary mental health professionals have recognized the role of stress in behavioral disorders. They have also isolated the types of stressful conditions that can have physical consequences. But their greatest achievements have been in the area of prevention. I suggest you carefully consider the techniques I have discussed. A little time spent in formulating a tension-release program may well prove the best investment you have ever made.

There are many variations on the themes mentioned here. Your physician, bookstore, or library can refer you to numerous courses, training schools, and books. Never underemphasize the value of a well-planned stress-release program. In fact, you may want to make it your greatest priority.

REVIEW

1. The role of stress is significant in the overall investment plan.
2. Serious and continued stress can have physiological correlates.
3. Stress can also lead to many inappropriate market actions thereby increasing losses.
4. There are many symptoms of stress. Several major ones are mentioned.
5. Relaxation techniques for coping with pressure and stress are discussed, and effective alternatives to tension release are mentioned.

23

Often-Asked Questions

During the course of my frequent lectures on the futures markets and investor psychology, many listeners have asked me the same questions. The question-and-answer section that follows answers many of the more frequent queries. Should you have any remaining questions about what I have covered in previous chapters, you will most likely find the answers here.

What Is the "Best" Way to Cope with Losses?

Although it is always necessary to take losses when investing or trading, this does not make a loss any more palatable to accept. It is nevertheless a mark of a successful trader to take losses just as soon as the trading system he or she is using so indicates. Any response that is either premature or tardy will lead to uncalled for consequences. Many investors refuse to take losses. The reasons for this inability or unwillingness have been discussed in previous chapters. Very often the fear of taking a loss arises from the pain one anticipates will come as a function of the loss. Whatever the reason, inability to take a loss when and as required is a psychological problem. There are, however, some investors who can take losses promptly, but who have difficulty in dealing with the pain, rejection, shame, and other negative feelings that accompany such losses.

There are a number of ways in which one can cope with losses more successfully. Here are just a few suggestions:

1. Make certain that you have set your total loss limit. In other words, when you start your investment program make note of exactly how much you can afford to lose. Assume, for example, that you set a $10,000 total loss limit on your investment program. By setting the limit before initiating any trades, you will know how bad things can get. Each loss will not seem like part of an endless series. As a consequence, you will find a loss much less threatening.

2. You may wish to incorporate the various suggestions that I made in the section on treatment of trading problems. For example, rewards might be given for taking a loss on time. This will help you cope, since you are being rewarded for making the correct decision at the proper time.

3. Practice some of the relaxation techniques discussed previously. It is a good idea to "relive" each loss in a nonthreatening environment. By placing the body in a relaxed state the loss will be more readily acceptable and tension will be relieved. This is the same principle that is employed in behavioral therapy and systematic relaxation. My best recommendation is to practice relaxation after each and every loss. Frequently, such a program will virtually eliminate the pain of taking losses within a brief period after it has been initiated.

How Can an Investor Cope with Nonspecific Fears about the Market?

The method described in answer to the previous question is advised. Where diffuse anxiety or tension exists it is best to use relaxation techniques several times each day. Keep a record of when and in response to what your anxiety occurs. Perhaps the best information you can have is when the problems begin. After keeping such a record for about a week, begin a program of systematic relaxation shortly before the expected "anxious time." Only several minutes of deep relaxation are necessary. Perhaps four or five ten-minute sessions each day will be enough to provide the necessary relief. There are some investors who exhibit symptoms that can be treated only by a professional therapist.

If you have attempted some of the methods described in this book (and in others), but still find either that you are unable to relax or that your functioning is affected to a serious degree, then I suggest you consult a psychiatrist or psychologist. You can obtain help by getting a referral from your family physician, a local chapter of the American Psychological Association, or the American Medical Association. Bear in mind that fears which totally prevent your effective functioning are most likely a reflection of more deep-seated problems which have nothing to do with the market. Typically, an individual who is well adjusted and has no serious conflicts in his or her home life will not exhibit more than occasional anxiety in the market.

Is There an Effective Way to Deal with Greed?

Many investors would be successful were it not for the forces of greed. Although many positions are correctly entered at the appropriate time, they are often kept too long once they show profits. Objectives are ignored, and the basics of rational trading fall by the wayside. There are many investors who would otherwise be successful. The problem here is one of poor discipline. As in most cases, inability to take profits once an objective has been hit is purely a function of poor organization and lack of discipline. I therefore recommend some of the methods outlined earlier. Objectives, once determined, should not be altered other than by dictate of the trading system. It may be helpful to obtain assistance from a second party when it comes to taking profits at stated or predetermined objectives. The key to avoiding greed's effects is organization, discipline, and trading by objective.

How Can I Find a Broker Who Will Best Suit My Needs?

This is a topic on which I could spend several weeks. Certainly there are many brokers who are quite capable at their work. And there are many brokers who are excellent market analysts as well. The difficulty for most investors lies in selecting a broker who will be compatible with the investor's personality and needs and who will not—either directly or indirectly—interfere with the investor's plan.

There are several ways in which the process of selection can be approached. First and foremost, I recommend that you get to know your broker, or potential broker, prior to dealing with him or her. Make certain that you both understand what is expected of the relationship. Each party has needs, rights, and expectations. Some brokers want to be called frequently, whereas others do not wish to be disturbed after an order has been placed (unless it is for the purpose of changing the order). Some brokers will help insecure traders, whereas others want no part of the insecurity. Some brokers enjoy making recommendations to their clients, whereas others do not wish to assume the responsibility of doing so. Here are several guidelines that I believe should be followed by all investors in selecting a broker:

1. If you plan to use a broker's recommendations in your trading, make certain that you follow all of his or her recommendations. Trading on the advice of a broker is in no way different from following a trading system. If you do not intend to follow through exactly as specified, then do not insult your broker by second guessing him.

2. Make a list of precisely what you expect of a broker. When you go looking for the right person, make certain that your requirements are met.

3. Your expectations should be specific. Don't just expect a broker to get you "good information"; rather, indicate what you mean by "good information."

4. Let the broker know what you expect. Show him or her your list of requirements and see if they meet with approval.

5. It is also important to make a list of what the broker expects of you. In so doing, you will not fall prey to the many pathological relationships that can occur in broker-client interactions.

6. Do not burden your broker with emotional problems. You are most likely not his only client and he does not have time to counsel you. Should you seek his assistance in a particular program as described earlier in this book, make certain that it does not infringe on his time and ability. A broker should not be depended on for consolation, support, or confidence building.

7. I would suggest that you look for a broker who has the following qualities and skills:

    a. Ability and willingness to promptly execute orders correctly and without hesitation.

    b. Willingness to avoid making recommendations either in agreement with or in opposition to your opinions of trades.

    c. Ability to secure technical and/or fundamental market information as required by client.

    d. Good record of work attendance and being on time for work. When a broker is needed, he must be there!

The best way to determine how a broker-client relationship will work is the test of time. If you find that a broker is not making things less difficult for you, then look for a new broker. Always make certain that you are not to blame. My greatest successes have been with brokers who do not talk unless asked to do so. By letting a broker do his job as best he can, you will also derive the maximum benefit.

It is not possible for me to overstate the important role a broker plays in the total investment picture. There are many investors who blame brokers for getting them into positions or getting them out of positions. For many years, the broker has been a scapegoat of the undisciplined investor. It is time we stopped blaming brokers for our own lack of discipline. Therefore, I suggest a reappraisal of your current relationship with your broker. Don't be too quick to affix blame that might, in reality, be yours.

Which Markets Should I Trade?

Not every market is suited to the temperament of every investor. Some individuals do better with stocks, where others might do better in commodity futures. Certainly the decision of which markets should be traded is one that must be based on three distinct factors: experience, temperament, and financial ability. Even though experience and financial ability may be present, temperament may not be sufficient. For the beginner, I would advise no trading in the futures market. It takes time to acquire the necessary skill and emotional strength to trade in this area.

There is a tendency for small traders to take on positions in obscure, low-priced stocks and thinly traded issues. This is not, in my opinion, an advisable approach. If you are a small trader and you think small, then you will remain small. This does not mean that you should assume a position above and beyond your financial ability. You can, however, put on trades in the stocks or commodities you wish, so long as the amount of shares or contracts is within your limit. When a signal is triggered by your trading system, you should take the signal. You need not, however, "plunge" into the trade with an unacceptably large position. Although many errors have been made in the overly bold direction, more have been made by those who were too weak.

At this time, it is also reasonable to discuss how many markets should be traded. If you are a full-time trader and do not have other responsibilities, then there is no problem in establishing several positions at one time. If, however, you are not totally committed to the market, then you had best assume only a limited number of trades. The best index for determining how much is too much is by the degree of concern or anxiety you feel when the market does not move in your direction. If you become extremely anxious, then you have instituted too many positions. In the long run, only experience will be the guide. Start slowly, trade carefully, and do not overtrade on limited funds.

Would It Be Advisable to Have Several Individuals Participate in the Decision-Making Process?

Trading "by committee," as it is called, is not a valid or effective procedure for most traders. Where a specific trading system exists, it may be useful to have several inputs regarding the signals themselves. But if the system is effective and clear-cut, there will be no need for interpretation or judgment of any kind. Thus, it is not necessary to have more than one or two individuals decide on a given trade. Generally, there will be too much disagreement if more people are involved in the ultimate decision. The democratic process may work well when it comes to long-term fundamental researching of stocks and commodities, but it may not yield good results where fast decisions are required.

Moreover, the various personalities involved may clash. The entire process can easily become a power struggle that will cloud objective features of the system. Investment clubs usually have a number of members who put forward their points of view. This process will work if those who participate are mature enough to stick to the facts and avoid the personalities. All too often this is not possible. I have long believed, based both on personal experience and observation of successful traders' methods, that one must trade one's own line, make one's own decisions, and accept all the glory or grief alone. There is much to be said in favor of the "loser" when it comes to investment. I have indicated how and why too much information can be a dangerous thing in the market. And so it is with too many "cooks" in the decision-making process.

Is Long-Term Investing Better Than Short-Term Trading and Speculation?

This depends on the individual. Historically, the greatest amounts of money are made in riding large moves. But it is not always possible to do so. For one reason or another, many investors feel that they should enter and exit a market many times, in order to protect what they have. They are afraid their profit will disappear. This is a type of insecurity that generally reflects poor discipline and technique. There are many investors who trade only for the short term. They somehow need the satisfaction that comes with immediate gratification of needs. This stems from psychological factors and may cause many losses. The best course for each individual is the one that causes the least anxiety. Since stress, tension, anxiety, and panic can lead to more than the necessary number of losses, any act that increases these tendencies is not advised. For well over 90 percent of the investment community, long-term trades are the only ones to consider. By long term I mean specifically trades that are kept for a minimum of several months. It is not always possible to keep a trade for this length of time, particularly if your loss point is hit. The trades held for brief periods of time will most frequently be losers, whereas those held for longer time spans will be winners. This is typical of most successful systems. There are few traders who can "scalp" or day trade the market with any consistent degree of success. Those who consistently do so profitably are pit traders or specialists on the exchange floor. When you attempt to compete with these people, you are working at a disadvantage that will almost always cause you considerable grief.

Long-term investment is favored over short-term speculation. Even trades that are carried for several weeks are preferable to those held for shorter time spans. I recommend that 90 percent of all investors carry long-term positions. Speculation should be reserved for those who make it their life's work.

How Does One Know When to Seek Help from a Mental Health Professional?

There are many individuals walking the streets who feel they need psychiatric treatment. And there are many individuals walking the streets who need treatment but are not receiving it. How does one know when, why, and where to seek help? Are there signs and symptoms that a mental health professional should be consulted? The best single indicator of necessary treatment is the ability to function.

If a behavior disorder is so intense that it affects functioning, then it is time help was sought. It is, for example, relatively normal to suffer some periods of mental depression; it is, however, a very serious problem to be so depressed you cannot leave for work in the morning. This occurs very late in the history of the behavior disorder, and there is no longer any choice about treatment. Hospitalization may be necessary. Early in the course of a disorder, there are many warning signs. Any increase in symptoms over an extended period of time is perhaps the first clue. Dependence on alcohol or drugs is another symptom of impending trouble. The things to watch for are primarily an increase in symptoms, an intensification of symptoms, and/or the development of new symptoms.

What precisely do I mean by "symptoms"? Typically, symptoms include intense anxiety, depression, mental confusion, forgetting, sleeplessness, delusions and/or hallucinations, use of drugs or alcohol, intense irritability, high blood pressure unrelated to a medical condition, attacks of colitis and/or ulcer pain, tics, stuttering, feelings of depersonalization (i.e., not knowing who you are or where you are), inappropriate laughter. There are many other associated symptoms reflecting even more serious mental conditions. My advice would be not to delay if you notice any problems cropping up. An ounce of prevention goes a long way when it comes to mental health. Do not attempt to be your own therapist. Consult a professional if you find that your functioning is being hampered. Some of the simple methods described earlier are intended for the treatment of trading problems that are not indicative of more serious difficulty.

Where Do You Find Professional Help If You Have Decided You Need It?

Assuming that you or a friend requires treatment, where do you start to get the help best suited to your needs? Assuming you have not waited too long, I would suggest a consultation with your family physician. He or she may decide to help you through the bad time with some medication. Although I cannot dispute this authority, I would not recommend drugs for more than a brief period of intense crisis (see next question). In most cases, your family physician will make referral to a mental health professional. Either a psychiatrist or psychologist will be recommended. If you are at a loss as to where you might turn, contact any local chapter of the various mental health treatment organizations. They will help you get the right kind of help. In this respect, I would also suggest you not "shop around" for the least costly therapist. Regardless of price, I advise you seek help from an individual who is respected and capable.

How Do Drugs Affect Personality and Investing?

The 1970s have witnessed a sharp increase in drug use among individuals of all ages and backgrounds. Whereas the most common drug at one time may have been alcohol, this is slowly changing. Other drugs have taken its place. No matter what the drug, its effect on personality will be negative. There has also been an increase in prescription drugs, such as mood elevators, tranquilizers, and diet medication. These also tend to have a negative effect on performance in all areas. Benefits may be far outweighed by the side-effects, and I suggest you never mix drugs with investing.

Isn't the Market Just Another Form of Gambling?

Depending on the manner in which it is used, the market may be a tool of either the investor or the gambler. If used in a predetermined, applied, consistent, and well-researched fashion, the market will protect the investor from inflation, help money grow at an above-average rate, and provide retirement security. It is neither the goal nor the ability of gambling to provide these. Motivation is at the heart of this issue. The investor who allows long-term objectives to become obscured can easily become a gambler. The incessant need to trade is one symptom of gambling in the marketplace. Losses that mount and are not cut short tend to cause more caution in the serious investor. But in the gambler they inspire more chance taking, less rational behavior, borrowing, and an almost frenzied attachment to the trend of prices. Savings are taken from the bank, home furnishings may be sold, and money may even be stolen to support a gambling habit. If things become this bad, then the investor has become a gambler and professional help is necessary.

Should I Manage My Own Money or Should a Professional Do It for Me?

There are many individuals who refuse to admit that they cannot "make it in the market." They continue to take loss after loss and will not allow one who may know better to manage their money. The only real difference between most individual investors and professional money managers is that the money manager does this work as his livelihood. His approach tends to be more organized, concise, objective, and professional. More often than not he can do a better job than the investor. Certainly there are financial managers who will lose more money than any investor can lose on his own. This is why the decision to employ a manager is so very important. Not only is it necessary to know the manager's "track record," but it is also necessary to know the person who is doing the managing.

There are those investors who wish to "backseat drive." Although they do not want to accept the responsibility and effort that come with investment planning, they do want to supervise the money manager. They frequently call the manager and question the moves that were made. This angers most professionals and is not a suggested form of behavior. There are, therefore, several questions that should be asked before you decide to have another manage your money for you:

1. Am I capable of emotionally accepting the fact that another is in control of my money? Will I be grief stricken if it is lost? Will I be ego-deflated if money is made?
2. Can I give the money manager the "breathing room" necessary for him to do his job?
3. Am I satisfied that I cannot do the job on my own?
4. Will my tension and stress be relieved by having another manage my funds?

I suggest you evaluate these questions before making the decision.

Are There Any Personal Qualities That Differentiate Losers from Winners?

This is another question that could take an entire book to answer. I believe that there are many specific qualities of the market winner. To name but a few:

1. Discipline and organization.   Decisions are made from a base of secure attitude, organized investment objectives, and disciplined application of trading rules.

2. Persistence.   The winner must be willing to try and try until he succeeds. One of the best traders I ever met refused to accept failure in any aspect of his life. If there was something he could not do, he would learn how. When his trading system failed, he would go "back to the drawing board" and start over.

3. Positive attitude.   This is an important quality. The willingness to say that you will be successful is important and has been discussed.

4. Independence.   There is a tendency for successful traders to ignore the advice and opinions of others. Their own work is regarded as best, and they implement decisions that have come from their own trading system. Even if information is gathered from other sources, it is recombined in a unique way and implemented with confidence.

5. Self-confidence.   This is a combination of positive attitude and persistence. The belief that you can do what has to be done is a mark of self-confidence.

6. Contrary thinking.   Quite often the successful investor is moving contrary to the crowd. When the trend is strong in one direction or another, he is moving with it. At major changes in trend, he is one of the first to change course, no matter what others may say or do.

7. Isolation.   Many successful investors tend to isolate themselves from the public world. Although some are eccentric and peculiar in their mannerisms, this is not a necessary requisite to success. There are many information inputs that cloud thinking and pervert judgment. These are systematically excluded from the repertoires of successful traders.

8. Well-rounded personal life.   Many investors are so tuned into the market that their personal lives suffer. Eventually their trading will suffer as well. Those who live well-rounded lives—socially, interpersonally, physically, and professionally—are among the most frequent and lasting market winners.

I have outlined some of the most important qualities. Certainly there are many more. The readings recommended in the Bibliography of this book can help you learn about the more subtle characteristics.

Can My Home Life Really Affect My Market Performance?

Just as your home life can affect your job and interpersonal relationships, it can also affect your investing and trading. If you have experienced trauma, intense personal loss, or serious quarrel in the home, you will find your ability to make decisions of all kinds affected. The best thing at such times is to back away from the market, making as few decisions as possible. If the home situation is an ongoing aggravating factor, your overall performance will decline even further. Good trading begins in the home. Solve whatever the crisis may be before you begin a serious program of trading.

In the same way, trading problems can affect home life. Take the necessary steps to leave your problems in the office. It is important to make the separation as soon as possible, particularly if you trade the market for a living.

Can "Self-Improvement" Courses Help?

Yes. They can be of immense value if you are serious about what has been taught. There are many individuals who tour the country giving self-improvement seminars. Only a few are worthwhile. Without mentioning names, I suggest you carefully look into the background of each such course. Only those that are well established and have a record of longevity should be considered. As with most skills, you must use them or lose them. If you intend to spend your hard-earned money on a trading course in self-confidence, self-discipline, and positive mental attitude, do not enter the class with the misperception that all the work will be done for you. Much effort is required during and especially after.

Is It Helpful to Attend Trading/Investing Seminars?

I have led many market seminars over the last 15 years. In most cases, the individuals who attend these meetings are sincere, interested, and well intentioned. However, they are often ignorant of the best way in which to use the information that has been presented. Instead of taking notes, listening intently, asking good questions, of making cogent comments, they busily record my comments and safely tuck the tape in a back drawer when they get home. If you spend the time and money to be at one of the many expensive market seminars, make certain you get your money's worth. How to do this? I have a number of suggestions:

1. Take notes, ask questions, make comments, and participate actively.
2. Get plenty of rest the night before and make certain that you follow the speaker at all times. If you get confused, ask questions.
3. Attempt to know something about the subject matter before entering the meeting.
4. Have a list of prepared questions. If they are relevant but not answered, then ask them.

5. Don't be intimidated or shy. Ask as many questions as necessary. If you have a question, chances are many others have the same question as well.

6. Find out where you can acquire a transcript of the talk.

7. Obtain an address where you can write if still confused or unclear about some issues.

8. Attempt to integrate the material with what you already know or do.

9. Test the material before using it in the market. Just because a person speaks on a given subject does not mean that he or she is always right.

10. Obtain written material from the library to supplement your learning.

11. Be suspicious about those "sure fire," "get rich quick," "ultimate trading system" seminars. Generally they are expensive, hard to implement, and even harder to disprove. You will most likely be disappointed.

What's the "Best" Trading System for Me?

Previously, I indicated that no single system contains all of the answers necessary for success. Perhaps no one method can give any investor all of the required self-control and discipline that leads to profitable investing and speculation. There are certain types of individuals who are naturally attracted to particular trading methods. Engineers, for example, tend toward mathematical and technical trading systems. Academicians and economists are inclined in the fundamental direction. A majority of novice traders are enchanted with technical systems, which are less time consuming and easier to grasp than fundamental types of methods.

Regardless of the system employed, results are almost always a function of the user. This I have indicated many times, and you, most likely, have observed it to be true. It is one thing to have a good trading method; it is yet another to use it appropriately. As a result, the "best" trading system for you is the one that helps you maintain the greatest amount of discipline. Some techniques easily lend themselves to such regularity; there are others that leave too much room for interpretation and judgment. I advise you to utilize a particular system based on your level of self-discipline and confidence. If you have a history of poor adherence to trading rules, then a very rigid system is what you need. If you have mastered the basics of trading discipline, practically any system will work for you.

Finally, the last few years have seen a marked increase in the number of trading systems offered for public sale. This has been true primarily in the commodity futures market. Typically, these techniques are sold at very high prices. The buyer agrees to keep the system secret. The seller often guarantees the system to be effective and offers a refund if this is not the case. Many books have made similar offers and claims. All appeal to a very basic lust and greed within the human psyche. Effectively written advertisements for such systems can draw an exceptionally large response within a matter of days. More often than not the buyers are sorely disappointed. This does not reflect upon the value of the system they have purchased. A large majority of the losses taken following such systems is due exclusively to trader error, emotion, poor judgment, lack of discipline, and disorganization. The system itself is never fully given the opportunity to function as advertised. Guarantees made by promoters of the systems often offer a complete refund, if it can be shown that the system did not work over a period of, for example, one year. Certainly there can be no refund given for a system that has not been implemented as required. This is not a defense of such system sales. I do not believe that anyone who has an infallible system will sell it, if indeed there exists such a beast. There are many techniques I use in the market that I do not intend to reveal to anyone, at any price. Although I have my doubts about the systems offered to the public, I have more doubts about the public that buys them.

Should I Subscribe to an Advisory Service?
If So, Which One(s)?

This decision is similar to those previously discussed in the sections on managed accounts and broker selection. There is nothing wrong with subscribing to an advisory service. Many of the issues relating to services have been discussed in a previous section. Here are several additional guidelines that should be considered in subscribing to a service:

1. Does the service provide specific recommendations, and do they fit into your financial limits? If too many trades are recommended, you may not find it financially possible to follow all of them. As a result, you will not be trading according to a total system.

2. Is there follow-through on each recommendation? Is every recommended position updated until closed out? If this is not done, then you may not wish to subscribe.

3. Do you really want to have the input of a service that may interfere with your own system, or one that may dissuade you from making trades based on your own work? It might be best to try your own hand at investing before allowing input from other sources.

4. Before subscribing to any service, make certain you understand why you want to subscribe, what you believe you can get from the service that you cannot do for yourself, and what factors will be used in deciding that you are actually obtaining the desired results.

5. How widely read is the service? Frequently, there are disadvantages in following the recommendations of a service that is too widely distributed. You may be entering orders along with thousands of other investors. This will often result in relatively poor order fills.

There are many advisory services, both in stocks and commodity futures, that do an excellent job of market analysis and recommendations. The majority are run by honest, hard-working, and dedicated advisors. Typically, their performance records are above average, and they help many investors who would otherwise not have the time to study every market opportunity. They cannot, however, help those who are unwilling or incapable of disciplining themselves. This point has been made many times before. If you intend to subscribe to an advisory service, make certain you use it! Even if you find a service which has a poor record and do the opposite of what it says, make certain you are consistent in your approach and actions. There is more to be said for consistency than there is for all of the sophisticated technical work I have ever seen.

Is It Possible to Become Overconfident?

Absolutely! Any emotional extreme is an unwelcome quality. Just as lack of self-confidence can lead to errors, so can overconfidence. After making a number of highly successful investments, there is a tendency for many individuals to become complacent, cocky, conceited, and careless.

When profits come in quickly and one's trading system is working well, there is a natural human inclination toward feelings of infallibility. As a result, judgment is often impaired and decisions are made based strictly on "gut feelings." This, as you know, is not a sign of good trading and will, more often than not, result in losses. I have personally known several investors who made large amounts of money in a brief period of time, only to give it all back after falling prey to overconfidence and its accompanying evils.

It is always best to observe the "golden mean" in your investments. Nothing should be carried to excess in either direction. When you begin spending too much time on either extreme, this is an indication that something has gone wrong. The most effective action that can—and should—be taken at this time is to return to basics with even more self-discipline than before. You must act firmly and intensely to correct an overreaction. Another indicator that you may be in an overconfident state is your willingness to put on too many positions. The list of "symptoms" provided next can help you recognize the problem early in its development:

Symptoms of Overconfidence

1. Willingness to take larger than normal risks.
2. Accumulation of a much larger than average position in one market.
3. Accumulation of more than the usual number of positions in different markets.
4. General decline in adherence to trading rules.
5. Disregard of indications contrary to your present positions.
6. Willingness to ride losses longer than usual.
7. An increase in the "let's take a chance" type of attitude that accompanies rapid growth in profits.
8. Unwillingness to take profits as previously determined objectives.
9. A general euphoria and an accompanying belief that the best is yet to come.

Many individuals have specific syndromes of overconfidence. You are advised to study your attitudes and behaviors for a more thorough understanding of how you act when you feel overconfident. As with many other behaviors, friends and loved ones can alert you to the fact that something is wrong.

My Results in the Market Affect My Home Behavior;
How Do I Make the Separation?

There are many individuals who take their work home with them. When they have had a good day at the office, all's well at home. But when they've had a bad day, those around them become the object of their work-related frustration. This is very common in the market as well. For the investor or trader who is very active in the market, this is an even greater problem. It is very normal to experience such a "spillover" of emotion, and many things can be done to prevent its ruining your home life. Many investors and active traders resort to liquor. This is not the answer. Although it may provide temporary relief, it simply masks symptoms and does not permit proper ventilation of feelings. In addition, there are physical side-effects that make their presence known before too long. I recommend, instead, a series of steps that should be taken before entering the home. If this is not possible, then I would take the necessary action as soon as possible after arriving home. First and foremost, I suggest you employ any or all of the relaxation techniques described earlier. These will help ventilate the locked-in feelings. The resulting release of stress will decrease the possibility of your striking out at the nearest human being.

Second, I advise you to think through the actions of each day in light of your trading system. Discover exactly what went wrong. You must pinpoint the cause for whatever the problem may have been. If it was due to poor execution of trading rules, then accept the error, enter it appropriately in your trading record or diary, and make a commitment to rectify the error in future dealings.

Third, make yourself aware of the fact that you have had a difficult day. Be cognizant that you are frustrated, anxious, and/or irritable. This will act as a signal to your self-control mechanisms.

Fourth, let your family know that you have had a difficult day. Warn them that you may be on edge. This will help them keep out of your way. Fifth, take the opportunity to relax when you get home. A hot bath, a slow and leisurely meal, or soft music may be in order. Sixth, get to sleep early. Let the naturally healing process of sleep relieve the tension and frustration. Your dreams may be troubled but they will help release much of the pent-up pressure.

The importance of preventing the market from influencing your home life is obvious. In addition to the domestic difficulties that can result, there can be a reverse effect. Once problems in the home have started, they will affect your trading. This will add to the stress, and more diffi-culty will be precipitated in the home. This is why it is important to break into the progression of events as soon as possible. It is very common for emotional problems to feed on each other. The best way to prevent the consequences of such a situation is to take preventive measures promptly.

How Can the Average Investor Take Advantage of Market Psychology?

There are two distinct ways in which the small investor can use market psychology to his or her advantage. First and of greatest importance, in-vestors should know themselves. Their objectives and expectations must be clearly stated. As things change and goals are attained, new objectives should be formulated. The guidelines presented in previous chapters are designed to help you in this process. In addition, there are many books available that help improve insight.

The second way in which an average investor can take advantage of market psychology is by understanding the psychological functioning of other investors. The meaning of such things as panics, climax tops and bottoms, contrary opinion, and news should be clearly understood. The lessons of history are many, and history tends to repeat itself in the mar-kets time and time again. Each investor must take some independent ac-tion to learn the necessary market indicators. Although it is becoming increasingly difficult for many investors to profit through traditional types of securities, there are still many opportunities.

How Can I Overcome Depression Which Sets in after Several Losing Trades?

Depression is perhaps one of the most difficult symptoms to overcome. There are some theories that severe depression may have its basis in bio-chemical factors. As a result, intensive treatment is required to eliminate the effects of serious depression. From time to time all individuals are subject to the effects of sadness, remorse, and depression. The best treat-ment I know is preventive rather than curative. In order to prevent depres-sion from setting in, it is vital to maintain as disciplined and organized a program as possible.

Depression has a way of keeping you from acting on matters of importance. It is a way of saying that you will not take any action at all, since all actions lead to failure. For those who fall deep into the pit of depression, the inability to act is almost a relief. If you are permitted to remain in the depths of inactivity, your depression will become increasingly resistant to change. This is why some societies treat depression with immediate action. The best thing you can do is to keep working, keep trying, and keep studying the market.

In some cases, there are specific physical causes for depressive states. I would suggest that a physician be consulted promptly when such symptoms arise. He or she will determine if there is any systemic cause for your feelings. Many individuals cannot distinguish between physical feelings of tiredness and clinical depression. Consultation with a physician can help rule out any organic cause.

How Do I Know If Disorganization Is One of My Major Market Problems?

Many problems can be minimized, if not totally eliminated by making some very minor changes in your approach to investing; the most important of these is organization. Have you ever missed a market move because your charts were not up to date? Have you ever failed to liquidate a position because you did not know you still had it? Have you ever looked for some market data which, although important, were misplaced in a pile of papers on your desk? These are all symptoms of underlying disorganization—all of which will contribute to market losses. I believe that most of the poor investors would become much more successful if they had the wherewithal to become organized. I recommend the following remediative steps:

1. Take stock of your current situation. Being totally honest with yourself, can you say that you have not suffered losses as a result of disorganization?
2. Ask yourself the following questions:
    a. Is my market work and related material all accessible within a matter of seconds, or is it scattered throughout the house (office)?

  b. Do things disappear? Are charts or statistics you worked on several days ago stashed into a drawer or folder never to be seen again?

  c. Are your trades planned daily, weekly, or monthly? Do you have a set time for your studies? Is your market work done on a regular basis? Do you have a specific time for entering orders?

  d. Do you feel organized? Do you feel as if you have a good grasp on the market long term, intermediate term, and short term? Do you have a long-range plan on paper—or is it formulated piecemeal?

The answers to these questions will help you realize the degree to which you are organized. Most likely you will be unpleasantly surprised with the answer. If so, I have several suggestions:

1. Read the earlier section on scheduling.
2. Keep a daily log of what you do with your time. Write down all activities, time started, time completed, and things accomplished. You will rapidly discover where your time is going and how much time is spent in compensating for disorganization.
3. Set up a program which is highly precise, specific, and organized. Implement it for a given period of time and see how it affects profits. A positive result will most certainly let you know if disorganization has been standing in your way.

24

Sex and the Markets: Fact or Fantasy

Let's briefly review some of the previous material on psychosexual development. Sigmund Freud placed considerable emphasis on sexual conflicts and feelings in the understanding of personality and its dysfunctions. In fact, his theory is so heavily weighted in this area that it is termed the "psychosexual theory of development." According to the tenets of this school, sexual feelings begin at birth and pass through several changes as the child grows to adulthood.

The details of Freud's theory are available in many publications, particularly his own writings. The essence of what psychosexual theory teaches is that sexual feelings, experiences, anxieties, and fears have a profound effect on us in later life. Many of the conflicts between child and parent are sexual. Many of the issues regarding authority, punishment, control, and achievement are closely related to sexual development. Following "childhood amnesia," a concept that was mentioned earlier, many of the sexual conflicts and feelings are locked away deep within the unconscious mind. Accordingly, they tend to influence our behavior without our being aware of their effect.

As mentioned earlier, the theory presented by Freud has been disputed by others throughout the years. Although there is little experimental evidence to support some of Freud's conclusions, his work has passed the test of time. Many of the concepts he proposed are still highly regarded by psychiatrists and psychologists. In addition, there are numerous branches of his original theory, all of which are in some close way related by the common thread of psychosexual development. Patients who suffer from various neurotic and/or psychotic behaviors have often been helped through the application of Freudian therapeutic techniques.

Certainly no methodology is without its flaws or limitations. Behavioral therapists criticize the psychoanalytical technique as unscientific and not founded on empirical fact. They also claim that classical Freudian treatment of emotional problems takes too long. Whereas it may take a psychoanalyst several years or longer to treat a phobic patient, behavioral methods can accomplish the same result in a matter of months, quite often more effectively, and most often with less expense. Psychoanalysts retort that the behavioral therapist is treating only the symptoms and ignoring underlying causes. They claim that the behavior that was treated in such a mechanical fashion (see some of the behavioral methods described earlier) will recur in a different form. This is called symptom substitution. Clinically and experimentally there is no evidence that a well-applied behavioral course of therapy will lead to a recurrence of the dysfunction, or a symptom substitution. And so the debate continues. Behaviorists have experimental data and effective technique and results on their side, and classical analysts have tradition, longevity, and results on their side. Both techniques work. I have my personal bias, but I will present you with both sides.

Turning back once again to Freud's theory of psychosexual development, we will see why it is important to understand one's deep-rooted sexual feelings and conflicts. If, indeed, they influence our overt adult behavior, then we must be aware of their effects and consequences at all times. Perhaps we are engaging in a certain behavior that could be avoided were we to understand or have insight into the unconscious motivation. This is, to be sure, one of the key elements of classical analytical (and many other) theories. It is necessary to unlock pent-up feelings. It is necessary to dig deeply into the unconscious mind, probe the experiences and feelings, bring them into consciousness, experience them, and put them into their proper perspective. Some of the examples that follow will, no doubt, be deemed incomplete by those who are avowed followers of Freud. I cannot, however, do justice to the immense theory of this man within the limited amount of space available. I can, however, present you with the information necessary for a good overview of the topic. Many readers, with insights previously not experienced, and investors, not blessed with these insights, may be inspired to take up the study of Freud and his theories.

A trader has just experienced the greatest single profit he has ever made. He is elated that his trading system has functioned so well. Everything he did was correct—the profit was expected, he liquidated near the indicated objective, and the desired result followed. Several hours after his victory, he begins to experience a gnawing feeling in the pit of his stomach. As the day grows later, he becomes aware of his increasing anxiety. By evening he is extremely tense, jumpy, has a nervous stomach, and cannot get more than several hours of sleep. The thing that distresses him most is the fact that he cannot understand why he feels as he does. He should be pleased with the success, and yet he cannot enjoy it. But to add insult to injury, he soon begins to lose the money back. It takes several days of persistently poor trading, but he manages to achieve his goal and the money is soon gone. Now he feels a sense of relief. At the same time he feels depressed. Within a matter of days, he becomes anxious once again, this time because he does not understand why he lost the money back, why it did not make him feel good, why he is depressed, why he has undone his success, what he can do about it, and why he is so very confused. This is a classic case of sexual conflict. You may be surprised to see the word "sex" enter into the discussion at this point. After all, there has been no mention of sex throughout the brief story. How does it now enter into the picture?

This trader is suffering from an unconscious sexual conflict. Ideally, this one situation should not be removed from the total picture of his personality, but for the sake of example I will do so. Freud wrote a great deal about the feelings of "castration anxiety" and the sexual attraction of the male child to his mother. He theorized that a male child is attracted to his mother and a female to her father. The sexual attraction that is experienced leads the child to begin to fear reprisal by the father (or mother for female children). Fear is related primarily to the body organ that experiences sexual pleasure, namely the genitalia. Armed with only a very elementary understanding of the world, the child begins to fear that his father, on learning of the attraction to mother, will remove the child's penis and/or associated parts as a punishment. In female children, the feelings run in generally the same direction. They realize that they do not have a penis and feel that it has been removed as punishment for attraction to father. Both cause what is called *castration anxiety.* But the fear does not stop here. As the child matures, the feelings remain. In some cases, the fears are intense and buried deep within the unconscious mind. In other situations, there has been resolution of the fear through positive experiences between father and son or mother and daughter. When the child becomes an adult he is no longer aware of the basis for such feelings. All he knows is that he feels anxiety. During the course of his childhood, the fear of castration becomes generalized into a fear of authority.

Often the child begins to feel that if he is successful at conquering, or overcoming, a great task, this will bring upon him the wrath of his castrating father. Through the process of generalization, fear then becomes associated with any major achievement. The individual becomes anxious that he will be punished, or castrated, and this generally results in guilt, depression, and a series of losses. The losses are an unconscious way of repenting for the victory. It is as if the investor is saying, "Now that I have succeeded in conquering my mother, I had better undo the damage, give her back to my father, and hope that he will not castrate me."

Sexual Conflict in Dreams

Frequently the conflict may express itself symbolically in dreams. During his sleepless night subsequent to being victorious, the sufferer may have a dream which, although he does not fully understand, feels to him as if it relates to the problem. An example of how such a dream might be related by the trader to his therapist is:

> I am in a car traveling up a mountain road. The climb is long and steep. My father is driving. My mother is sitting in front with my father.
> I am sitting in the back seat. Suddenly the car begins to swerve. My father is injured as the car hits a large rock. For some reason or other, we decide to put him in the trunk of the car (patient laughs), that seems funny to me now; I wonder why we had to put him in the trunk . . .
> Well actually . . . well it seems that there was some sort of a hospital in the trunk . . . sounds funny . . . but there was some first aid there. Can't understand why . . . but then my mother asked me to drive the car. Even though I was very young in the dream, I took the wheel and drove the car all the way up the mountain . . . my mother was happy . . . then I woke up.

There is deep symbolism in this dream. The subject has injured his father, removed him from the picture by locking him in the trunk, and then he has assumed the "wheel" or control of the car, thereby making his mother happy. He has conquered the mountain, his mother, and his father, all at the same time.

The dream expresses in symbolic, or unconscious, laughter how the trader feels about his victory in the market. In fact, the dream might have continued with the father leaving the trunk and punishing the child for assuming control of the car. In any event, the dream was created from the unconscious feelings of the individual. By understanding how the dream relates to his current situation, the trader might gain some insight, thereby relieving his anxiety and castration fear.

Sexual Inadequacy and the Market

There are many other situations in which sexual feelings might dictate market behavior. It should be said that market behavior is not the only thing affected by sexual conflicts. The entire personality can be shaped by these events, according to Freudian theory. Its effect on investment behavior is merely one aspect upon which I have chosen to focus. Here is another example of how sexual feelings can mediate or influence market behavior. Assume the following situation: An investor is very aggressive in the market. He seeks to acquire as much wealth as possible, within the shortest period of time. Meanwhile his attitude is one of self-centeredness, conceit, and blatant immodesty. He believes that he is the market Messiah (if there is such a thing). Not only does he trade actively and aggressively, but he seems to have no regard for caution, conservatism, or common sense. There are times that will be enormously profitable for such a trader, and there will be occasions that bring him to the brink of ruin. His overall behavior is one of a "chance taker." He is confident to a pathological extreme; so much so, that he ignores many of the realities in a situation. How can we understand his behavior from an analytical point of view?

In my opinion, such behavior is typical of one who is attempting to compensate for feelings of inadequacy. Most likely he feels that he has either been castrated and must compensate, or that his sexual equipment is inadequate to do the job. Such feelings typically arise from childhood experiences that either were threatening or instilled a sense of smallness and/or worthlessness in the individual. In adulthood, there are several response styles that could have developed. In this case, our subject overcompensated for his internal feelings of inferiority. Internally he most likely feels negative about himself, is afraid of the market, and does not believe he will ever succeed. This type of behavior is typical of many who suffer from the same feelings. Men who, for example, are extremely "macho," who are inveterate bachelors and women chasers, who feel that they are the Lord's gift to women, are often compensating for unconscious feelings of sexual inadequacy and, possibly, homosexuality.

Linguistic Clues and Sexuality

There are, in addition, many popular expressions and attitudes relating to the market that reflect an unconscious sexual orientation. Freud was a student of behavioral symptoms that reflected underlying feelings. Not only was the dream important, but such things as associations, slips of the tongue, jokes, and daydreams were also taken to be symbolic of internal feelings. There is a tendency for most traders to relate to the market in a sexual way. This is reflected in their behavior as well as in their verbal expressions about the market. Based on a purely Freudian interpretation of what transpires on the floor of an exchange, or in the trading pit, we can see how sex might become a factor. For many years, pit traders and floor specialists were primarily male. Fortunately, this is beginning to change and more women are participating actively. The competition that transpires relates very closely to the competition between father and son for mother's affection, or mother and daughter for father's affection. Hence many of the emotions aroused in the competitive act, whether on the floor or behind a desk, are seen unconsciously as sexual. A loss is not seen unconsciously as a loss but rather as castration. Those who have had serious traumas in early childhood are particularly subject to such feelings. Typically they develop neurotic disorders. Women are subject to many of the same feelings.

Considerably more evidence can be cited. The common expression, "we really got screwed in the market," although not necessarily reflecting good taste, is typical of the manner in which some investors view the market. They feel as if the market has taken sexual advantage of them. There is no objective reason to relate to the market in such a fashion. The only realistic explanation is the one that has been presented here as an overview of Freud's work. There are other popular expressions about the market that have sexual overtones; they will not be repeated here.

This chapter is only a small indication of the manner in which classical psychoanalytic concepts apply to the marketplace. Certainly there will be those who have other interpretations. There will also be those who feel that I have not provided sufficient coverage of the topic. Since this is only a general text, I do not have sufficient time or space to delve into any one topic as deeply as might be desired. Those who wish to take the plunge, however, can find enough information at the public library to provide a lifetime of study.

REVIEW

1. Freudian theory stresses the importance of psychosexual development as an integral part or aspect of adult personality.

2. The many feelings to which a child is exposed can help create various unconscious reactions and attitudes to sexual experiences.

3. Such feelings are generalized and in adulthood become part of overall behavior.

4. Dreams, jokes, expressions, slips of the tongue, and attitudes are all symbolic of underlying sexual attitudes.

5. By helping a patient understand these feelings, the therapist can affect a cure.

25

Using Psychology to Maximize Investment Success

I am, both by profession and attitude, interested in only one thing: results. All that I have attempted to tell you, and all that I have sought to teach you, both by example and by instruction, will amount to nothing unless it is faithfully employed. Provided your investments are legal, the technique you have used does not matter so long as profits result. As indicated at the outset, my focus has therefore not been on the system but rather on the trader. Let us examine briefly where we have been, what we should have learned, what we can still learn, and how we can implement what has been expressed.

There lies a vast expanse of intellectual wilderness between education and expression. Lessons learned from a book will perhaps never be translated into action. Were we capable of internalizing and integrating all we have read and heard, many of our life's problems would be readily solved. Unfortunately our capacity to act on information is limited. There are, however, a number of proven psychological techniques that will help in the profitable implementation of what has been expressed here. Review, repetition, and reaction are the three R's of learning. Thus I advise you now to proceed to review, in outline form, each chapter of this book. I suggest you treat it as a textbook. Make an outline of what has been discussed, study the outline, examine the review at the end of each chapter, and internalize the concepts. You need not agree with what I have said. You need only observe the market to see that what I have said is valid.

Next, repeat the process. Attempt to put yourself into the picture as much as possible. In so doing, you will have personal contact with the concepts. You need not jump into the change process with both feet. Test some of the ideas on a limited scale. Acquire a feel for what has been

230

presented, and see if it has potential. Certainly the market will let you know very quickly if you are correct. If an idea appears to have merit, then follow up and take further action.

Finally, react to the more specific sections of this book. Set goals, implement them, design your own programs, read some of the recommended texts, ask relevant questions, but above all, act. Don't be content to just sit there, losing money, making bad investments, feeling sorry for yourself, and being jealous of others' success. Put your ideas to work and they will work for you. They will bring you the investment profits you seek. But you will never know if you don't act.

I have said on many occasions that it is a relatively simple matter to determine whether a market will go up or down. It is yet another to implement, with success, what has been decided. It is fortunate that the rules that must be followed in attaining market success are so simple; otherwise many basically average investors, myself included, would never have achieved wealth. In fact, the personal rules for investment success are so (deceptively) simple that they could all be overstated on half of an $8\frac{1}{2} \times 11$ inch piece of paper. We have all heard these rules over and over again. They do not bear repetition.

Let's step back and take a look at what has been discussed. First and foremost, the point has been repeatedly made that market prices are a function of supply and demand over the long run, but related to investor psychology over the short and intermediate term. The basics of market theory and psychology were discussed. Attention was given to the psychoanalytic versus behavioral methods as opposite ends of the continuum. An analogy was made between fundamentalist versus technician and medical versus behavioral models of human behavior. The basics of both major psychological theories were discussed with close consideration of their individual concepts relating to investor psychology. Sample programs for change were discussed along with key concepts such as interpersonal relationships, sex and the market, stress, the use of trading systems, losses and how to take them, broker-client relationships, the use of advisory services, and scheduling. A number of frequently asked questions were answered.

And now the rest is up to you. Within the limits of what I can transmit via the written word, I have provided you with many of the basics as well as directions to try in looking for answers. I would, in closing, leave you with several final suggestions I believe have merit in any trading program, for any individual, regardless of financial ability, and independent of experience.

Before investing in any market—stocks, commodity futures, options, real estate, or collectibles—make certain that the market you have chosen has the potential to lead you to the desired goal. If you seek the satisfaction that comes from social service, then you must not expect the market to bring you what you need. The market can only yield profit and the pleasure that accompanies being right. Expect more, and you will most likely be disappointed. Investments such as antiques, coins, or stamps can yield aesthetic satisfaction as well. Each avenue of investment, therefore, has its unique ability. You must make certain that your goals are realistic and, above all, within the scope of your selected area of endeavor.

After having decided where and when to invest, be certain to approach your program with all the seriousness of a neurosurgeon involved in a life-or-death operation. There is a tendency for many investors to be flippant, disorganized, casual, and unconcerned about their investments. This often leads to losses. Investing, trading, speculating, forecasting, money management, and advising are serious businesses. Unless given total consideration, their end result will not be positive. Dedication, persistence, thoroughness, and hard work are the keys to investment success.

Your most difficult task will not be prediction, but rather self-control. Expect to encounter some of the most difficult and frustrating personal experiences of your life. You will find that you are the most important element of the success equation.

In addition, you will rapidly discover, if you have not already done so, that attitude, state of health and emotion, interpersonal relations, stress, tension, and work environment will all have a market effect on your investment success. The more active your trading, the more susceptible you will be to these influences. Keep investment goals firmly in mind at all times. Set new goals after current objectives have been attained.

In the coming years, economists will continue to make advances in forecasting methodology. Trading systems will come and go. Computer technology has only recently made its mark in the area of econometric analysis and mechanical trading methods. But through it all the basic substance of price change will continue to be human emotion. Panic, fear, greed, insecurity, anxiety, stress, and uncertainty will endure as the primary forces of short-term price change. Success in the market is, in my opinion, not as complex or difficult as it appears to be. There are time-tested rules that, if religiously applied, will lead to profits. It's as simple as that and, at the same time, it's as complicated as that. The answer to investment success lies within.

26

Writings of the Masters: Study History to Learn about the Future

I maintain that the best and most meaningful lessons are learned from direct experience, yet there are ways in which we can acquire certain types of knowledge without suffering the attendant pain. One of these less painful methods of learning is through vicarious experience. Although indirect learning such as this in no way compares to the strength and power of direct stimulus-response reinforcement, there are many behavioral cues that can reach us through the indirect route. By watching others trade, we can learn a particular style and vocabulary. And by reading about how others have been successful in the markets, we can learn a great deal about our own technique.

My personal experiences have led me to the conclusion that all investors, traders, and speculators must include, as part of their market education, an intensive reading of works produced by the great "trading masters." To name but a few, these include the writings of Cutten, Pugh, Baruch, Livermore, Gann, and Wyckoff. Certainly there are many other individuals whose words of wisdom should be taken to heart. And there are many other texts of a technical nature that have made major contributions to the field. My concern is, however, with the psychological aspect of what has been experienced and recorded by those who have traded profitably through the years. If we can learn even one lesson from their experiences, if we can gain even one insight, or one inspiration, then the effort will have been well worthwhile. This is why I always recommend such reading as the first step in market education (or re-education). What exactly can we learn by spending time studying the masters' works? How can we apply their learning to our own? Is there a way in which we should approach the study of their writings? Have we indeed spent enough time learning from their errors? Should their teachings be read more than once? Here are some of my thoughts regarding these questions. I will attempt to give you some general rules of a psychological nature.

Why Read What They Had to Say?

There are those who believe that the markets of today are not like the markets of yesterday. There was less volatility in those days; there was more price manipulation; and there was considerably less volume. The fact remains, however, that investors and speculators were as much governed by their emotions as they are today. The common element in all great masters' writings is their repeated reference to psychological principles. Despite differences in technique, the net result of their achievements was almost exclusively a product of several key personality traits—patience, perseverance, determination, and rational action. These are all skills trading systems cannot teach us. They are all personal qualities that come with experience. And they are, in fact, the most basic and important tools a trader can possess. By vicariously experiencing the trials and tribulations of those who have been successful before us, we can gain the inspiration to help us carry on. We can acquire a general idea of the qualities that have helped others on the road to trading and investing riches. By reading what they had to say, we can shorten significantly the discovery process.

In addition to the indirect learning that may result from such readings, the investor who seeks to acquire new trading techniques can be so inspired. Frequently one develops original ideas about the market while familiarizing one's self with the approach of others. The synthesis of many readings can help formulate what appear to be totally unique technical and/or fundamental approaches. Not only can new systems be created, but old ideas, which may not have worked for others, can be avoided. In reading about the losses resulting from the use of certain concepts, we can avoid them, refine them, or study them closely before we implement them.

Last, and by no means least, the writings of successful investors can help encourage us when times are bad, and caution us when times are good. It helps to know that we are not alone in our struggle for success. It helps to know that others before us have experienced the same defeats and enjoyed similar successes. For the uninitiated, the rags to riches stories Jesse Livermore reports can provide goals and directions as well as comfort. When one realizes that the road to vast profits is a long and difficult one, any one profit or loss can be put in its proper time perspective. It is important to remember that most market wealth is acquired steadily over a period of years. This message will be clearly conveyed by the masters' writings.

Reading for Pleasure—Reading for Facts

There are many different ways in which your readings may be approached. For simple entertainment value, it is not necessary to maintain any organized study program. And there is certainly nothing wrong with reading for enjoyment! In fact, I strongly recommend that your first time through any market text should be primarily for enjoyment. Following this initial reading, return to the text for a more thorough, learning-oriented examination of the material. I suggest you use the following specific and time-tested method to achieve the maximum benefit from your reading:

1. Underline in the book.   If you do not wish to mark in your book, buy two copies, one for the shelf and one for repeated use. By underscoring relevant passages, concepts, or observations, you will highlight their importance. After the reading has been completed you may wish to scan through the underlined sections as a quick review. It would also be a good idea to categorize the underlining in different colors, according to topic. Technical trading rules might be underlined in blue, and psychological concepts in red, for example.

2. Make an outline.   I suggest that you make a topic outline of the book. If you do not know how to do this you can consult almost any text on English grammar or composition to learn how. The object of this lesson is organizational. By having a topic outline of what you are reading, you can gain some insight into the transitional events in the writer's life and experiences. This will provide you with a perspective and framework within which to evaluate your own experiences. Having an outline will also help you find key topics quickly when you wish to refer to them.

3. Make a list.   List the 10 most important psychological trading rules you have extracted from the text. These rules may not be the same for all individuals. They may, in fact, be different from the main points the author has stressed. The only important consideration should be their relevance and importance to you, the reader. Each book and author will have a unique set of rules. I suggest you keep them close at hand for ready referral.

4. Make note of common rules.   In your readings, it should become obvious that some trading rules are common to most successful investors. It is especially important to indicate these on your list. In fact, I suggest you draw up a list of those rules or observations that are common to all or most traders whose works you have read.

5. Take referrals.   If, in your readings, an author refers to another work of importance, note the reference and place it on a list of things to read. In so doing, you will broaden your base of readings. I advise you to study as many of the works on your list as possible; at times they may be more helpful than the book you are reading. They will, in turn, lead you to other useful sources.

6. Review rules frequently.   This will help "burn" the rules into your memory. It is no simple task to acquire a functional set of trading rules, and it is even more difficult to learn how and when to apply the rules. Constant exposure will keep them foremost in your mind. This will allow you to apply them frequently, which in turn will help you learn.

7. Your favorite author.   As you progress in your readings, you will begin to find favorite authors. Pursue your readings of these authors. Most likely you have identified with their experiences for a good reason. When you study their trading in greater detail, you may find additional reasons for your interest. Because you are attracted to what they have said and done, there is reason to believe that you either strive to duplicate their successes or strongly identify with their experiences. If you are especially interested in a certain "master," then make it one of your goals to study his work intensively.

8. Look for similarities and differences.   If you have a particular handicap or repetitive market error, attempt to determine how others have solved similar difficulties. This is perhaps one of the most efficient and effective ways of finding solutions to recurrent market problems. By drawing on the experiences of others, you can save yourself time and often money. Note also any large differences between your trading rules and those of successful traders. If there are too many radical differences, then you may be on the wrong track and a change could be helpful.

9. Reread them often. Although I have read most of the great works many times over they never seem to lose their appeal. And they never lose their instructive ability. It seems that there are new bits and pieces to be learned with each additional reading. It is for this reason that I recommend frequent reading. When I have suffered some losses in the market and feel my spirits getting low, I read my favorite market book to help inspire me. And it does!

Like most traders I have my own ideas as to which market readings are best. I do not wish to impose my own bias on you. Nevertheless, my list is the result of considerable experience and investigation. Certainly there are many other writings. I would advise you to read all of them if you have the time. Let me make clear precisely what I mean when I tell you to read writings of the "masters." I am not making reference to the rash of "How to Make a Million Dollars" books that have appeared on the market. I am referring strictly to the writings of those who actively traded the markets, with success, from the early 1900s through the mid-1950s. There have, indeed, been many capable traders since then. I have found, however, that lessons learned in the early 1900s have more of an impact on the individual trader than those of recent years. Note also that I am not referring to texts that explain various or specific trading systems. The type of book I suggest you look for is autobiographical, and not trading-system oriented. There are too many trading systems, each claiming to be better than the next. There are too few good traders to implement these systems.

Pages 279–285 provide you with a brief overview of trading masters whose works I suggest you read. I cannot do justice to the totality of their experiences or writings, but I believe that I can offer you some additional understanding of how important proper attitude and effective psychology can be in the overall attainment of success. In providing only brief coverage, I have chosen to place virtually no emphasis on the trading system each individual employed. My orientation is, as you certainly know by now, almost purely psychological.

REVIEW

1. Every investor should be familiar with the experiences and philosophies of those investors who have been successful.

2. Most of the market masters had their own psychologically based trading rules.

3. Many of the opinions and philosophies of famous investors are similar, even though they had different backgrounds and experiences and traded at different times.

4. By reading what they had to say about the emotional side of the market, and their experiences with it, we can help limit some of the losses that might be part of the learning process.

5. Several readings of each book can yield a wealth of information. Notes should be taken to maximize the learning process.

27

Creative Visualization and Guided Imagery

Several years ago my futures trading results began to deterio-rate. I found myself making foolish mistakes; mistakes I had not made in many years. I was riding losses contrary to the dictates of my systems. I was jumping out of profits quickly for fear they would disappear if I waited too long. My insecurity led to dissatisfaction with my trading signals and methods when in fact they were not at fault. In vain I searched for new approaches, spending many hours at the computer. Eventually I turned to other traders to ask for advice; to inquire as to what systems they were using. The more I looked, the less I found. The harder I searched, the more frustrated I became. The more I attempted to blame the system, the markets, the economy, the government, and other traders, the farther I traveled from the truth. For well over a year, the struggle and anguish continued, finally resulting in a pervasive feeling of despair and helplessness.

I called a psychoanalyst for help. "Come in and we'll talk about it," he said.

We talked about it. He suggested to me that I had fallen out of touch with conflicts and issues from my childhood which had apparently not been fully understood and resolved in the early 1970s when I had concluded several years of traditional psychoanalysis.

"Since then," he surmised, "you've married, become a father, enjoyed wealth and success in business, and you have, therefore, opened the way for new experiences with which you've never had to deal before. As a result, these new experiences have led to new conflicts that have affected your perception, self-confidence, and judgment. This has affected your trading negatively." It all sounded logical to me. I inquired as to what it might take to get me back on track, knowing all the while that there was no answer a psychoanalyst could provide to this question. And of course he refused to commit.

Naturally, I wanted a quick cure, a fast recovery, an immediate answer so that I could get back on track with my trading. I investigated several alternatives, the most intriguing of which was creative visualization and guided imagery. I'd like to share with you some of my experiences with these techniques.

The Basics of Creative Visualization and Guided Imagery

For many years, we've been told that the human mind has potential that is by far greater than its actual performance. We've been told that we use perhaps 10 to 20 percent of our mental capacity. And we have been advised to develop our mental powers more fully in order to make use of the marvelous mental computer that we possess. But we've rarely been told exactly how to do this. I find it most incongruous that so much of what we learn in our formal education depends on rote memory work but that, at the same time, we receive no specific instruction on how to achieve an outstanding memory. There are specific memory techniques that permit near total recall; techniques which have been handed down since the time of the great Greek and Roman Empires. These tried and true methods are not taught to students in spite of the fact that their success in school and their success in life depends on a vast amount of memory work. Medical students, whose training consists of heavy memorization, have developed mnemonic devices to facilitate their laborious task; however, these techniques are, as I've already pointed out, *not* part of their formal education. It is a sad commentary on the Western system of education that we place so much emphasis on results but that we provide so little in the way of training that will ensure success. To the motivated seeker of wisdom, memory techniques are available as near as the closest library; however, that's really not the way things should be. Memory methods should be taught as a formal course in every grade of elementary and high school, but primarily in the elementary grades where they can help form a solid structure for what will be added in the future.

Our educational system has also been guilty of failure to fully develop other aspects of the human mind as well. Such vital areas as dream analysis and control, hypnosis, biofeedback, unconscious processes, reflexive behavior, extrasensory perception, and near death experiences have received only minimal attention in the academic world. In fact, virtually any concept of methodology that is not in the mainstream of traditional Western education has been rejected as either unscientific, unacceptable, unpalatable, uncouth, untestable, un-American, unhealthy, or a host of other "un's."

Another victim of the "un" crowd is guided imagery and creative visualization, two related techniques that have the potential to facilitate the development of new ideas, techniques, relationships, and methods of thought. While both methods have been given a significant amount of attention in the so-called "New Age" literature of the 1980s and 1990s, they have not found their way to the level of public education and, I suspect, never will. Their rejection by pedagogues and social scientists rests upon their loose system of concepts and structures which, in the minds of their detractors, make them unfit for educational consumption. The motivated student is, as usual, left to draw upon his or her own efforts in order to acquire the necessary knowledge and skills in these areas.

Guided imagery (GI) and creative visualization (CV) are essentially the same techniques. In both cases the subject calls upon his or her powers of imagination in order to creatively structure new mental images for the purpose of achieving any or all of several goals. These goals are as follows:

1. Relaxation.   By creating through mental imagery certain images, scenes and/or vignettes, either independently or with the assistance of a facilitator, the individual will induce a state of mental and physical relaxation whose purpose is nothing more than deep relaxation and stress relief. In many ways, this application of CV and GI is similar to the end result of Transcendental Meditation which can be extremely valuable in tension relief and which has been repeatedly demonstrated scientifically as a stress-reducing and blood pressure lowering technique.

2. Problem solving.   By mentally attacking a particular problem using a systematic approach based on creating mental images, the individual can arrive at potentially new and powerful solutions to specific problems whether these be personal, financial, creative, or scientific. Various mental exercises allow the individual to perceive potentially new solutions to problems whose solutions may have been obscured by a variety of factors such as personal conflicts, negative interpersonal relationships, or a host of classic defense mechanisms. Typically such problem-solving aspects of GI and CV require the assistance of another individual (i.e., therapist, guide, teacher, facilitator) who will direct the process.

3. Creativity.   This is yet another area that can be greatly enhanced through the use of CV and GI techniques. While this can be achieved without the assistance of a guide, it is often helpful to recruit the assistance of a trained professional who can help you maximize the experience. I will describe this and other approaches later on.

4. Fears and phobias.   By detailed visualization of the fears and/or phobias in a nonthreatening environment, the individual may find that his or her fears are not nearly as bad as imagined or that there is a logical answer to the fears that will prevent their recurrence.

5. Self-confidence limits the performance of many individuals not only in business and investing but in interpersonal relationships as well. GI can help the individual come to grips not only with the cause or causes of their confidence crisis but with solutions to it as well.

6. Medical problems have reportedly been either cured or significantly improved through the use of CV methods that focus upon enhancing the body's ability to fight disease and that attempt to fortify the immune system. While there is considerable controversy regarding the efficacy of such methods, I believe that these techniques can have positive results. I will give a specific example later on.

While these are some of the more common uses of creative visualization and guided imagery, there are myriad other applications limited only by the imagination of the individual. As I've noted earlier, the methods of CV and GI are not scientific and, hence, subject to the usual criticisms of such techniques. But science and progress are not necessarily synonymous. Science may be contraindicated in psychological and spiritual growth. Imagination transcends the traditional boundaries of science and often leads to scientific discovery. In 1909, for example, Newcombe, then one of the world's greatest mathematicians proved scientifically that a heavier than air craft carrying human beings was impossible. Three years later, the Wright brothers, beginning with a dream, proved him wrong.

Techniques of Guided Imagery and Creative Visualization

The basic methods of CV and GI are very simple and direct. Typically the subject sits comfortably in a chair or rests quietly on a recliner or couch. The guide talks while the subject listens and visualizes the scene or scenes being presented by the guide. The first task is to become as relaxed as possible. This is achieved by using a method such as systematic muscle relaxation or deep breathing exercises. The goal is for the subject to create a mental scene that will either stimulate solutions, facilitate solutions, or prompt entirely new understandings of situations. The relaxed atmosphere helps unlock creative energies of the individual in ways which would not be possible in a different situation.

A session can last from just a few minutes to over an hour depending upon the complexity of the imagery or task and the response of the subject. There is no one-to-one correlation between the length of the session and the positive or negative results of the session.

In addition, there are many variations on the theme of the subject matter used to create the images. These are, to a great extent, a function of the session's purpose. Here is an example of what the therapist might say to the subject. With the subject seated or resting comfortably, the therapist or guide begins to speak in a slow, steady and soft voice. A typical GI session for the purpose of relaxation might proceed as follows:

> Relax. Take a deep breath and feel the relaxation spreading through your body from the top of your head to the tips of your toes. Concentrate on your breathing and know that with every breath you are becoming more and more relaxed; more and more relaxed; more and more relaxed. Now imagine that you are resting comfortably in a lush green forest. You look up and see the dense green trees. You smell the forest smells and feel the cool, damp air around you. In the distance you hear many different bird sounds as you see little creatures scurrying back and forth along. You feel relaxed and at one with the forest. With each breath you are becoming more and more relaxed. You see the blue sky through a few cracks of light in the forest roof. Soon the sky begins to darken as dense, dark clouds roll across the sky. The forest becomes dark as the smell of rain pervades your realm. At first a few cool sprinkles of rain fall on your face . . . .

The preceding was just a brief example of how CV might be used in order to induce a state of relaxation. After approximately 15 to 30 minutes of this "treatment," the subject feels extremely relaxed. The visualization exercise has achieved its purpose. Following several such sessions, the subject will be able to achieve the relaxed state independently and at will.

Now let's look at an example of CV that's more closely related to our area of concern. Early in this chapter I told you of how I came to discover the use of these techniques as a means of helping me overcome some difficulties I was experiencing in my trading. By chance I was referred to a psychologist, Dr. A, who had an office in her home, not too far from mine. She was among the first to use these techniques in virtually all areas of treatment. Following a lengthy telephone conversation with Dr. A, I felt very confident in her ability and I was certainly willing to try something new in my search to eliminate the trading problems I had been having for many months.

In our first meeting, we discussed the exact nature of my difficulties. Dr. A was unwilling to accept general statements from me, rather she probed and prompted for specifics. This is, in my experience, an important initial indication of success in treatment. You will find, as I have, that specificity is always necessary as a first step in remediating problems whether they are related to interpersonal situations, the markets, or business. The road to success is unclear unless you make it clear—and the only way to do that is to know exactly where you're going. In order to change behavior, whether by behavioral or more traditional means you need to know exactly what the behavior is, under what conditions it appears, and its consequences. Different treatment modalities will focus upon different aspects of the chain; however, a truly effective and efficient program will focus on all components in order to provide total and prompt relief and improvement. My impressions of Dr. A were, therefore, very positive which, of course, will facilitate improvement in any therapeutic situation.

My first session with Dr. A was designed to acquaint me with her techniques and to acquaint her with the specific nature of my problems. Since I practiced as a psychologist and had considerable experience in the area of clinical psychology for a number of years prior to and during my career change to futures trading, I had already prepared a specific list of the behaviors which were responsible for my failures and which were limiting my successes. The list I discussed with Dr. A was as follows:

1. Riding losses. My biggest problem was failure to close out losing positions when my system(s) indicated that the loss must be taken. Losses were, therefore, too large and destroyed the statistical validity of my systems' test results. While I knew that the logical thing to do was to close out the losers by the rules, I found excuses each and every time. I had fallen into the "give it some more time" trap which, on occasion worked to my advantage and which, as a result, conditioned me to avoid taking losses.

2. Finding new rules to justify riding losses. I observed that when I was in a losing position that should have been closed out, I quickly enlisted the help of my computer in order to reinforce my desire to avoid taking the loss. I was intellectualizing the losing position by hiding behind the computer tests. The availability of affordable hardware and software for system and indicator testing has helped create new problems for traders and investors, one of which is the "let's see what the computer says" syndrome. I found myself searching feverishly for a technical excuse to maintain my position. And eventually I found one. It is almost always possible to find an excuse for anything if you look long and hard enough. And a computer will definitely make the job easier while making the results appear more valid.

3. Loss of self-confidence. Naturally, this led to a complete deterioration of my self-confidence. I found myself unwilling to trade, fearful to enter positions, and afraid of the markets. I began to feel that every trade I made was a loser from the start and I felt that my many years of market experience were useless. Naturally, I blamed virtually everyone and everything for these problems including the economy, government policies, floor traders, the exchanges, the trading public, and, of course, myself.

4. Loss of discipline as another natural outgrowth. While loss of discipline was certainly responsible for my riding losses, it was also an after effect of the primary problem. Once you have made a mistake you are more likely to make others. Unless you break into the chain of events very early in the life of the problems you will continue to blunder until you eventually break every important rule in the book. This is why it's so very important to get back on track as soon as possible.

This was the list that I discussed at length with Dr. A. She was interested in assessing my feelings prior to, during, and subsequent to the errors. The simple act of airing my problems (called ventilating in psychological terminology) was helpful; however, I knew that this was not a final solution. Once she had acquired a good understanding of my difficulties as well as some basics about the markets that were necessary in order to provide a framework within which to understand my behavior, we began to work on several CV and GI techniques, the first of which was a simple relaxation exercise similar to what has already been described. Following a few sessions on relaxation the work began in earnest. Here is an example of the way the problems were "treated."

Session 6

Dr. A: Today we'll focus on taking losses when the system indicates that this must be done. Since you've been having difficulty closing out losing positions we'll focus on a visualization that will help relieve the problem. First I'd like you to get comfortable and relax. Take a deep breath . . . hold it . . . good . . . now let it go. Now I'd like you to visualize the following scene. You are standing in a large field. It's summertime and the air is warm. The sky is a clear blue and a few lazy clouds roll by as you gaze slowly upward. You see the trees swaying as the warm wind blows lightly, brushing your face with its healing energy. In the distance you see a mountain rising high against the plain, its peaks white and base dense with green vegetation. You are feeling driven now to walk toward the mountain in order to appreciate its majesty from close up. You begin your walk. As you walk you see the mountain becoming larger as the terrain begins to change from flat to hilly and then from hilly to a slow and steady incline. You stand still for a few moments and admire the scene which now appears before you; the dense green forest of towering evergreens; the rocky mountain sides and snow-capped peaks.

Suddenly you feel an intense urge to scale the mountain; you seek to overcome the challenge, knowing intuitively that in overcoming this immense obstacle you will find an answer to obstacles which have been plaguing you for many months now. You decide that you must climb the mountain and find the answer.

You know that the climb will not be achieved without considerable effort, but you know that you can do it as long as you apply yourself. You begin the arduous task. You climb for many hours and your task becomes more difficult as the incline of the mountain increases. You perspire profusely and you realize now that the temperature is dropping. You are hot and cold at the same time. Soon the ground is covered with snow and the air is thin. Although you find it difficult to breathe you are inspired as you see the peak in sight, knowing that an answer awaits you.

At long last you arrive at the apex. Your legs and arms are shaking partly in fear and partly in weakness yet you overcome both in order to enjoy the wondrous beauty of the flat and distant land below. You appreciate also the distance you have traveled in your quest for progress.

As you scan the world below, you notice what appears to be a human silhouhette in the distance, also scaling the peak. At first you dismiss the figure as a shadow, yet it continues to move and grows larger as it comes closer. Soon, to your great surprise, you realize that it is, indeed, another climber. You watch intently as the form begins to take shape; it's an elderly gentleman who appears to possess great wisdom. He glances your way as if to indicate that he's on his way to see you. And indeed, as he reaches the peak he begins to walk toward you. As he does, you notice that he carries in his hand a small book. He approaches. On his face you discern a knowing look. You feel a sense of peace in his space; a self-awareness and a self-confidence which is difficult to describe verbally. Without words you exchange a common knowledge. You know that he knows you are deeply troubled; that you are searching for an answer. Without warning he hands you the book he has been carrying and as you accept it he turns to leave. You watch him disappear slowly in the distance as he begins his descent from the mountain. Within a few moments he is gone and you have only the book he has given you as a remembrance of this peculiar event. You glance at the book. The title reads "Answers." You sense that the "answers" it contains are important to you and you hasten to open the book. As you turn the cover page you see that the book does not contain many pages, perhaps ten at the most and that the pages do not contain much print. Yet you know the "answers" to be valuable. You turn the pages slowly, one by one and assimilate the knowledge contained therein. Here are the answers for which you have been searching these last six months; answers which are clear, concise and to which you can relate. You take your time to read each and every answer slowly, carefully, and methodically. You study them, first in sequence and then randomly. You see them clearly now and they make great sense to you. Yet you also realize in your reading that they are all answers you have had before but, for reasons which may never be known to you, you have repressed or suppressed them. You examine the answers one by one. You can see them clearly and in considerable detail. In reading them you realize that the answers are simple and that they are answers you have known all along.

You feel a great sense of relief and peace as you close the book and place it in your backpack. You begin your trek back to civilization. The book and its answers will be with you to read and refer to whenever and wherever you need them.

This trip has come to an end now. Open your eyes and feel relieved and at peace with your knowledge.

The session was over. While I did not utter a single syllable during the visualization experience, my mind was focused and extremely active. The process of my journey had rekindled insights and repressed knowledge which came to the surface in the form of concise answers. During the next few weeks, I did not consciously apply the answers in my book, however, I found myself employing the answers automatically, reflexively, as I had done for so many years before. The visualization experience had helped me rediscover what I already knew but had, for one reason or another, forgotten.

Additional Suggestions for Using Creative Visualization and Guided Imagery

I am certain that CV and GI will arouse positive feelings in many of my readers but that others will be repulsed by the idea as either magical, unprofessional, or otherwise unpalatable. This is understandable. Traditional psychologists and psychiatrists as well as individuals who are not sufficiently open minded to experiment with new techniques will not find the energy to attempt such processes. I have, however, found both techniques to be very valuable in all types of treatment. This is true for simple relaxation, control of blood pressure, or the resolution of trading problems. I have had sufficient experience on the receiving end of CV and GI to give you the following suggestions should you be interested in pursuing them for your own benefit:

1. Seek out an experienced therapist to assist you in the process. This is very important. While there are many books and tapes that purport to provide the necessary assistance, success is difficult to achieve without professional guidance.

2. Be certain that you practice what you learn in your sessions. The knowledge you have gained will only be helpful if it is translated into actions.

3. Don't expect magical answers. While many problems can be resolved very quickly, some are resistant to change and require many sessions.

4. Don't restrict yourself to resolving only trading problems. Many personal and family problems can interfere with your trading. And you may not be aware of what is happening. Therefore, don't be afraid to take a "back door" approach to trading problems by dealing with these difficulties first.

5. If you try these methods and they don't work for you within several sessions, then don't continue. It's senseless to waste time and money on something that's not working for you.

6. Once you have made some progress with a professional therapist you may record your own instructions and play them for yourself, in effect, becoming your own guide.

7. The best advice I can give you is to be open minded. Many things can be achieved if you keep an open mind. However, if you are rigid and unwilling to accept new ideas, or even to try them before you reject them, then you will not succeed in life. Naturally, if you have found answers that serve you well, you need not look too hard for new techniques and knowledge; however, if you find that what has worked for you in the past is no longer effective, then you must search out the new and unusual.

28

Overcome Your Worst Fears: How Psychology Facilitates Success

My personal experiences during more than 20 years as a futures trader have led me to the inescapable conclusion that the worst thing a trader can do is to run from problems. This is, as you know, true in our personal lives as well. Problems can be avoided and swept under the rug for only so long before the rug gets lumpy and you can no longer walk on it safely. While most trading problems are self-limiting, that is, they come and go without becoming too serious, some are chronic and become worse if left unresolved, untreated, or unsolved. While fear of failure is a potent fear, it is also a fear that can feed on itself. You become afraid of fear and the fear is magnified. You are so afraid to fail that you magnify the consequences of failure many fold until you are unwilling to attempt any solution. Most fantasies, whether good or bad, are not nearly as great as are the realities. Fantasies are most often gross exaggerations of the truth. Therefore, if you fear losses and allow this fear to affect your trading, your fear will be worse than will be the actual loss. You will avoid trading in order to avoid the fearful fantasy. And the end result will be worse than it would have been if you allowed yourself to come face to face with the fear.

Types of Fear

Although many traditional psychologists will tell you that most fears originate in early childhood as castration fear, both in men and in women, it is difficult for most of us to relate to this concept. While I am

250

not suggesting that this may not be a real fear among many individuals, there are still other fears that are more easily recognized as originating in the here and now or even in childhood. Such concerns as the fear of rejection, fear of failure, fear of success, fear of disapproval, fear of losses, fear of trading large positions all are very specific fears, each and every one of which may be overcome by the application of many different psychological techniques. There are many different ways to overcome these problems or to minimize their negative effects, however, taking action is more important than the actual actions which are taken.

How to Recognize Fear

Fear can take many forms. It can express itself physiologically in the form of cold hands, a racing heart and elevated pulse, profuse sweating, and a tight anxious feeling in the pit of your stomach. The fear syndrome is a by-product of the "fight-flight" response which is one of the most primitive emotions known. It dates back to archetypal man—to the days of cave dwellers whose survival was often a direct function of their ability to defend against human and animal predators. The rush of adrenaline that results in these feelings causes us to either stand up and fight or to turn and run. Although we no longer face the same struggle every day, the fight or flight response remains. While this response can be exceptionally helpful in a true life or death crisis since it mobilizes our defenses, it is not helpful in the trading situation. It is important for traders to realize that we do not face visible adversaries in the markets; that we cannot overcome these invisible market enemies by brute force. Nor can we avoid our invisible market foes by running from them. The fear that we face as traders involves fear of intangible foes which can be even more threatening than a tangible enemy since it allows one to conjure up infinitely more monstrous fantasies inspired by our active imaginations.

Face the Challenge

The only way to overcome the fear is by facing it. However, the method is considerably different from the one used by our prehistoric forebears. Running from the challenge will not solve the problem. It is not an option. I suggest that whenever you find yourself attempting to avoid a trading problem by running from it, you immediately rule this out as an option. If you intend to trade tomorrow, then every error must be systematically eliminated and every fear must be faced and overcome today. As soon as the urge to run presents itself, you must face the problem and fight it— not in the traditional sense, but with common sense, understanding, insight, discipline, skill, and consistency. Frequently, you cannot overcome your worst fears by yourself. However, if you become aware of the fear early enough and if you admit to it early enough, it will not grow, and you will overcome it while it is still very weak. But if you wait too long, you will allow it to grow strong and it will be impossible to eliminate without professional help.

I've faced many market challenges since the 1960s when I made my first trade. And I've run from many fears as well. I have come to understand first hand how fears rarely vanish on their own. While the methods I've used to analyze and overcome my own fears is not highly systematic, I feel that I can offer you a number of concise suggestions that will help you face the challenges rather than run from them. These suggestions are not necessarily in order of importance or implementation. They will be given following a more detailed examination of the different types of trading fear and their origin.

Fear of Losses

Fear originates both from profits as well as from losses. This may seem surprising to you, however, I know it to be the case. Most traders become fearful of trading following a series of losses or after one large loss. Few traders can withstand the pressures of more than three consecutive losses. After the third loss they begin to doubt their trading system, their money management principles, their trading skills, and/or their wisdom. Yet logic and an understanding of trading systems clearly indicates that some trading systems will experience as many as 25 consecutive losing trades before getting back on the road to success. This is especially true of moving average-based systems (as I demonstrated in my book *Timing Signals*). Intellectually the trader knows that numerous consecutive losses can occur when following trading systems, however, emotionally this knowledge is insufficient to overcome the fear that all of one's capital or more will be lost before the system gets back on track.

The fear of loss is associated mentally with the loss of ability, the loss of power, the loss of masculinity, the loss of femininity, and/or the loss of nourishment. We fear that losing money will diminish our power or that it will leave us homeless, without sustenance, or without sexual ability. To a certain extent, there is some truth behind some of these fears, however, they are grossly exaggerated fears. If the money you are using for trading is "scared money" then you have every reason to be fearful. By "scared money" I mean money that should not be used for trading. If you have broken one of the cardinal rules of trading by risking capital which you cannot afford to risk, your fears are justified and they may very well be realized, sooner rather than later. If, however, you have been sensible in your decision to trade by using risk capital only, then your fears are clearly illogical and given their lack of rationality they must be totally ignored or they will become your undoing. Accept the fact that the capital is nothing but risk capital and that it was gone before you started trading. If you assume at the outset that the money you have put up for the purpose of speculation is lost before you even begin trading, then you will not fear losses and they will not cause you to act irrationally. The best way to overcome the fear of losses is to be prepared for the worst before it happens. The best defense for fear of losses is a strong offense.

Another way of overcoming the fear of losses is to be familiar with your trading system. If you have thoroughly researched your trading system, you will know its limitations. Specifically, you will be aware of how many losses your system has taken in the past and what its worst dollar drawdown has been. *Do not assume that this will be your worst case scenario.* You must assume that your worst case will be worse than what the hypothetical system test has revealed. *Always assume that things will be worse.* In so doing, you will be prepared for what may come. And the preparation will help you avoid the fear.

Fear of Profits

Are you surprised that I mention fear of profits? Most traders assume that they will have no problem handling profits, yet in practice many traders commit some of their worst blunders when they're riding a profit.

If you know the markets and trading systems, you know what the accuracy of even the best systems is, at most, 75 percent. And 75 percent is a rare case indeed. The fact is that most systems run between 25 and 60 percent accuracy with the vast majority in the 30 to 45 percent range. Logic dictates that more than half your trades will be losers. We also know that of the trades which are winners, about half will be small to mediocre winners. This leaves about 20 percent of the trades as fairly large winners. Of these only about half will be very large winners. The fact is that about 80 to 90 percent of the profits in many trading systems are derived from a relatively small number of trades. It is impossible for the trader to know a priori which trades will be the big winners.

Now consider the fact that most traders become extremely anxious when they're riding a profit. They have frequently suffered numerous losses and then, when presented with a profit, they are fearful that it will disappear. They cling anxiously to the profit. And when it appears that the profit may be deteriorating, they exit the trade, contrary to what their system dictates, relieved to have the profit. All too often they then sit and watch, without a position in the market, in disgust, as the trade they were in becomes immensely profitable.

The fear of profit is actually the fear that a profit will disappear. In fact, this is a fear that can be totally eliminated when the trader understands the nature of his or her system and of the market. Edwin Lefevre in his classic book *Reminiscences of a Stock Market Operator* said it best when he said that "you can't get poor taking profits but that you can't get rich either." What he really meant was that you must do everything in your power to ride profits as long as possible. You must avoid the temptation to take a small profit regardless of what you want to do impulsively if your system tells you to hold on to the position. This is the only way you will ever be successful unless you have mastered the art of short-term trading without a trading system.

I do not discount the fact that there are individuals who can do extremely well second guessing or intuiting the markets. I would be among the first to agree that extrasensory perception and clairvoyance can be used to discern the future direction of prices, however, it is the rare individual indeed who possesses the gifts of precognition. And even then the ability to predict is inconsistent.

If, therefore, you rely on a trading system to pinpoint market entry signals for you while relying on your own judgment or whim to get you out, you will be doing yourself a disservice in the long run because you will not be allowing your system to achieve its full potential. The fear of losing a profit, even a small one, will be your undoing.

In order to help overcome this fear, I suggest you trade multiple positions instead of single lots. In other words, instead of buying one contract of soybeans, for example, buy two. Trade one of the contract strictly according to the rules and signals in your trading system. Trade the other contract as you wish. This may satisfy your natural impulse to circumvent the system and to avoid the fear of losing a profit. After you have done so for a while compare the results of what you have accomplished following your fear, and what you have achieved by following your system(s).

Fear of Disapproval and Fear of Rejection

These are both normal and natural fears that are common to all individuals no matter what their position in life, social class, race, color, or creed; they are equal opportunity fears, however, they vary in intensity from one individual to another as a function of personality, achievements, insight, and interpersonal relationships. Each and every human being fears that failure will result in rejection and disapproval by peers, spouses, family, and society in general. The desire to succeed, particularly in capitalist societies is intense. It can create pressures that lead to a host of psychological, physical, and psychophysical consequences. The intense pressure for success during the 1980s and 1990s in Japan, for example, has taken its toll on Japanese students, resulting in an outbreak of suicides. In America, teenage suicides have increased markedly due to social pressures and the fear of rejection by peers. And fear of failure has driven even some of the world's most well-known industry leaders, politicians, and financiers to crime and deception. The fear of disapproval and the rejection it usually brings are powerful negative forces that can create a host of serious difficulties.

Understanding the Fear of Disapproval and Rejection

Both of these fears are related inasmuch as rejection is usually the result of disapproval. Both originate in early childhood as outgrowths of parental childrearing techniques which, in all too many cases, rely much too heavily on negatives rather than on positives. Children are told that if they do not do as their parents wish, they will not be loved, or that they will be punished, or that they will be ridiculed. The wish to avoid the removal of love and the need to avoid disapproval force involuntary compliance and exert unnecessary pressure on children. A great deal more can be achieved by maintaining positive attitudes rather than by using negatives to shape behavior. Failure is a negative in and of itself. It does not require additional negative response from parents and teachers. Unfortunately, we have all experienced too much of the negative and not enough of the positive. As adults we find ourselves doing things we do not want to do. We continue to carry old learning and find ourselves dissatisfied with the things we are doing but we are not certain as to why we are unhappy. Certainly not all unhappiness is caused by the negative effects of disapproval and rejection as used during the formative years of childhood, however, many of the things we do today are motivated by the desire to avoid rejection and disapproval, and this does not foster positive relationships. We continue to pursue a profession we do not want because the fear of disapproval and rejection, originally perpetuated by our parents, has been generalized to society and spouse. The source of such fears is, therefore, deeply rooted in childhood and, in reality, has no rational bearing on our current situations. Furthermore, they have nothing to do with the markets except in our own minds. A study of great traders shows that many have experienced numerous setbacks and failures on the road to success. Very few were instant winners. The fact is that you can't succeed unless you fail many times along the way.

How Fear of Rejection and Disapproval Can Affect Your Trading

Some fears can motivate positive behavior but most don't. Behavioral psychologists have demonstrated that learning as a function of grossly negative consequences can occur after a single exposure to the intensely negative consequences. A severe burn on a hot stove, for example, will be enough to make you careful for the rest of your life. Such "one trial learning" can be effective if the alternative to the negative behavior is very clear. In other words, if you touch a hot stove and suffer a severe burn you will know that you must not touch the stove. The way to avoid the burn is very clear—don't touch the hot stove. In some individuals, such an experience can develop into a phobia to stoves. A phobic reaction to the traumatic event of being burned on the stove would cause the individual to avoid stoves altogether. The person so afflicted might never enter a kitchen; might generalize the fear to objects that look like stoves, or even to all objects that emit heat.

An intensely negative experience in the markets, on the other hand, will not, in and of itself teach you anything. There are only a few things you can do right in the market but the list of errors is, by comparison, immense. By adding disapproval to the already negative experience of a loss, you have added nothing constructive. In fact, you have added a destructive element since it may cause you to generalize the fear into a fear of trading. Fear of trading is just that; you will avoid the disapproval and rejection that comes with losses by avoiding the markets entirely. But your response may be more subtle than a complete avoidance response. You may intellectualize the process by becoming extremely selective about trades, by rejecting trades on the basis of what you have conjured up in your mind as a good reason, or by not following your system and, thereby, not having up-to-date information on which to trade. The human mind is capable of unlimited self-subterfuge. If there is a way to deceive yourself, you will find it.

How to Avoid the Negative Effects of Rejection and Disapproval

I have a few simple suggestions for you if you are suffering from fear motivated by rejection and disapproval.

1. Don't discuss the markets with anyone, particularly with those who are supposed to be close to you. Stick to this rule rigidly if the people in your family or if your closest friends are inclined to be negative toward you when you fail. You are sufficiently negative toward yourself and don't need any additional disapproval.

2. Make an assessment of the "negative" individuals in your life. Be especially careful to avoid any negative comments from them by avoiding issues related to the markets, your trading, your successes, your failures, and so on. Negative individuals can give you negative ideas about yourself whether you accept these consciously or not.

3. Endorse yourself. In other words, reward yourself for your successes and accept your failures for what they are. Failure is a very important and very real part of the trading game. Success in this game without failure is impossible for all but very, very few.

4. Understand the worst aspects of your trading system. If you know the worst case scenario in terms of drawdown and consecutive losses then you'll be more patient with the system, not allowing it to affect you negatively.

5. Be very careful in your selection of a broker. Brokers can influence their clients in many subtle and not so subtle ways. If your self-confidence is at a low point, a few well chosen words, bad or good can prompt you to change your behavior. Most often changes inspired by such comments are not for the better.

6. Understand that fantasy is often much better or much worse than reality. Our minds can construct the most positive and unrealistic scenes as well as the most negative and fear-inspiring fantasies. Fear of disapproval and rejection can be made worse by destructive fantasies. Don't spend much time fantasizing what could happen because when it finally does happen, it won't be nearly as bad as you have imagined it would be. Nor, for that matter will things be as good as you fantasized them to be.

7. Train yourself to recognize the onset of all fears, whether their source is the external world or your own harsh self-judgment. The best time to avoid the destructive effects of responding to failure or feared failure is to act as soon as you see them developing. If you remain aware of your reactions and realize that rejection and disapproval can set in, you can squelch them immediately.

8. Make a list of your worst market fears. Consider the following broad categories: Fear of losses, failure, rejection, disapproval, bankruptcy, ridicule, success, giving back profits, too many successive losses, trading system failure, large positions, specific markets, limit moves, unexpected news.

Once you've made a list of your worst fears (perhaps your fears don't even appear on the preceding list) make a few notes and attempt to understand the source of your fear. Once the source or stimulus is recognized, take decisive action(s) to limit the source or to avoid it if it is impossible to eliminate it.

I have found fear, regardless of its source, to be one of the most destructive emotions to which a trader can fall victim. It forces a host of losing behaviors; it paralyzes traders, it distracts from constructive action and thinking and it forces traders to actions they might not otherwise take. Do your best to understand it and to minimize its destructive influences on your behavior. And remember that fear of virtually anything in life most often arises from lack of understanding or ignorance. While many fears are reasonable and justified, reality is often much less fearful than fantasy.

29

Why Too Many Traders and Investors Lose

If you've traded stocks or futures even for a relatively brief period of time, then you understand how very difficult it is to be successful at this game. Reason and knowledge tell us that the rules of stock and futures trading are relatively logical and that success should not be too difficult to attain. We are shamelessly barraged daily by advertisements, claims and testimonials that consistent profits are not only possible, but relatively easy to attain. As an exercise, I surveyed the advertisements in a recent issue of *Futures* magazine. There were 61 advertisements in total. Of the 61, more than half, about 35, were for futures exchanges, data vendors, brokers and/or non-advisory related services. Of the remaining 26 advertisements, 21, or over 80 percent, promoted products, systems, seminars, or services that claimed to improve trading results or offered "outstanding" systems. An advertisement for one trading system went so far as to guarantee profits within the first 60 days of its use or the entire purchase price of the system would be refunded. An examination of the less expensive, classified advertisements showed an even greater percentage of fantastic claims.

On the surface, it would appear that there are many trading systems, methods, and timing indicators that have profit potential. Those of us who have developed and tested trading systems know that although profitable systems are not easy to find, they *do exist.* But as the Zen philosopher said, "every front has a back . . . and the bigger the back, the bigger the front." Simply stated, every trading system, no matter how well it performs in hypothetical testing, has its limitations. The greater the rewards promised by the system, the greater the risk exposure. Stock and futures trading involve risk. There is no system, method, or indicator that does not entail some degree of risk. We accept this as a fact of

259

trading life. As strange as this may sound to you, many traders and investors fail to understand the true meaning of risk. They feel that risk is for other traders. Only when confronted with the reality of risk and loss do they comprehend its full impact. Only when the threat of loss is real can they respond. And when they do respond it is, all too often, an inappropriate response.

Traders and Investors Are Not Created Equal

It is the nature of a trader's individual response to risk that separates winners from losers. My studies of trader behavior as well as the analysis of my own behavior during 23 years of trading and investing have led me to the inescapable conclusion that trading systems, methods, and indicators comprise perhaps 25 percent of the total equation for success; that 15 percent is good fortune; and that the remaining 60 percent depends on trader response to the system he or she is using; and to the markets themselves.

All traders are not created equal when it comes to trading discipline—some are more reactive than others; some more tense than others; some too confident; others too sensitive; and others too detached. It is the response of the trader which constitutes the single most important variable in the equation for trading success. Too many traders lose money in the stock and futures markets simply because they *do not possess the skills necessary to implement a trading system effectively, systematically, or in a consistent fashion.*

It Doesn't Have to Be This Way

The sad and frustrating fact is that this deplorable situation needn't exist. I contend that by following some of the very basic rules presented in this book, traders and investors can easily improve their results. Although the important rules are considerably more difficult to learn and to follow consistently, they are well within reach of virtually all traders and investors. The first step to internalizing the rules is to recognize that an immediate change in behavior is necessary. The next step is to eliminate certain behaviors. And the final, but crucial step is to replace these behaviors with new ones. This is, of course, the most difficult step. Once this process has been completed, it is vital to maintain the new behaviors through practice, and to avoid regression to old and counterproductive habits.

There Are Many Ways to Achieve the Desired Results

Regardless of what you may have read in some books or articles, there is no single best way to change trading behavior. There is no single method that works for *all* individuals because each trader has a different market personality. The best way for you is the way that brings results.

Before giving you some suggestions, I'd like to remind you that a good trading system in the hands of an undisciplined trader is frequently a losing proposition, just as a mediocre trading system in the hands of a disciplined trader can be a winning proposition. A trading system is like a race car. While a trained driver can win races and perform incredible maneuvers, an untrained driver can crash within a few minutes of driving. It is important to be familiar with the workings of your machine, to know its pitfalls, its strengths, and its shortcomings. And it is important to capitalize on the assets of the system—becoming aggressive when the system is in a period of strength.

These skills are not developed instantaneously—they take time to form. In conjunction with an intimate knowledge of your system, you will need to acquire and nourish the following skills:

1. Consistency. This quality covers a multitude of behaviors and includes everything from placing orders to enter and exit by the rules, to keeping your system data updated as required. Consistency is a quintessential aspect of all learning. In order to achieve consistent results, consistent behavior is necessary. If you do not follow a system with consistency, you will never know whether the system works or not. You'll only have the hypothetical results—and they won't mean much to you viscerally. Consistency will give you the feedback you need in order to be successful. Whether the feedback is a profit or a loss, it's still important feedback that relates directly to the behavior.

2. Control of emotions. " . . . emotion is the chief enemy of the speculator . . . always boring from within . . . " said Edwin LeFevre (alias Jesse Livermore). Too much pessimism will cause you to either get out too soon or to not get in when you should. And too much optimism will cause you to hold on when you should be getting out and possibly reversing position. Emotions can be controlled by the use of relaxation techniques, brute force (i.e., forcing yourself to control your emotions), external force (i.e., having a partner who won't let you break the rules no matter how good or bad you feel), or by isolating yourself from the situations that will cause you to act emotionally. Of the available methods, I prefer isolation. Total isolation from market information is, to a technical trader, the optimum situation. The ultimate is to isolate yourself from everything, including prices, once your decision has been made.

3. Persistence. There are few traders who have the persistence to trade their system by the rules once it has experienced more than three consecutive losses. If you know your system, however, you will know that it may take up to seven consecutive losses before getting back on track. Persistence is the ability to go with the system through bad times as well as good.

4. Honesty with self. The eminent Russian philosopher Ouspensky claimed that self-deception was the root cause of virtually all personal and interpersonal problems. When it comes to trading, he is most assuredly correct. If you can be honest with yourself about every aspect of your trading then you will refuse to break the rules of your system or, if you do break the rules, you'll do so under very well-defined circumstances. Self-honesty is one of the most valuable qualities a trader can possess.

The next quality is so very important that I've devoted an entire section to it.

Implementation—The Key to Everything

Without implementation, there can be nothing. When I was a practicing psychologist, I helped many patients achieve great insights into their behavior. I helped them understand the whys and wherefores of their behaviors. These understandings, unless followed by actions, were nothing more than romantic exercises. There are futures traders who spend hours and hours developing systems that appear to have great profit potential; systems that backtest beautifully, but which remain nothing more than works of art, never traded due to the fear or indolence of their developer. Once you have pinpointed the reasons that you have failed to realize your full potential, you must act *immediately* or the opportunity will be lost— you will fail to seize the opportunity and time will be lost. The longer you wait the less capable you will be of taking action because lack of action will become comfortable to you.

Why Do So Many Traders and Investors Lose?

The answer is a simple one indeed; they lack the skills necessary to succeed at this most demanding of all games. The vast majority of traders and investors fail to follow a reasonably disciplined and organized approach to their task. All too often they expect their profits to be the result of following the right advice, the right market letter, the right broker, or the right trading system. While all of these can help, none of them will be effective unless the individual who is following them exercises the right mix of discipline, judgment, and consistency. Without the skills I've reviewed earlier in this chapter, there can be no consistent success, no clear victory in the battle for investment survival. There will only be small victories and numerous losses.

I have touched on this subject only briefly. There is enough material here to fill several books. There is a disproportionately high number of traders who lose in the futures and stock markets. It need not be so. It takes work—but the skills that must be learned and known and they can be acquired—not by all individuals but by many.

30

Modeling the Behavior of Successful Traders

In days of old, it was common for those who wished to enter a given profession to become an apprentice to one already established as successful in the given field. Following an appropriate period of "hands on" instruction, usually several years, the trainee, provided that the lessons had been learned, was granted the right to go off and begin practicing as a journeyman in the given profession. It was an effective system for passing on the knowledge acquired from one generation to another.

As technology increased, however, and as the number of students increased substantially, the system was generally abandoned in favor of a more formalized method of classroom instruction through colleges, universities, and trade schools. One teacher could instruct literally hundreds or thousands of students. This was a considerably more efficient method, however, it was not as effective and failed to pass on the more intuitive aspects of the given profession. Today, the student is left to his or her own experiences to learn the finer details of the skill and this often takes a lifetime. In many cases, it is never learned.

In the 1980s, as the so-called "New Age" movement began to spread, many alternatives to traditional education became popular. Hopeful "new agers," primarily in response to a clearly failing Western educational system, began to explore such methods as subliminal learning, psychocybernetics and neurolinguistic programming. Proponents of these techniques claimed that they were new methods when, in fact, a little examination of their techniques revealed them to be reincarnations of tried and true methods which have been known for many years. By being presented as new concepts with new lingo and new interpretations these old teaching approaches were sold to the public.

Among these I include the various modeling methods which became popular in the late 1980s. Several well-known prompters held hundreds of seminars, selling books and tapes at high prices, which taught their methods to thousands of hopeful followers. While I do not find fault with what was taught, I feel that the information is essentially old information which has been available for many years. The concepts are valid and relatively easy to apply. This chapter is devoted to a relatively brief but concise discussion of the various modeling techniques as they apply to trading and investing.

A Review of the General Principles

Earlier in this chapter I discussed the apprenticeship method which was used to pass on knowledge many years ago. Essentially the modeling methods, regardless of their name, are based upon mimicking the behavior of an already accomplished professional. Here are some general principles about such techniques:

1. Successful behaviors are primarily learned behaviors. Losing behavior are either learned or they are the result of ignorance or emotional problems.

2. Because successful behaviors are learned behaviors, regardless of profession or vocation, they can be taught and they can be learned.

3. There are many ways in which these behaviors can be learned and taught. Some are more effective than others. And some are more time consuming than others.

4. Formal education is not necessarily the best method of imparting the knowledge necessary for success in business. Stimulus-response training such as behavior modification is not necessarily the best method of doing so either.

5. The most efficient and economical method of teaching the skills necessary for success in any field of human endeavor is by modeling.

6. Modeling means precisely what its name implies. The student models the behaviors of the teacher as closely as possible. In so doing the student will learn by doing.

Modeling in Practice

While the theory of modeling is reasonable and valid, in practice it is not as simple to achieve as one would hope. The issue is further complicated by the fact that a number of individuals have held themselves out to the public as experts in teaching the necessary skills. But they do so at a very high dollar cost which is often not within the reach of those who are most in need of the knowledge. Yes, there are books and courses, but books and tapes are dreadfully inadequate. If the object is to model then the object is to model a live human being, not a tape or a book. The results of directly modeling the successful individual can be very disappointing, and this will reduce the urge to learn.

Another problem is that of finding the individual to model. Yes, you can prepare a list of well-known or even not so well-known individuals who are successful in the field, however, this does not mean that they will permit you to intrude into their personal and professional lives so that you can learn how to do what they do. Nor are many of them willing to divulge what they perceive to be their secrets. What's in it for them? A number of aspiring students have asked to come into my office and model my behavior. But in every case the proposals were entirely one sided and I have refused.

What to Do?

While I have heard great success stories, I am still not convinced that this approach is the best or the most effective due to the problems I have cited earlier. I do feel, however, there may be ways to achieve the desired results by employing a few relatively simple methods which are part-way measures. They will not appeal to the purist, however, who feel that they have great potential. Here are my suggestions:

1. Study the behaviors of successful traders. When I say study, I mean STUDY. It is not enough to simply read about the individuals. You'll need to conduct intensive research into the lives and behaviors of these people. You may even want to interview them, provided they will cooperate.

2. If there is one individual in particular whose success you would like to model, you must spare no effort in gathering as much information on this individual as you possibly can. Books, articles, and

newspaper stories should be collected and studied, provided, of course, that they are available.

3. Attempt to establish a writing relationship with these people. While they may not be amenable to interviews, they may be willing to answer questions in writing.

4. Set your goals high but don't be unrealistic.

5. Watch for positive changes in your own trading. If you see that your results are improving then be certain you know why. You can only do this by keeping thorough notes on the behaviors you are modeling.

6. Don't stop once you're on the right track.

7. Ask direct questions. If there's something you want to learn then don't be afraid to ask very direct questions. You may be surprised at the concise answers you'll get.

In conclusion, I feel that there's a great deal to learn from successful traders. The age-old apprentice system would be ideal for learning the kind of knowledge traders need so badly. But it is, unfortunately, generally not available in the field of stock or futures trading.

31

Facing the Challenges of Today's and Tomorrow's Markets

Many traders and investors erroneously believe that technology will alter the nature of the markets. They have been convinced that the availability of computers and sophisticated investment software will mean more profits and less risk. But they are wrong. Although the markets of tomorrow will, in some ways, be very different than the markets of today or yesterday, they will, in many basic aspects, be the same as the markets of today. If this sounds like double talk, you have probably missed the most important points in this book. Markets are ruled by emotion; if they were not, there would be no markets. If the markets functioned as perfect economic systems, prices would always be at the right level and there would be no need to anticipate market direction. As long as human beings are involved in the process and as long as such important factors as the weather are not totally predictable, there will be uncertainty, and uncertainty will prompt emotionalism. Emotionalism will, in turn, stimulate volatility and significant price swings. Volatility will complete the circle, affecting traders and influencing them to act emotionally. Ultimately it will be the rational, self-disciplined trader who will emerge from the battle of speculation victorious.

What Tomorrow Holds in Store

Just a little future-oriented thinking will help us know a great deal of what the markets of tomorrow may bring, how they will act, and how they will be traded. My more than 20 years in the futures markets have taught me much about changes and how they can affect the behavior of traders. Here are a few of my thoughts regarding the future of the markets, traders, and what is likely to influence them.

1. New futures contracts. During the 1980s, there was a shift away from activity in tangible futures contracts to intangibles. Bellies and beans gave way to Tbonds and S&P. I suspect, however, that the 1990s will usher in a new era of interest in the old "standby" markets such as the agricultural futures. The stock market of the late 1980s was characterized by a plethora of leveraged buyouts. Time has proven this method of buying corporations both ineffective as well as highly risky. Some big names have fallen victim to bad strategies. This has brought more sensibility to the stock market. Hence, I feel that the 1990s will witness a return to the basics in many markets.

Furthermore, I feel that many new futures contracts will be introduced both in the United States and abroad. The course of action taken by futures exchanges clearly suggests an interest in trading futures contracts on items that do not exist. The Goldman Sachs Commodity Index (GSCI) is yet another newcomer to the nontangible futures game. In the near future, the Chicago exchanges are expected to begin trading "clean air" futures. Hence, the trend is clearly away from tangibles to intangibles, and I expect that this trend will continue. New futures contracts in other abstract commodities will be introduced, however, regardless of the market, its basic principles of operation will be based upon human response and emotion.

2. Computerized trading will likely replace the current open outcry system. The pit brokers and floor traders of today will likely be replaced by computers and computer terminals, however, this will only make the system more efficient, not more predictable in terms of determining the direction of prices. The individual speculator will still be the weakest link in the chain. Those whose income depends on the current "floor-trader" system in futures might be well advised to prepare for what is coming. Exchange members will fight progress, but in the long run, computers will win. Those with a vested interest by virtue of their owning exchange memberships which sell for hundreds of thousands of dollars will be threatened and will, therefore, defend the old ways. There will be nothing to fear; the exchanges will still remain closed societies that can only be entered by the purchase of memberships.

Stock trading which works on the specialist system will also change, however, securities firms are considerably slower to change their ways than are futures trading firms. The specialist system is so strongly in control of the markets that it may not change for many years in spite of the demonstrated ability of computerized systems to complete the task of matching trades more quickly, more efficiently, and without error.

The move toward computerization will create a host of emotional responses and considerable controversy. This will affect traders both on the inside of the markets as well as those on the outside. The already difficult task of achieving consistent profits as a trader or investor will be made even more difficult by the uncertainty which the move toward computerized floor trading will create.

3. Artificial intelligence and neural networks. Computerization will also affect the individual speculator investor as well as professional money managers. Computers are rapidly finding a role in virtually every area of life. The use of computerized robots in automobile assembly lines has led to the development of artificial intelligence (AI) programs that can mimic some functions of the human mind. AI has prompted yet another sophisticated mathematical approach to programming called neural networking or neural networks (NN). Some developers of NN programs have made strong claims for their programs suggesting that they possess the ability to reason and to "learn" from their experiences. While in some cases this is true, the jury is still out regarding the ability of NNs to benefit from experience in the markets. The promise of NNs is that they will be able to develop highly effective trading programs by analyzing numerous aspects of market behavior that influence prices and apply the knowledge thus gained to actual trading models. Some traders are concerned, therefore, that NNs may become so good at trading the markets that the general public as well as those unable to afford the extremely expensive NN hardware and software will lose their ability to compete with professionals. These are unrealistic fears. Ultimately emotions will rule the markets regardless of how advanced or effective the technical strategy may be. Furthermore, there will always be unexpected events that force the emotions that accompany losses. During such crises, many market professionals will err just as does the general public. I expect, therefore, that bigger, better, faster, and smarter computers will not positively affect the results of the vast majority of traders. Emotion, consistency, discipline, self-control, and persistence are the qualities that count now and will count tomorrow as well.

4. Global influences will become more pronounced as the world grows "smaller." This means that what happens in Zimbabwe or Shanghai will have more of an impact on prices than it does today. The speculator and investor will, therefore, have more opportunities. Concomitant with these opportunities will be more risk. And more risk will mean that speculators and investors will have to be more disciplined.

5. Speed of communication will also increase markedly in the years ahead. Not only will the news from the distant countries have more of an impact on world markets, but it will reach the markets faster. The rapidity of news dissemination will impact markets more quickly than it does today and this will, in turn, also call for greater self-discipline on the part of the trader.

6. Global consumption will increase as all nations advance technologically and economically. There will be more demand for industrial commodities, agricultural commodities, money, fuel, and so on. The futures and stock markets will grow not only in participation, but in the stocks and futures contracts traded. There will, therefore, be more opportunities for traders and, as I've noted above, more risk.

Tomorrow's Success Will Require the Same Skills as Today's Success

In my extensive studies of the stock and futures markets, I've reviewed historical trading literature that spans literally hundreds of years. The pervasive theme is that markets change but traders don't; the same qualities that facilitated success one hundred years ago are the same qualities which lead to success today. And I would extrapolate that the same qualities will also lead to success in the markets of tomorrow, no matter how these markets may change.

In short, I feel that there is nothing to fear about the markets of tomorrow since the ingredients for success will be the same as those of today. Yes, it's true that reaction time may need to be shorter; that actions must be more decisive; and that the incoming events influencing prices may be more numerous than they are today, but the raw ingredients will be similar.

32

Some Closing Thoughts: Facing the Challenges of Today and Tomorrow

The goal of achieving and sustaining market success is more difficult to attain today than it was yesterday. And it will be more difficult tomorrow than it is today. As the economic world grows larger, encompassing new nations with unprecedented political and social changes, it also grows smaller as worldwide communications become more instantaneous. News of changes in China which, for example, once took days or weeks to influence traders in the West, now reach the trading pits within minutes. Their impact is virtually immediate. Computers now monitor price changes continually, alerting traders and arbitrageurs to short-term opportunities which might not have been perceived in the past. Professional traders compete aggressively with the average investor. Mutual fund managers devote their full time to finding opportunities and capitalize upon their research quite often before the average investor can do so. And finally, market volatility has become more pronounced than ever before resulting, at times, in violent price movements that create both great risk and unprecedented opportunities.

It's been said that trading is a loner's game. It's also been said that successful trading is one of the most challenging things in life. I believe that both are true. They are more true today than they were yesterday, and they will be even more true tomorrow than they are today. In the long run, you can only depend on yourself and your own actions in this toughest of all games. True success, lasting success, and consistent success can only be achieved by those who know how to play the game. I have done my best to give you the insights, understanding, and tools that will facilitate success, however, only you can implement them. Only you can make them work. I have often considered the task of the trader to be akin to that of a race car driver. The tools of the trade, such as market lingo, charts, timing indicators, trading systems, timing signals, computers, are your vehicle. The race car driver has a fast and powerful automobile as his vehicle. The inexperienced driver may not even know how to start the motor. However, assuming that the motor has been started, the novice could easily drive the car as fast as the professional as long as the track is straight. When the road begins to twist and turn, and when it becomes necessary to shift gears, apply proper braking, pass other cars, and do all of these safely, the novice may crash the car while the professional will most certainly reach the finish line, even though he or she may do so slowly.

The goal in trading is to finish the race without crashing your car. You must, therefore, learn how to drive your vehicle carefully and skillfully. You must learn the nuances of your vehicle so that you can drive it fast when necessary and so that you can avoid the many obstacles you will encounter along the way.

Furthermore, you have a choice of different vehicles. You can select the systems and timing indicators that are consistent with your personality and trading style. You can day trade, position trade, spread trade, or "scalp" markets in the trading pits. You can go as fast or as slow as you want. The main idea is to finish the race without a life-threatening crash or without a crash that disables your vehicle. You will need to keep your car in working order (in other words, you'll need to preserve your capital) and you'll need to stay in control of your vehicle (in other words, you'll have to remain in control by making the correct split second decisions). There are many more parallels which can serve you well. Think about them.

Prepare for the Worst, Not the Best

All too often traders are disappointed with their results. They are unhappy with themselves. They are unhappy with the markets. They are dissatisfied with virtually everything that relates to the markets. Frequently their dissatisfaction is the result of unrealistic expectations. Traders test systems often without regard for the worst case scenario.

They fail to understand that there is a world of difference between what is produced under the ideal conditions of a computer-generated back test and real life. In a computer test, orders are filled at perfect prices. Traders do not interfere with their own systems. Brokers cannot talk you into or out of trades, and emotions do not play even the slightest part in the decision-making process. But in real life everything is a potential complication. Fantasy is greater than any reality. Results in real time cannot be expected to match the ideal results of a hypothetical test, no matter how many adjustments are made in order to compensate for the ideal conditions. Accidents will happen. You must be prepared for them. Expect the worst, not the best. This does not mean you'll have a negative attitude, rather you'll have a realistic one.

Find Your Niche

The markets are many and varied. There are literally hundreds of things you can do to make a profit. You can trade, you can invest, you can be a broker, a floor trader, a trading advisor, an author, a systems developer, or a money manager. It takes time to find the things that you really want to do, but when you have finally found them I advise you to stay with them. How will you know when you've found what's best for you? The answer is simple. You'll make money and you'll be happy. Both elements must be present. And one does not necessarily lead to another. You can make money but you may not be happy. You can be happy with what you're doing but it may not make you any money.

Be Flexible But Don't Change Too Quickly

While some traders change too slowly, others change too quickly. There's nothing wrong with being flexible in response to changing market conditions, but there's everything wrong with changing too quickly. The problem with changing your trading system or method too quickly is that all trading systems need time to work. There's no hard and fast rule as to how long a system may take to do its work. It's very much a function of the system and its average trade length. So don't be too quick to abandon a system which has worked in the past in favor of a new system which you've never used before. All systems need time to work. It's good to be flexible; you need to know when to quit. But don't quit too soon.

The Virtue of Isolation

Few traders are able to make themselves immune to outside influences such as news, world events, market reports, brokers, family pressures or the advice of "experts." Such pressures can affect us in subtle ways. At times we are affected by external influences without knowing that we are being influenced by factors outside our conscious awareness. The best way to avoid such problems is to become an isolationist when it comes to trading. Here are a few suggestions that will help you:

1. Don't listen to the news either on television or the radio. The news will confuse you. It will prey on your unconscious mind, influencing your behavior in negative ways.

2. Don't listen to your friends. Their opinions are a function of their own perceptions. They will not work for you.

3. Don't believe government reports; they tend to be the most bullish at tops and the most bearish at bottoms. They won't help you trade unless you are a fundamental trader who can understand these reports within the context of all other available fundamental data.

4. Avoid the opinions of brokers, newsletter writers, market analysts, and so on unless you have found one or two whose methodology and style are compatible with your work. If you're a newcomer to the markets, you might be best off employing the services of a knowledgeable broker and/ or advisor. Either rely totally on your own work or find a professional with whom you work well and proceed accordingly.

5. Don't discuss your positions, opinions, results, or research with anyone. Keep all of these to yourself. Talking about your work will either give another individual an opportunity to undermine your self-confidence or, by agreeing with your conclusions, give you false confidence. We always feel better when someone else agrees with us and we feel worse when someone disagrees with us.

Have the Confidence to Play Your Own Game

My last word of advice is to be confident in your decisions. I could elaborate on this final point, however, I would simply be repeating what I've told you in the preceding chapters. Now, go forward with confidence, self-knowledge, and persistence. Do so with consistency and discipline and you will succeed!

Bibliography

Altman, L. L. (1969). *The Dream in Psychoanalysis.* New York: International Universities Press.

Bernstein, J. (1982). *The Handbook of Commodity Cycles: A Window of Time.* New York: John Wiley & Sons.

Bernstein, J. (1986). *Seasonal Concepts in Futures Trading.* New York: John Wiley & Sons.

Bernstein, J. (1987). *Short-Term Trading Futures.* Chicago, IL: Probus.

Bernstein, J. (1987). *Facts on Futures.* Chicago, IL: Probus.

Bernstein, J. (1988). *Cyclic Analysis in Futures Trading.* New York: John Wiley & Sons.

Bernstein, J. (1988). *How the Futures Markets Work.* New York: New York Institute of Finance.

Bernstein, J. (1989). *The New Prosperity.* New York: New York Institute of Finance.

Bernstein, J. (1991). *Cycles of Profit.* New York: Harper Business.

Bernstein, J. (1991). *The Handbook of Economic Cycles.* Homewood, IL: Richard D. Irwin.

Bernstein, J. (1992). *Timing Signals in the Futures Market.* Chicago, IL: Richard D. Irwin.

Binet, A., and Simon, T. (1908). "Le Development de l'Intelligence Chez les Enfants." *L'Anige Psychologique 14:* 1–94.

Brenner, Charles. (1974). *An Elementary Textbook of Psychoanalysis.* Garden City, NY: Anchor Books.

Caplan, Ruth B. (1969). *Psychiatry and the Community in Nineteenth Century America.* New York: Basic Books.

Capra, Fritjof. (1975). *The Tao of Physics.* Boulder, CO: Shambhala Publications.

Capra, Fritjof. (1982). *The Turning Point.* New York: Simon & Schuster.

Capra, Fritjof. (1982). *Uncommon Wisdom.* New York: Simon & Schuster.

276

Dollard, J., and Miller, N. E. (1950). *Personality and Psychotherapy.* New York: McGraw-Hill.

Eriksen, C. W. (1958). Unconscious Processes. In M. R. Jones (Ed.), *Nebraska Symposium on Motivation.* Lincoln: University of Nebraska Press. pp. 169–227.

Escalona, S. K. (1950). The Use of Infant Tests for Predictive Purposes. *Bulletin of the Meninger Clinic 14:* 117–128.

Ford, D. H., and Urban, H. B. (1965). *Systems of Psychotherapy—A Comparative Study.* New York: John Wiley & Sons.

Franks, C. M., and Wilson, G. T. (1974). *Annual Review of Behavior Therapy: Theory and Practice.* New York: Brunner/Mazel.

Freud, S. (1953). *The Interpretation of Dreams. Collected Works. Vols. 4–5.* London: Hogarth.

———. (1957). *Three Essays on Sexuality: H-Infantile Sexuality Collected Works.* London: Hogarth.

Gann, W. D. (1923). *Truth of the Stock Tape.* Pomeroy, WA: Lambert-Gann.

———. (1942). *How to Make Profits in Commodities.* Pomeroy, WA: Lambert-Gann.

———. (1943). *How to Make Profits in Puts and Calls.* Pomeroy, WA: Lambert-Gann.

———. (1949). *45 Years in Wall Street.* Pomeroy, WA: Lambert-Gann.

Gesell, A., and Amatruda, C. S. (1962). *Developmental Diagnosis.* New York: Harper.

Gibson, Eleanor J. (1967). *Principles of Perceptual Learning and Development.* New York: Crofts.

Gittelson, Bernard. (1976). *Biorhythm—A Personal Science.* New York: Arco.

Gold, Gerald. (1975). *Modern Commodities Futures Trading.* New York: Commodity Research Bureau, Inc.

Goldberg, F. H. and Fiss, H. (1959). Partial Cues and the Phenomenon of Discrimination without Awareness. *Perceptual Motor Skills 9:* 243–251.

Henry, William E. (1956). *The Analysis of Fantasy.* New York: John Wiley & Sons.

Laffal, Julius. (1965). *Pathological and Normal Language.* New York: Atherton.

Lefevre, Edwin. (1965). *Reminiscences of a Stock Operator.* Larchmont, NY: American Research Council.

London, Perry. (1977). *Behavioral Control.* New York: Meridian.

Marx, M. H., and Hillix, W. A. (1963). *Systems and Theories in Psychology.* New York: McGraw-Hill.

Masson, Jeffrey Moussaieff. (1990). *Final Analysis.* Boston, MA: Addison-Wesley.

McCleary, R. A., and Lazarus, R. S. (1949). Autonomic Discrimination without Awareness: An Interim Report. *Journal of Personality 18:* 171–179.

Meyer, William J. (1964). *Developmental Psychology.* New York: Center for Applied Research in Education.

Mikvlas, William L. (1974). *Concepts in Learning.* Philadelphia: Saunders.

Mounier, Emmanual. (1956). *The Character of Man.* New York: Harper.

Natenberg, Sheldon. (1988). *Option Volatility and Pricing Strategies.* Chicago, IL: Probus.

Ouspensky, P. D. (1957). *The Fourth Way.* New York: Random House.

Packard, Vance. (1961). *The Hidden Persuaders.* New York: Pocket Books.

Pavlov, I. P. (1927). *Conditioned Reflexes.* Oxford: Clarendon Press.

Plotzl, O. (1960). The Relationship Between Experimentally Induced Dream Images and Indirect Vision. *Psychological Issues 2(3),* Monograph 7: 41–120.

Pugh, B. (1948). *A Better Way to Make Money.* Pomeroy, WA: Lambert-Gann.

Schwager, Jack D. (1989). *Market Wizards.* New York: New York Institute of Finance.

Secord, P. F., and Backman, Carl W. (1964). *Social Psychology.* New York: McGraw-Hill.

Selye, H. (1950). *The Physiology and Pathology of Exposure to Stress.* Montreal: Acta.

Skinner, B. F. (1953). *Science and Human Behavior.* New York: Free Press.

Watson, J. B. (1913). Psychology as the Behaviorist Sees It. *Psychological Review 20:* 158–177.

———. (1919). *Psychology from the Standpoint of a Behaviorist.* Philadelphia: Lippincott.

———. Behaviorism. (1924). New York: Norton.

Watts, A. W. (1972). *The Book on the Taboo Against Knowing Who You Are.* New York: Vintage.

Watzlawick, Paul, et al. (1967). *Pragmatics of Human Communication.* New York: Norton, 1967.

Weinstein, Stan. (1988). *Secrets for Profiting in Bull and Bear Markets.* Homewood, IL: Dow Jones-Irwin.

Wiener, M., and Schiller, P. H. (1960). Subliminal Perception or Perception of Partial Cues. *Journal of Abnormal Social Psychology 61:* 124–137.

Williams, L. R., and Noseworthy, M. L. (1977). *Sure Thing Commodity Trading.* New York: Windsor Books.

Williams, Larry. (1988). *Futures Trading.* New York: Windsor Books.

Wolman, Benjamin, Ed. (1973). *Handbook of General Psychology.* Englewood Cliffs, NJ: Prentice-Hall.

Overview of "Trading Masters"

I have attempted to provide you with a brief overview of some "trading masters" whose works I suggest you read. I cannot do justice to the totality of their experiences or writings, but I believe that I can offer you some additional understandings of how important proper attitude and effective psychology can be in the overall attainment of success. In providing only brief coverage I have chosen to place virtually no emphasis on the trading system each individual employed. My orientation is, as you certainly know by now, almost purely psychological.

W. D. Gann

SUGGESTED READING: *Truth of the Stock Tape*
                                  How to Make Profits in Puts and Calls
                                    How to Make Profits in Commodities
                                    45 Years in Wall Street

Available from: Lambert-Gann Publishing Co., Box O, Pomeroy, WA 99347.

Of all the well-known traders, W. D. Gann was perhaps the most prolific writer and the most active researcher. His trading systems were detailed, innovative, extensive, and in some ways almost mystical. But more than technique itself, Gann recognized the overriding importance of psychology in the marketplace. Despite his considerable coverage of historical price behavior, methodology, and seasonality, his observations of human nature and its relationship to the market were not overshadowed or given a back seat. Even his closing remarks in *45 Years in Wall Street* were tinged with comment on the emotional state of traders and investors:

279

We cannot escape it [emotion] in the future. It will cause another panic in stocks. When it comes, both traders and investors will sell stocks, *as usual, after it is too late* or in the last stages of the bear market. . . . (1949, p. 94, emphasis mine)

We can learn a great deal about Gann's market psychology by examining his list of "24 Never Failing Rules" (1949, p. 16). The following are those rules that apply to investor psychology:

14. Never get out of the market just because you have lost patience or get into the market because you are anxious from waiting. . . .
16. Never cancel a stop loss order after you have placed it at the time you make a trade.
17. Avoid getting in and out of the market too often. . . .
23. Never change your position in the market without a good reason. When you make a trade, let it be for some good reason or according to some definite plan; then do not get out without a definite indication of a change in trend.

In addition to these specific rules, Gann commented extensively on the human element and his belief that it is the trader's greatest weakness. His basic belief is similar to what I have been telling you throughout this book. Simply and concisely stated his point is as follows:

Therefore, in order to make a success he (the trader) must act in a way to overcome the weak points which have caused the ruin of others. (p. 25)

Gann writes additionally:

When a trader makes a profit, he gives himself credit and feels that his judgment is good and that he did it all himself. When he makes losses, he takes a different attitude and seldom ever blames himself or tries to find the cause with himself for the losses. He finds excuses; reasons with himself that the unexpected happened, and that if he had not listened to some one else's advice, he would have made a profit. He finds a lot of ifs, ands, and buts, which he imagines were no fault of his. This is why he makes mistakes and loses the second time.

The investor and trader must work out his own salvation and blame himself and no one else for his losses, for unless he does, he will never be able to correct his weaknesses. After all, it is your own acts that cause your losses, because you did the buying and the selling. You must look for the trouble within and correct it. Then you will make a success, and not before. . . .

I can give you the best rules in the world and the best methods for determining the position of a stock, and then you can lose money on account of the human element which is your greatest weakness. You will fail to follow rules. You will work on hope or fear instead of facts. You will delay. You will become impatient. You will act too quickly or you will delay too long in acting, thus cheating yourself on account of your human weakness and then blaming it on the market. Always remember that it is your mistake that causes losses and not the action of the market or the manipulators. Therefore, strive to follow rules, or keep out of speculation for you are doomed to failure.

These words, taken from years of experience in stocks and commodities, are well worth the price of Gann's book. Bear in mind that Gann had extensive experience in the markets. Keep also in mind the fact that his main point was similar to what has been stressed throughout my writings as well. The speculator, trader, investor—the human factor—is the weak link in the chain. This alone is the instrument that can guide the trading system to success or failure.

I will close my commentary on W. D. Gann with some words from *How to Make Profits Trading in Commodities:*

Hope and Fear: I have written about this often in all my books, and I feel that I cannot repeat it too often. The average man or woman buys Commodities because they hope they will go up or because somebody advises them they will go up. This is the most dangerous thing to do. Never trade on hope. Hope wrecks more people than anything else. Face the facts, and when you trade, trade on facts, eliminating hope.

Fear causes many losses. People sell out because they fear commodities are going lower, but they often wait until the decline has run its course and they sell near the bottom . . . never make a trade on fear. . . . (1942, p. 17)

Burton Pugh

SUGGESTED READING: *A Better Way to Make Money*
                      Mastering Cotton
                      Science and Secrets of Wheat Trading
                      Trader's Instruction Book

Available from: Lambert-Gann Publishing Co., Box O, Pomeroy, WA 99347.

Another "master" of the markets was Burton Pugh, who ran a successful market advisory service and pioneered many new technical market concepts. Although Pugh's work was highly technical, he also found it necessary to comment on the fallibility of man in the overall success of a trading program. In his 1948 publication entitled *A Better Way to Make Money,* Pugh covers many trading techniques and commodity market indicators. His words are concise and his concepts specific. And his concluding "Epigrams and Observations" is rich in psychologically oriented trading rules. Here are a few of his observations:

Enter the market with the belief that you *will win.*

Surrender no advantage to the natural human indolence. Money is made by aggressiveness and determination. If in doubt, learn more about what you are doing. . . .

All the crop news and political events will be of little use. If it were possible to trade successfully by good and bad weather conditions, it would be unbelievably easy to make money. When the news filters through ten or twenty thousand minds interested in wheat, the major opinion may be quite different from the opinion of an individual. . . .

If a trader fails to come out right, the error will be found in the operator—not the market. . . . A loss makes one thoughtful. It is the losses that makes the operator studious—not the profits. Take advantage of every slip to improve your knowledge of market action. It will be found that, no matter how erratic the action of either stocks or grains, they are still conforming to the laws of market movements. Practice is a greater renovator. It enables us to discard wrong ideas. . . .

There is a very simple *philosophy of loss* in all trading.

The reason traders lose readily *is* because there is no one to make them accept a profit, and there *is* someone to make them take a loss—the broker. . . .

Success is the most desirable thing in the world, but it is an eliminating contest. The one who wins must try and try until he is able to pass the test. . . . (pp. 299–303; emphasis in original)

Jesse Livermore

SUGGESTED READING: *Reminiscences of a Stock Operator*

Available from: American Research Council, Larchmont, NY 10538.

A reflection of my fondness for the writings of Livermore is the frequency with which he is mentioned throughout this book. Most certainly the man had his own "trading system," as did other speculators. But his technique was not as much a part of his story as was his psychology. *Reminiscences of a Stock Operator,* written under the name Edwin Lefevre, is perhaps the greatest single compilation of psychological market wisdom contained in one work. It is thought to be biographical although it is presented in a fictional format. Regardless, it is, in my opinion, a must on any serious investor's list of reading materials. The greatest justice I can do this work of art is to quote for you several of the significant passages. Others have been quoted extensively elsewhere in this book. I would not want to limit, in any way, the possible benefits and enjoyment that can be obtained through your independent reading.

In fact, I always made money when I was sure I was right before I began. What beat me was not having brains enough to stick to my own game. (p. 14)

I know from experience that nobody can give me a tip or a series of tips that will make more money for me, than my own judgment. It took me five years to learn to play the game intelligently enough to make big money when I was right. (p. 31)

Finally there came the awful day of reckoning for the bulls and the optimists and the wishful thinkers and those vast hordes that, dreading the pain of a small loss at the beginning, were now about to suffer total amputation—without anaesthetics. (p. 110)

A loss never bothers me after I take it. I forget it overnight. But being wrong—not taking the loss—that is what does the damage to the pocketbook and to the soul. (p. 118)

Additional Readings

In addition to the works of "great masters," many books contain a wealth of historical information about the markets. I believe that every investor, whether interested in stocks, commodities, bonds, real estate, or options, should have a firm knowledge of market history. A great deal can be learned from studying the action of investors in past bull and bear markets, fads, crashes, and panics. Such information will supplement much of what I have discussed in this book.

I therefore recommend you either purchase or, at the very minimum, read most of the publications described here.

BARUCH, B. M. *My Own Story,* New York: Holt, 1957.

Baruch was one of America's most outspoken and successful speculators. His writings are a must, particularly the one mentioned. More than most well-known investors, he recognized the importance of emotion in the market, and gave specific recommendations as to how it might be used to one's financial advantage.

SMITH, ADAM. *The Money Game,* New York: Random House, 1967.

This book is also a must for those who enjoy laughing at themselves. In a humorous and purportedly fictional series of tales, many of the markets' foolish goings-on are discussed.

There are also historical works that should be read, and possibly studied. The major bull and bear markets, as well as some of the well-known investors who helped make them, are discussed at length. Two important books are:

MOTTRAM, R. H. *A History of Financial Speculation,* Boston: Little, Brown, 1929.

THOMAS, D. L. *The Plungers and the Peacocks,* New York: Putnam, 1967.

In the general category of market books I advise the following:

LOEB, G. M. *The Battle for Stock Market Profits,* New York: Simon and Schuster, 1971.

SOBEL, R. *Inside Wall Street,* New York: W. W. Norton, 1977.

SPERANDEO, VIC. *Trader Vic,* Wiley & Sons, New York, 1991.

TEWELS, R. J., et al. *The Commodity Futures Game: Who Wins? Who Loses? Why?,* New York: McGraw-Hill, 1974.

I have by no means covered all of the major works. Certainly there are many others that can provide the information necessary to successful investing. All things considered there are relatively few books in the investment area that are truly worthwhile reading. Those that focus on trading systems, techniques, and methodology are generally lacking in the area of investment psychology. The well-rounded investor should make it his or her goal to read every significant market work. In so doing, several favorite authors will emerge. I advise you to follow up on the works of the "masters" whose stories appeal to you.

Suggested Psychology Readings

In addition to the market texts recommended previously, I also believe you can find some guidance in the psychology texts listed in the references at the end of this book. There are several other sources you might find interesting. I have not used them as references for this book but recommend them as informational sources:

FREUD, SIGMUND. *The Interpretation of Dreams,* New York: Avon, 1965.

GELLERMAN, SAUL W. *The Uses of Psychology in Management,* New York: McGraw-Hill, 1960.

HARPER, ROBERT A. *The New Psychotherapies,* Englewood Cliffs, NJ: Prentice-Hall, 1975.

ORNSTEIN, ROBERT E. *The Psychology of Consciousness,* New York: Penguin, 1972.

Index

A

Abreaction, 198
Adler, A., 172
Adlerians, 27, 172
Advisory service, 114–122, 216
Assets, 115
Attitude(s), 123–127

B

Baruch, Bernard M., 6, 14
Bear (eternal), 153–156
Bearish, 110
Behavioral learning, 45–49, 102
Blavatsky, 11
Bottom out, 107
Breakouts, 105
Brewer, Josef, 27
Brokers, 110, 125, 205
Brute-force, 131–132
Bull (eternal), 156–157
Buy or sell, 118
Buying climax, 183

C

Castration complex, 32–33, 225
The Character of Man, 130
Chartist, 24
Chicago Mercantile Exchange,
    18–19

China, 272
Computerized trading, 269
Commission, 121
Conditioned seeing, 176
Consecutive losers, 121
Consistency, 261
Contrary thinking, 213
Cope with losses, 203–204
Coué, Emil, 129
CTA, 119
Cycles, 105
Cutten, Arthur, 6, 233

D

Daily diary, 199
Daily price limit, 15
Depression, 220
Diet, 200–201
Disapproval, 255–256
Discipline, 212, 245
Disorganization, 221
Dollard and Miller, 59
Drugs, 210–211

E

Earnings reports, 105
Egg futures, 2–3
Entry and exit prices, 118
Equity drawdown, 121

Estes, W. K., 95
Extrasensory perception,
    191–192

F

"Fade out" rewards, 96
Fear, 250
Free association, 199
Freud, Sigmund, 27–28, 35–39, 54,
    87, 190–198, 223–224
Futures contract, 17–18
Futures magazine, 119

G

Galvanic skin response (GSR),
    190
Gann, W. D., 6, 233, 279–280
Goals, 232
Goldman Sachs Commodity Index
    (GSCI), 269
Greed, 205
Guided imagery, 240
Gurdjieff, G. I., 11

H

Head and shoulders bottoms, 105
The Hidden Persuaders, 189
Historical tests, 120

I

IBM, 107
Id impulses, 31
Independence, 213
Intellectualization, 34–35
Investors, 9–11
Isolation, 213

J

Jungians, 27

K

Key indicator, 107
Key reversals, 105, 107

L

Leadbetter, C. W., 11
Learning to trade, 116
Lefevre, Edwin, 59, 67, 77, 104,
    105
Leverage, 17
Liabilities, 115
Limitations, 115
Limit moves, 121
Linguistic clues, 228
Livermore, Jesse, 6, 14, 67,
    233
London Sunday Times, 189
Long-range goals, 102–103
Long-term patterns, 105
Long-term trends, 104
Losses, 244

M

Market-by-market basis, 121
Market indicators, 105
Market preparation, 101–102
Market psychology, 220
Market trend, 110–113
Markets, 14–16
Modeling, 264–266
Moving average systems, 105
Mounier, Emmanuel, 54

N

National Futures Association
    (NFA), 119–120
"New behavior," 95
Neural networks, 270
Nonspecific fears, 204

O

Objectives, 118
Oedipal complex, 32–33
Operant seeing, 177
Operational definition, 93
Optimized, 121
Ouspensky, 11
Outline, 230
Overconfidence, 217–218

P

Packard, Vance, 189
Pavlov, 29, 40–41, 177
Perceptions, 178–179
Persistence, 212
Personal life, 213
Physical exercise, 199
Pleasure principle, 32
Plotzl, 190
Pork bellies, 4–5
Positive attitude, 212
Potential, 115
Psychology, 21–30
Profits, fear of, 253
Professional help, 210
Pugh, Burton, 6, 261–262

R

Rankians, 27
Rationalization, 34–35
Reaction-formation, 34
Rejection, fear of, 255
Real estate, 16–18, 23
Record keeping, 102
Regression, 34
Relaxation, 200
Reminiscences of a stock operator,
  77, 104, 192
Repression, 34, 131
Russell, Richard, 110
Risk, 7–9

S

Scalpers, 105
Schedule, 200–201
Science and human behavior,
  176
Self, 12
Self improvement courses, 214
Sell, 118
Selye, Hans, 195
Sexual conflict, 225–226
Sexual inadequacy, 227
Shaping, 79–80
Short term, 104, 105
Skinner, B. F., 28–29, 43, 45, 49,
  176–177
Signals, 105
Sleep, 200–201
Slippage, 121
Soybeans, 107
Speculation, 10, 13, 105
Stock and futures trading, 7,
  16–18
Stone, W. Clement, 7
Stop losses, 118
Stress, 196–198
Sublimation, 33–35
Success, 9–11, 18–19
Suppression, 34

T

Target behavior, 95
Technical trader, 104
Technician, 23–24, 40, 104
Theosophist philosophers, 11
Thorndike, Edward Lee, 28–29
Tomorrow, 268
Traders, 9–11
Trading by committee, 208
Trading rules, 112, 164–167
Trading seminars, 214–215
Trading system, 6–7, 75–76, 146

Trend, 104–105, 110
Trend reversals, 105

V

Vacations, 201–202
Ventilation of feelings, 198–199
Visualization, 239

W

Watson, John B., 28–29, 41–43, 57
The Wall Street Journal, 46
Working conditions, 201
Wright-Hargreaves mines, 1
Wykoff, 14, 233